This miracle journey belongs to

_____

_____

Start Date

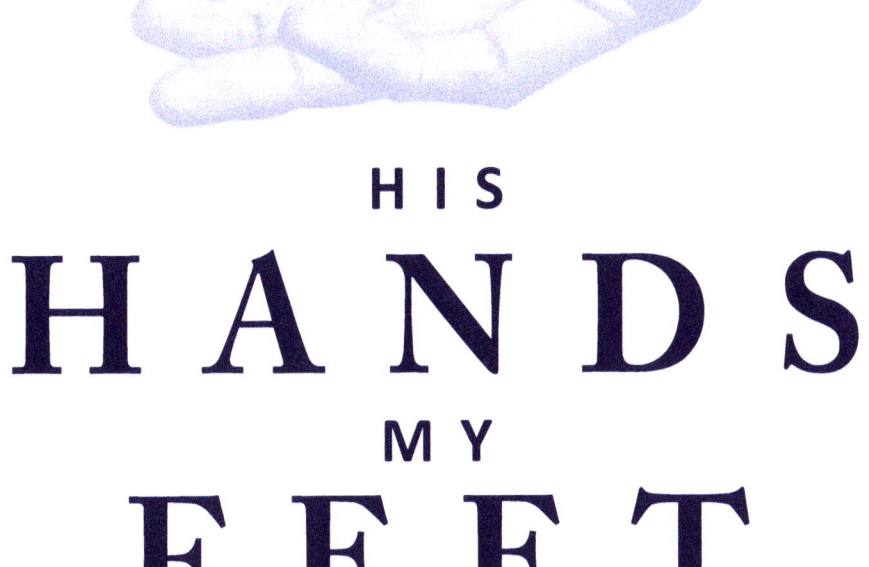

HIS
HANDS
MY
FEET

JOURNEY THROUGH THE MIRACLES OF JESUS

by
GAIL OKULEY

Copyright ©2025 by Gail Okuley.
His Hands, My Feet: Journey Through the Miracles of Jesus.

Published by Leadership Books, Inc.
Las Vegas, NV – New York, NY

LeadershipBooks.com

ISBN Hardcover: 978-1-951648-47-3
Paperback: 978-1-951648-52-7
eBook: 978-1-951648-56-5

All Rights Reserved. No part of this publication may be reproduced, distributed, or transmitted in any form or by any means, including photocopying, recording, or other electronic or mechanical methods, without the prior written permission of the publisher, except in the case of brief quotations embodied in critical reviews and certain other noncommercial uses permit-ted by copyright law.

Leadership Books, Inc. is committed to publishing works of quality and integrity. In that spirit, we are proud to offer this book to our readers; however, the story, the experiences, and the words are the authors alone.

The conversations in the book all come from the author's recollections, not word-for-word transcripts. All of the events are true to the best of the author's memory. The author, in no way, represents any company, corporation, or brand mentioned herein. The views expressed are solely those of the author.

Unless otherwise noted, all scriptures are from the NEW KING JAMES VERSION®. Copyright© 1982 by Thomas Nelson, Inc. Used by permission. All rights reserved.

Scriptures marked KJV are taken from the KING JAMES VERSION (KJV): KING JAMES VERSION, public domain.

Scriptures marked NIV are taken from the NEW INTERNATIONAL VERSION (NIV): Scripture taken from THE HOLY BIBLE, NEW INTERNATIONAL VERSION®. Copyright© 1973, 1978, 1984, 2011 by Biblica, Inc.™. Used by permission of Zondervan.

Scripture quotations marked TPT are from The Passion Translation® Copyright ©2017, 2018, 2020 by Passion & Fire Ministries, Inc. Used by permission. All rights reserved. ThePassionTranslation.com.

All Greek references are from the *Greek Interlinear Bible* at Scripture4all.org.

Cover design and artwork by Haley Okuley.

DEDICATION

To my amazing and adventuresome husband Gordon, who lovingly and persistently encouraged me to complete this work; who willingly stretched alongside me in these unexpected revelations; and who landed my first consultation with the publisher.

ACKNOWLEDGMENTS

The Lord is full of blessings and surprises that will change the trajectory of our lives. I could not have been more unsuspecting, as I began taking notes during a sermon by my pastor, Kent Yorgey. He posed two gripping questions that ultimately sparked this entire book!

Another special blessing has been a *Jonathan and David relationship,* with my friend Sharon Mullay, who heard most of this *first* and has faithfully encouraged me to keep sharing these deep revelations.

Eric Bugbee, Blue Trail Productions, insisted that my *Along the Way* stories be in *every* chapter, not just the twelve I had originally planned to do.

I must express my deep gratitude to family and friends who eagerly contributed amazing stories and testimonies in the following pages, to supplement my own stories "Along the Way." *Thank you!*

Dr. Caroline Oda, (Oahu, Hawaii), surprised me one day when she graciously offered to edit this entire manuscript, much to my delight.

My sister, Marsha Cook, also came alongside me eagerly, for discussion and further editing.

My publisher, Leadership Books, graciously opened the door for my first consult at the National Religious Broadcasters conference in 2023. They readily accepted my manuscript within a few weeks! I appreciate their wise recommendation to "take the bridle off the horse" and expand my Along the Way stories.

Dr. Ed Silvoso and Dave Thompson, Transform Our World, radically transformed our mindsets since we first met in 2011, to accept our responsibility for the Great Commission on a daily basis and to live a lifestyle of peace and blessing.

ENDORSEMENTS

Come! Embark on a journey with Jesus as Gail Okuley's book, *His Hands, My Feet,* brings Jesus' miracles to life. Watching Gail's developing confidence in obeying God's daily instructions, you, too, will be encouraged to apply Gail's question: "What do You want to say to me today, Lord?" The rich harvest of attainable fruit that comes from Gail's growing intimacy with the Lord will touch and inspire both beginners and experienced Christians. *His Hands, My Feet* is a book to savor repeatedly as you build your own intimacy with the Lord and serve Him in tangible ways here on earth.

DR. CAROLINE WARD ODA, Transform Our World, Hawaii
Author, *Catch the Wave of Transformation*

This book will certainly excite us and make us appreciate what Jesus said in John 14—that we can do what He has done and even greater things than Him. Each chapter of every miracle Jesus performed is so inspiring that, as believers of Jesus, we too can become His miracle workers so that His will is done on earth as it is in heaven.

RICARDO "KING" FLORES, Chief Equipping Officer
Transform Our World Philippines

His Hands, My Feet is an amazing adventure that can be read in a relatively short time compared to Gail's lifetime of learning, listening, growing, stretching that it took to accumulate all this book contains. Gail is a gentle spirit who also possesses a fierceness for the truth. The reader will enjoy her unique facets shared in this beautiful portrait of Jesus and His miracles. With a deep humility of spirit, Gail shares remarkable insights into Jesus' miraculous ways, while encouraging the reader to discover deeper interaction with the Father. Her own communion reveals the expansiveness of the riches that are embedded in the Word waiting for the diligent lover to unearth. As her pastor, I have observed freedom in Gail's journey that allows the Spirit of God to dance with her daily, bringing obvious joy in her approach to life. You will be richly challenged to join the journey of *His Hands, My Feet.*

KENT YORGEY, Pastor
New Beginnings Fellowship, Allentown, PA

Gail has a unique gift to give you a guided tour of the miracles of Jesus as if you were there with him! Unlike a daily devotional, she doesn't just open a door to her revelation of God's word but lays out a path, with powerful activations to receive for yourself the "richness" available to us in these stories from the gospels. Get ready to engage in the power of the gospels as the reality of these miracles become evident in your own life through the blessings and challenges offered in each miracle of Jesus.

JILL ROBSON ALLEN
Author, *The Fire of Delay,* Santa Barbara, CA

Come have a seat at this powerful table-talk of miracles, where Gail has put forth her unique two-way conversations with the Lord. The loving kindness and power of Jesus springs to life, capturing all His miracle moments and bringing the reader right into the scene. As Gail asked the Lord the questions of all our hearts, He answered! As I read, it seemed like God was speaking directly to me. She also shares her own deep-unto-deep stories of miracles that will challenge you to pursue His power. Rich blessings *after* each miracle help to challenge the reader, requiring a response to become activated into a lifestyle of miracles.

SHARON MULLAY, General of Intercession for Okuleys
Transform Our World
Lehigh Valley, PA

Gail's meditation on the miracles of Jesus has something for everyone to glean from. Whether it's immersing you in the text through careful study, or through sanctified imagination and revelation, these stories come alive in a new way as you take the journey. The practical application and personal stories help to bring the reader, not only to a place of deeper understanding, but to the crucial precipice where the miracles of Jesus go from only being His history, to being our possibilities. This book is a tremendous tool for any who would seriously seek to be a disciple of Jesus.

JAMIE FITT, Director
Philadelphia Tabernacle of David

This book just shouts of the revelation available through intimacy with Jesus Christ. Gail makes Jesus' miracles come alive, so that we see, hear, and feel as though we are actually there. Deeper insight into these miracles reveals the heart and purposes of God. Gail's intimacy and insight drew me into greater intimacy and made me hungry for more! I'm thankful I could take this journey of discovery with my Lord through this Gail's own journey.

SUSAN P GIBSON, Founder & President
Vivolor Therapeutics Inc., CA

When Gail offered me the opportunity to review this book, I readily agreed, knowing her depth of insight into the Word and ways of God. As I read the first few chapters, I called her and said, "This is too good, I have to share it with others." With Gail's blessing, fifteen followers of Jesus who all needed their own miracles, embarked on this adventure together. Daily for eight weeks we pressed into the Lord, using Gail's revelations and the Lord's challenges to encourage one another. Now I realize how Jesus' life and ministry were naturally supernatural and that He wants ours to be as well. He lived in the present and ministered along the way, just as Gail shares her own "along the way" testimonies.

JOANNE TURNER Co-founder
The Caring Network, Pray For Newark
Co-Author, *The Street Adopter's Handbook*

TABLE OF CONTENTS

CHRONOLOGICAL[1] LIST OF MIRACLES

1. Water to Wine at the Wedding 25
2. "Unclean spirit" in the Synagogue 31
3. Rebuking the Fever 37
4. City Seeks Jesus at Peter's House 47
5. Miraculous Catch of Fish 53
6. Healing the Leper 59
7. Paralytic Lowered Through the Roof 67
8. Healing a Man's Hand on the Sabbath 73
9. Healing a Great Multitude 77
10. Centurion's Servant Near Death 83
11. Resurrection: A Widow's Son 89
12. Nobleman's Son Restored 95
13. Casting Out a Blind Mute demon 101
14. Wind and Waves Obey 109
15. Casting out the Legion 119
16. Twelve-Year Infirmity 125
17. Daughter's Resurrection 131
18. Restoring Sight to the Blind 139
19. The Mute Speaks 143
20. Pool of Bethesda on the Sabbath 149
21. Miracle of Impartation to the Twelve 155

---

[1] The chronological ordering of Jesus' miracles reflected in *His Hands, My Feet*, is based on the CHRONOLOGICAL STUDY BIBLE, NEW KING JAMES VERSION®. Copyright©2008 by Thomas Nelson, Inc. Used by permission. All rights reserved.

22	Feeding the Multitude: 5000 Men	161
23	Peter Walks on the Water	167
24	Multitudes Healed in Gennesaret	173
25	Daughter of a Gentile Woman	179
26	Healing of a Deaf Man	185
27	Healing and Feeding a Multitude Again	191
28	Blind Man Healed at Bethsaida	197
29	Boy with Epilepsy	203
30	Go Fish for a Coin	209
31	Blind Man Healed on the Sabbath	217
32	Miracle of Impartation to the Seventy	223
33	18-Year Infirmity Healed on the Sabbath	231
34	Dropsy Healed on the Sabbath	237
35	Ten Lepers Cleansed	243
36	Resurrection of Lazarus	249
37	Blind Bartimaeus at Jericho	257
38	Soldier's Ear Restored	263
39	RESURRECTION OF JESUS!	271
40	Another Miraculous Catch of Fish	281

EPILOGUE
HIS HANDS, MY FEET (PART 2)

1	Sudden Boat Transport	293
2	Transfiguration	297
3	Cursing of the Fig Tree	303
4	Jesus' Crucifixion	309
5	Kingdom Come!	319

| INDEX: Along the Way | 327 |
| STUDY JOURNAL: Sample Chapter | 331 |

FOREWORD

I know Gail and Gordon Okuley through their faithful and fearless participation as members of our Transform Our World family. We've prayed, worshipped, taught, done radio and TV programs, ministered in Argentina, shared meals, watched football, laughed and dreamed of kingdom exploits together—all of which is enough to be able to say that our Transform Our World byline fits the Okuleys to a "T." They are "ordinary people doing extraordinary deeds in the power of the Spirit to change the world."

I remember an early visit to their "homey" country abode near Allentown, Pennsylvania. The '71 Victory Red Chevy pickup sat prominently in the driveway, begging anyone who saw it to blurt out, "Wow!"—which was all Gordon needed to gleefully embark on the colorful history and tribulations that brought her to her current condition. I didn't have to beg much to get a countryside tour in that magnificent and loud machine!

Soon it was dinner time. Gail's turn! Mouth-watering steak and potatoes as I recall, but what was unforgettable was the apple pie served hot out of the oven in individual pottery bowls, topped off with a scoop of ice cream! The pie, along with non-stop, enthusiastic conversation about the goodness of God became the staple of every subsequent meal in their home.

Just off the dining room was what I call "The Worship Studio." The primary occupant was the grand piano that suddenly and frequently eased into soothing waves of worship as Gail's fingers gently glided across the keys. It was a complete and total antithesis of the sounds of Gordon's more charismatic truck!

Then came the tour of the backyard replete with flowers, a small forest of trees, ponds, flowers, foliage and the chirping of all kinds of birds. It was a mini paradise, no matter the season of the year.

I have said nothing about the prayer meetings and transformation initiatives that Gail and Gordon have initiated in their region, or the spiritual excursions and adventures they have been on, beginning with their own family and then extending to many others around the world to bring hope, help and encouragement. You will pick up on that and much more as you read the pages of this book.

What I want to point out is the melody line that has woven its way through all of this that I will call the manifest presence of the Lord. I found that presence impregnating every ounce of their being, corner of their home, every pot in the oven, every shift of the gears in the pickup, every chord struck on the piano and every breeze blowing through the back yard.

What Gail has captured so eloquently and seamlessly in this book is how to live life in the manifest presence of Jesus where miracles big and small take place. It is a symphonic masterpiece played on commonplace instruments that will draw you in, not to the audience, but as a member of the very same orchestra, to pick up the "instruments" that God has given you and to walk in step with the Jesus who meant it when He said, "I will never leave you nor forsake you." Yes, this book is your invitation to walk in miracles of your own. Read on. You are about to find Him in unexpected places!

DAVE THOMPSON
Vice President
Transform Our World

PREFACE

On May 12, 2013, in our morning service at New Beginnings Fellowship in Allentown, Pennsylvania, our pastor, Kent Yorgey, prompted us to take a quiet heart-to-heart moment with the Lord, in the middle of his sermon. It was life changing. "Tell Him where you would like to be in your relationship with Him."

Immediately I knew: *Lord, I want to be Your hands and feet for miracles! Also, I want to see YOU more! Would You open my eyes for visions?*

After Kent paused a few moments, he added this, "Now ask Him, 'What is one thing you need to do to start that process?'"

As he gave us time to listen, the Spirit spoke to my heart:

Seek Me. Wait expectantly to grow our friendship.
Watch and see what I will do.

Give Me your hands and feet—and anoint them with oil, in daily consecration!"

Then He added this: **Study the miracles of Jesus, to receive extra grace for miracles!**

Oh, I had never thought to take that direct approach in preparation.

Yes, Lord!

The next day as I began to read Matthew, the Lord reminded me of a testimony I had heard the previous year. A pastor had prayed the Lord would so reveal Himself in the Word that he would be allowed to see the Lord in the Bible stories, and He did! I excitedly began to read the gospels, meditate, listen, and felt challenged by His Spirit to boldly pray: *Lord, will you let me see You, in the miracles?*

He did! He began to open my eyes with brief visions within each of Jesus' miracle accounts in the Bible, to my continual amazement!

Receiving all those significant visions, my heart began to truly grow in expectation for Him to *use my own hands and feet* to do what He did. *I hoped* that His supernatural Kingdom power would break forth as a tangible reality in my world! He made me feel like a modern-day disciple sitting at His feet.

As I meditated about this new process, He spoke to my heart: **This is to teach you, prepare you, and train you! It is changing our relationship; as you are being allowed to experience the Bible in such a way, it will become ingrained in you. Have you not prayed that My Word would become living and active within you? I am answering your prayer.**

"No eye has seen, no ear has heard, what God has prepared for those who love Him!" (1 Corinthians 2:9 NIV)

As I heard this verse, I looked it up to read the rest. This passage is amazing: **"We do, however, speak a message of wisdom among the mature, but not the wisdom of this age or of the rulers of this age, who are coming to nothing. No, we declare God's wisdom, a mystery that has been hidden and that God destined for our glory before time began.**

"... However, as it is written: 'What no eye has seen, what no ear has heard, and what no human mind has conceived' the things God has prepared for those who love him— these are the things God has revealed to us by his Spirit. ... This is what we speak, not in words taught us by human wisdom but in words taught by the Spirit, explaining spiritual realities with Spirit-taught words."

Thank you, Lord, for this insight! Later, I reflected on how we all occasionally view Biblical screenplays at the theaters. In this study,

I loved observing some personal 'screenplays' offered to me in my mind's eye. The Biblical accounts came alive!

"For the word of God is living and active, and sharper than any two-edge sword." (Hebrews 4:12 NASB)

Now I invite you to embark on this unique journey with me, observing our Lord in these incredible miracles and emulating Him in my own "Along the Way" testimonies.

---

*For the Kingdom of God is not a matter of talk
but of power. (1 Corinthians 4:20 NIV)*

INTRODUCTION
NOTES ON COMMUNING

If you have not begun to listen for the voice of the Lord in your journey, begin now. Confess not listening. Confess unbelief. Thank Him for His indwelling presence and His desire to speak to you. The Lord has impressed me that "communing" is the most valuable type of prayer. It is seeking the heart of the Lord, to know Him better! This is often the most neglected type of prayer, however.

Simply cry out. "Lord, open my ears today! Thank You! I am ready to listen!"

As I began attempting to listen to Him several years ago, it became an evolving process, but so worth the time and effort! It has been an amazing journey to learn to recognize His voice. To hear Him speak personally to me quickly took our relationship to incredible new heights. I realized if He would speak to ME personally, He would speak to anyone else who would pursue the same.

"My sheep listen to My voice; I know them, and they follow Me." (John 10:27)

Although He began to speak to me as soon as I began to ask questions, I wasn't hearing much at a time. In the beginning, I literally heard only one word a day! That is simply what I had requested, and I felt thrilled about it! The greater breakthrough came once I began to pick up a pen, ask a question, and wait to write His reply. He knew I was expectant (faith, not doubt) and that whatever He would say would not be quickly forgotten.

Someone passed on a suggestion to me that they had learned. It's a great question to use as a tool in communing with God:

Lord, is there anything You want to say to me today?

That question brought the most incredible shift in my communication with Father, Son, and Holy Spirit! Rather than just asking a specific question for wisdom and guidance about a matter, I began to open my heart to listen to anything *He* wanted to discuss. Learning to seek His heart in this way quickly became an accelerated path to enjoy a measure of downloads —a new depth of hearing and understanding the voice of the Holy Spirit—that I had not yet experienced!

I soon discovered that His favorite subject is LOVE! You, too, will be amazed at the readiness of the Lord to speak and teach you once you begin asking that question with pen in hand. You will find this question incorporated in the "Communion" section of each chapter of the accompanying *Study Journal for His Hands, My Feet*.

Gail Okuley
Allentown, Pennsylvania

"He wakens me morning by morning, wakens my ear to listen like one being taught." (Isaiah 50:4b)

EDITOR'S NOTE ABOUT QUOTATION STYLES

- Gail's internal dialogue: *italicized, without quotation marks.*
- All dialogue from the Lord or the Holy Spirit with Gail: ***Bold, italicized, no quotation marks,*** when it is in God's voice.
- All spoken dialogue from others: "In quotation marks."
- All scripture quotations: **"Bold, in quotation marks, punctuation."** (Reference in parentheses)

1
WATER TO WINE AT THE WEDDING
John 2:1-11

His mother stated the problem: "They have no wine."

Jesus rebuked her gently. *"My time has not yet come."*

His mother said to the servants, "Whatever He says to you, DO IT."

Six stone water pots sat nearby, holding about 20-30 gallons each. Jesus said, *"Fill the waterpots with water."* They filled them to the brim. Then He added, *"Draw some out now and take it to the master of the feast."*

When the master tasted it, he said to the bridegroom, "You have kept the best till now!"

The master did not know the origins of the wine; only the servants knew the miracle of the wine.

This beginning of signs Jesus did in Cana of Galilee and manifested His glory!

His disciples now truly believed in Him.

REVELATION, LORD?

I saw a youthful, joyful Jesus with medium brown curly hair, grinning and enjoying the party! He loved weddings! I saw Him very lighthearted and happy.

When His mother spoke, He had always listened. But she surprised Him today. His beloved, revered mother, who had faithfully nurtured Him, had been granted the honor and privilege of getting the revelation first, from His heavenly Father—*Now was the time!*

Mother spoke to Him. Though He disagreed, He listened.

As He turned and looked into the eyes of His mother, He saw the resolute eyes of His Father looking back, eyes of permission and commission!

Time seemed to stand still. Eternity had come to the village of Cana. As an obedient Servant, He quickly responded to the sudden quickening of His spirit.

Now was the time! No more waiting to minister!

He quietly spoke to the nearby servants, and an unnamed bride and groom enjoyed the first miraculous sign of His deity. Just as the unexpected honor had been granted Mary to speak the will of the Father, so now Jesus gave unexpected honor to some humble servants, the least of these. They would be the hands and feet for His first miracle. They would be the first witnesses, much like the humble shepherds had once been to herald the miraculous birth of Deity upon the earth.

Obedient servants drew some water from the brimming waterpots and reached for the shining silver pitcher for the wedding. Pounding fear in the troubled hearts changed to startling faith as wine and grace poured out bountifully for the master servant.

I saw the dark eyes of the master servant gleaming with delight as he held the cup and swallowed; the taste surpassed anything he had ever known! The glory of the Lord had come! All the servants watched in awe.

Jesus saw Mother beaming and knew the Father would be well pleased. The joyful celebration resounded into the heavenlies.

Grace shone brightly on the face of Yeshua.

ALONG THE WAY

For several years in the 90's, I eagerly led a women's Bible study in our home each week. A handful of friends from various churches loved our country setting amidst a huge canopy of evergreens in the rolling farmlands of Pennsylvania. We challenged each other to go deeper in our faith, and we learned to be vulnerable in sharing our weaknesses and struggles.

After a few months, Kay invited us to a day-long women's retreat at her church. We all decided it would be fun to go seek the Lord together and be refreshed.

Admittedly, I went with no expectations of anything unusual, but the Lord had other ideas. At the close of the morning session, the speaker invited ladies to come up who wanted to receive the baptism of the Holy Spirit.

Oh no!

My parents had raised my sister and I in a conservative denomination, in the small, rural town of Prairie Grove, Arkansas. We had never learned about that belief. This unexpected turn of events made me feel somewhat annoyed. To my surprise, all my friends immediately went forward to receive this ministry. After a few minutes, Kay turned around and motioned for me to come. I quickly shook my head *"No!"* and she turned back around. I felt relieved and safe. I comforted myself that we could soon break for lunch.

As soon as I shook my head, however, I heard the Lord's familiar voice in my head asking me, ***Are you saying "No" to Me?***

His question jarred me. *No, Lord, I didn't think so.*

His question piqued my curiosity, and my annoyance began to vanish. *But Lord, didn't I receive all the Holy Spirit in my salvation as a child,* I queried.

I heard nothing but uncomfortable silence.

I loved the fact that His voice had become so familiar over the last four or five years. But now He seemed to want something for me I had never considered. The need for the baptism of the Holy Spirit loomed before me. I sighed, feeling caught in a great mental debate.

Now what?

The Lord, this lady, and my friends, all apparently wanted me to open my heart in a new way today. Finally, I came to a great conclusion. *Okay, Lord, if you want her to pray over me for this, then I'll let her, but she must come back here to me!*

It sounded so spiritual and safe. In a while she finished praying for the 20-30 ladies up front. Then she made a bold statement to the rest of us. "I believe there are others who didn't choose to come up front, so I'm going to walk around now to pray for the rest of you!"

Her words hit my heart with a thud! As I looked around at the 50-60 of us who remained, I felt sure she would run out of time, especially since she had started way across the room.

Lunchtime couldn't come soon enough! I kept looking at my watch, but she seemed completely oblivious to time for some reason. I clung onto a slender thread of hope, *I'm sitting in the last row!*

Eventually, it happened. This petite woman with coal black hair and a kind face stood gazing squarely into mine. She posed the dreaded

---

Notes about the text

Following each biblical account will be the author's own miracle story or account relating uniquely to that miracle. The author's personal account will be titled, "Along the Way."

Following "Along the Way" you will find a "A Blessing" from the author to the reader.

question ever so sweetly, "Have you ever received the baptism of the Holy Spirit?"

I could not escape those piercing green eyes, or the compassion I heard in her voice. "I received Him when I was saved," I responded, in the only way I knew.

"May I pray over you?" Eternity seemed to stand still in Macungie, Pennsylvania just then.

I paused to look at all the ladies, thinking, *Could a hundred ladies be wrong today?*

I had heard the Lord's question. He had heard my answer that *she must come*, and she came.

I felt *Love* standing before me.

An unexpected shift in my openness to the Holy Spirit began taking place in my heart.

I heard my own hushed voice of surrender, "Yes."

The moment I spoke, she began praying over me and the entire room disappeared!

Despite my feet of clay, I began to see myself in a realm beyond the whole earthly scene below. I saw myself seated alone up in the heavenlies somewhere, feeling enveloped by His love. I appeared to be all alone, seated in a simple wooden chair, in the presence of my Prince of Peace. His unmistakable peace settled over me, in me, around me, permeating the very air I breathed. I knew: He was pouring out an amazing blessing for me.

I had no clue that the Lord wanted to pour His new wine into my ordinary clay pitcher that day.

I never knew what happened to anyone else in the room. I only knew that His presence touched the core of my being with refreshment, love, peace, and unending joy! The wonder of this new wine swirled around inside this vessel. Without a doubt, He had just released a greater blessing for me.

Later, I discovered something in the scriptures which was very confirming. Paul the apostle posed a question to some of Jesus' followers in Corinth, **"Did you receive the Holy Spirit when you believed?"** (Acts 19:1-2 NIV)

They answered, **"No, we have not even heard that there is a Holy Spirit."** Obviously, they needed to receive more of the Holy Spirit.

I love John the Baptist's famous description of our Lord in Matthew 3:11 NIV, **"After me comes One who is more powerful than I ... He will baptize you with the Holy Spirit and fire!"**

His tangible, supernatural peace became a hallmark in my life that I have come to relish daily. Amazingly, the Holy Spirit has fresh fire and anointing for our weary vessels countless times in our lives. Through the years, I have learned to keep myself in a receiving position. *Fill my cup Lord, again and again! Baptize me anew and afresh today!*

Though the Spirit never leaves us, He certainly has times of fresh anointing and empowerment for us, subsequent to salvation.

Let Mary speak her words of wisdom to your heart today, **"Whatever He says to you, do it!"** (John 2:5)

A BLESSING

I bless you to receive the new wine of Jesus' anointing, love, and miraculous power. May the newness of His lavish love saturate your heart today, as you drink the new wine He has prepared for His precious bride. I bless you with expectancy to soar to new heights as you go deeper in the Spirit. I bless you with bountiful grace to simply say "YES" to the Holy Spirit today!

Note: See page 331 for a sample chapter from *His Hands, My Feet Study Journal*. Pause and commune with the Lord there for a few moments. Perhaps the Holy Spirit will lead you to journal your way through these miracles.

2

'UNCLEAN SPIRIT' IN THE SYNAGOGUE

Mark 1:21-28, Luke 4:31-37

Jesus went to Capernaum and immediately went into the synagogue to teach. His authority astonished everyone. A man in the synagogue with an unclean spirit cried out to Him: **"Let us alone, Jesus of Nazareth! Did you come to destroy us, Holy One of God?"**

Jesus rebuked the spirit, **"Be quiet and come out of him."** The man convulsed, screeching loudly, and the spirit left. Amazement filled the room. **"What is this? What new doctrine is this, who commands unclean spirits with authority, and they obey him?"**

His fame spread throughout the region of Galilee.

REVELATION, LORD?

I saw Him standing very still and resolute, in the place He had been teaching, open scroll in His hand. Turning His attention briefly to the man and speaking quietly but firmly to rebuke the foe, He was not concerned or threatened.

He simply put a stop to the commotion with His few words and blessed the man in need with deliverance. However, His words stirred the people watching. His rebuke ended the teaching lesson with a demonstration of the Spirit's power to confirm His message. This report went throughout the entire region.

I began to see Him unexpectedly again, in a secondary vision, this time standing there solemnly, facing ME, and speaking this scripture to me: **"Who is and Who was and Who is to come"** (Revelation 1:4).

The Lord spoke to me, **I have come to your temple. I am here. I came immediately to indwell you. You have My presence, My wisdom as the Teacher, My Word—the Living Word, My authority, My power. You have all you need to do these "greater works," greater in that I am multiplied exponentially throughout My body. If you know this, if you can understand this truth, you can do the same thing! Do not be alarmed at unclean spirits that will come to disrupt and try to take the glory. Silence the foe and set the captives free!**

What the enemy intends for evil, I intend for good (paraphrasing Genesis 50:20). **Do you understand?**

Yes, Lord.

There will be opposition, but...greater is He who is in you! (1 John 4:4b).

ALONG THE WAY

After being married 15 years, we made a major move from the deep south of Mississippi to the picturesque rolling hills of Pennsylvania. It had been our fifteenth move, encompassing eight states! We loved our first home in the country, and I loved being a stay-at-home Mom. But after a couple of years, I realized I needed to broaden my interactions with others somehow, hopefully in ministry.

I heard about the need for volunteers at the Pregnancy Center (now Pregnancy Resource Center) and my heart responded. So off I went, stepping out of my comfort zone. The training classes amazed me, covering many aspects of the counseling scene where I would soon be activated. To help women make the best choice, at such a critical junction in life, would be a great privilege.

The director herself began mentoring me once the classes wrapped up. She finally decided the time had come for me to sit in on some of her clients' sessions. Most the women came with desperate needs, not only for guidance, but sensitivity, compassion, and support. I realized they felt much further out of their comfort zone than I. The Lord's deep compassion stirred in my heart, as I watched and listened to those troubled hearts seeking difficult answers.

During the first week, I watched with astonishment as my trainer led a teenaged girl to Jesus quite effortlessly. The girl had simply asked a question about prayer, and somehow, we all wound up at the cross! I knew right then, I wanted to get to know this lady better! As it turned out, I discovered she would soon become my neighbor, building a new house out in the country not far from us. The hand of the Lord was clearly working to connect us. I was excited at the thought of having such a godly friend in the neighborhood.

Soon, the completion date arrived. Our new friendship grew deeply, as we sat in her living room watching the geese meander around their huge sparkling pond surrounded by a beautiful grove of trees. Slowly, her testimony emerged, between the geese honking and the hot tea brewing. I had no idea the roundabout journey through which this powerhouse woman had come!

She had found the Lord after many years of searching through quite a few other religions, such as Buddhism and eastern religions. After several years of searching truth, she finally found it and accepted Jesus as her Savior.

That same year, she decided she should put a stop to her long-standing nicotine habit. Although she attempted to quit countless times, nothing worked. She cried out for *help* in the Name of Jesus!

God heard her desperate cry and something unimaginable happened! A dark eerie spirit suddenly went out from her! She realized it was a spirit of nicotine! She had just been delivered by her Lord! Now she truly felt *free*!

That old bondage had just been broken. With it, the weight of oppression had been released. She could now enjoy a new life of freedom and power in the Name of Jesus.

How faithful our Lord is to set the captives free! **"He who the Son sets free, is free indeed!"** (John 8:36)

I felt very privileged that she had chosen to be vulnerable enough to share her deliverance testimony with me. Countless times I would share it later in our ministry at the Lehigh County Jail, in Allentown. So often the women would ask for prayer to stay free of drugs upon release. But most of the time they expressed that they "could not *wait* to start smoking again as soon as they got out!"

"It's not that bad," they assured me.

My friend's testimony helped give many of them a new understanding that to open any door to spirits of addiction would give them free reign to work in other areas too. This helped them to understand they must keep ALL the dark doors shut!

Though it's true a Christian cannot be possessed by the devil (since the Holy Spirit possesses us) we can give open doors to spirits of darkness that grant them access to defile our temples. When we embrace areas of darkness that rob the abundant life the Lord intends for His children, we invite oppression and powerlessness.

"For God has not given us a spirit of fear, but of power and of love and of a sound mind." (2 Timothy 1:7)

"It is for freedom that Christ has set us free. Stand firm, then, and do not let yourselves be burdened again by a yoke of slavery." (Galatians 5:1 NIV)

A BLESSING

I bless you with grace to recognize any areas of darkness that need to go. I bless you with willingness and wisdom to shut down all doors of darkness. I bless you with being filled fully with His great light. I bless you to be such a powerful light bearer that you will be able to help others to be set free.

Our Father loves a mother's prayers!

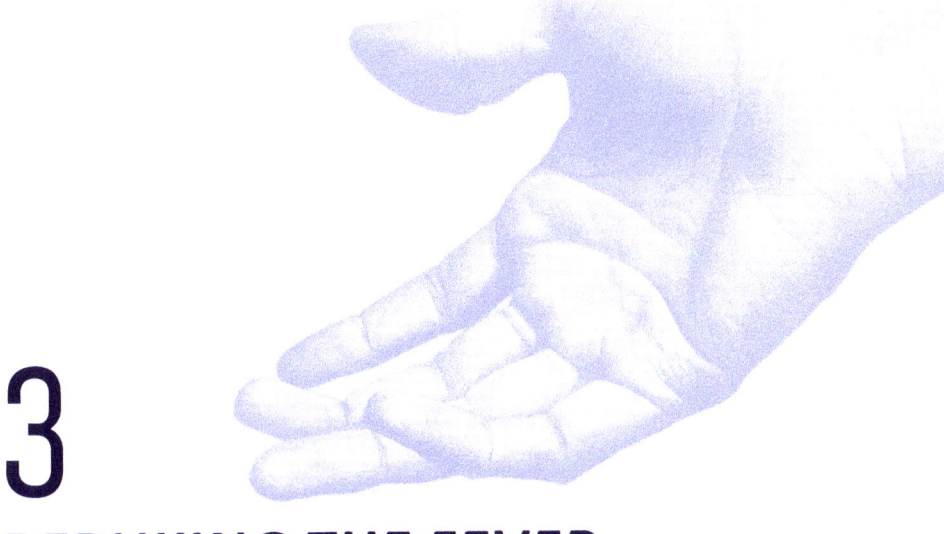

3
REBUKING THE FEVER
Matthew 8:14-17, Mark 1:29-31, Luke 4:38-39

After departing the synagogue, where Jesus cast out the demon, he went to Peter and Andrew's house with James and John. Immediately Peter told Jesus that his mother-in-law lay sick in bed with a high fever. Jesus stood over her, *rebuked the fever*, took her by the hand, and lifted her up.

She promptly began to serve them.

REVELATION, LORD?

I could see Jesus taking her by the hand with His powerful eyes of compassion arresting her in love and releasing her body and soul from pain.

The Lord spoke to me: **When she took My hand, and healing flowed into her, she unknowingly released her beloved 'son' into My hands, as we would soon depart on a journey. I let her know this One could be trusted. She saw My peace.**

Her heart would be united with our cause; another mother's heart would join my own mother's heart at the Throne, interceding for their sons.

Our Father loves a mother's prayers!

ALONG THE WAY

During a cold, blustery winter months in Pennsylvania, our 8-year-old succumbed to the flu, battling fever, chills, and nausea. Normally he loved sleeping up in his loft bed, with his new desk below, but making it down the ladder with a sick stomach proved to be a challenge. So, he had camped out in his sleeping bag until this bad bug would disappear.

Like any parent, when one of our three boys fell sick, we would run to the doctor, get some meds, pray a brief prayer, and hope for the best. But lately, my faith had been challenged to believe for more. Now, after his last bout with nausea, I had parked myself out on the couch alone, pleading with the Lord for relief. *Lord, please intervene! Take this sickness from him!* At that time, I had more faith to pray boldly by myself than in the presence of the sick one.

The Lord's quick reply startled me, **Get some oil and anoint him.**

Oil? Really Lord? His words stunned me.

I recalled the verses in James 5:14-15 (NIV), **"Is anyone among you sick? Let them call the elders of the church to pray over them and anoint them with oil in the name of the Lord. And the prayer offered in faith will make the sick person well; the Lord will raise them up."**

Did I qualify to anoint him? It seemed like such a shaky limb to go out on with my son. But I knew the Lord had spoken; I would never have come up with that idea. I had never known anyone (at that time) who practiced anointing people, except for one man, and his faith seemed a little too radical for me.

The longer I sat there, I knew I had to do it. *Wait, I don't have any anointing oil!* Maybe I could get out of this on a technicality! But the

Lord graciously impressed me that the olive oil in my kitchen would be fine. Oh.

I stalled a few more long minutes, hoping that faith and courage would arise, and put a stop to the debate still swirling in my head. *Okay, here we go ...*

Off I went in search of my olive tree blessing, pressed compactly into a bottle somewhere. Hmmmm, I found it there waiting for me between the baking soda and cinnamon. *Are you sure about this, Lord?* Bottle in hand, I let out a deep sigh and ventured cautiously into my son's campout scene. As I knelt, I began to explain the concept of anointing to our young son, trying to find words to convince us both.

Why is this so hard? Lord, you MUST help me!

My son's quick response interrupted my relentless questioning, "Ok, Mom, sure!" He sounded both desperate and hopeful. Clearly, his childlike faith sprouted more quickly than mine.

Thank you, Lord, I said, smiling faintly.

As I put the oil on his forehead and briefly prayed, he looked at me with eyes that suddenly grew very wide; his pale face covered in astonishment. I quit praying.

"What's the matter?" I asked.

"Mom, I really felt the power of God when you did that!" his eight-year-old voice sounded so bold!

About an hour later, I saw him dart quickly into the bathroom again. As I walked in, I expected to see him green with sickness. But instead, he looked up at me with a big grin!

"Mom, I thought I would throw up again, but I remembered your prayer, and just rebuked it in Jesus Name! It all just stopped! And my stomach feels pretty good again."

The Lord had healed him! I knew he would never forget God's sweet intervention, and neither would I. All his other symptoms left within the hour.

Thank you, Lord, for pouring out your loving grace through my simple obedience, despite my faltering faith.

"Truly I tell you, if you have faith as small as a mustard seed, you can say to this mountain, 'Move from here to there,' and it will move. Nothing will be impossible for you." (Matthew 17:20-21 NIV)

ANOTHER SON. . .

A few years later, one of our other sons became ill with fever and flu as a teenager. As I prayed over him on his bed, he opened his eyes in barely a squint, looking puzzled. "Mom, did you see anything just now when you prayed?"

"No, I didn't. Why?"

He hesitated and then explained he had seen some type of eerie red being with big muscles staring right at his face, with piercing eyes of hatred! He also said he could hardly open his eyes, but he knew he had to tell me.

What! I knew it was demonic, but how could that be? None of us had ever seen such a thing, especially in our home. We were both a bit unnerved. The Lord loves to stretch us.

Immediately, the Lord began to show us what to do. He reminded me of Matthew 12:29 (NIV), **"How can anyone enter a strong man's house and carry off his possessions unless he first ties up the strong man? Then he can plunder his house."**

The source of this fever became quite clear to us. We realized that we must use our authority to bind up the strong man, so we could stop this attack on his body.

"Yes, do it, Mom!" Our son sounded weak and desperate.

I prayed to bind up the strong man, and remembered to loose the healing power of Jesus, according to Matthew 18:18. It states, **"Whatever you bind on earth will be bound in heaven, and whatever you loose on earth will be loosed in heaven."**

After I finished, our son opened his eyes normally and let out a big sigh, taking some deep breaths. "Mom, I could hardly speak or breathe. It felt like something was pressing on my chest!"

I didn't know what to say.

We agreed the Lord wanted to teach us things we hadn't known about physical attacks on our bodies and how we must always take our authority over sickness.

MY TURN...

During another cold and flu season, I, myself, woke up sick with flu symptoms one Monday morning. All day long I kept running to the bathroom for every reason imaginable. I felt miserable the entire day and could think about nothing else.

By that night I was wiped out. Around 8:00 I thought to myself, *I just want to fall asleep for the night now, and hopefully wake up feeling better in the morning!* But since I had dozed off and on throughout the day, I realized I might not be able to go to sleep till late. I tried to shake that unwelcome thought.

The Lord decided He needed to help me process things a bit differently. He said something I had never heard before: **Put your spirit in control of your body!**

I had heard no teaching at all about that at that point.

What do You mean? How do I do that?

I did not hear anything else. So, I began to start praising Him, trying to activate myself on a spiritual level. I knew I had only been thinking about my physical body all day.

Thank you, Lord that You are here. You are my ever-present help in time of trouble! I praise you for your love. Thank you that this too shall pass. Thank you that "nothing is too difficult for you!"

I tried to keep my words going as quickly as possible, not to think about my misery. After just a couple of minutes, I paused to take a deep breath. *Wait a minute! I feel better. In fact, I didn't feel bad at all!*

I suddenly realized that my horrible symptoms had vanished!

How can this be? I decided I better keep my praise going, so the symptoms wouldn't come back. Soon, I fell fast asleep and slept all night.

In the morning, I felt completely well, except for one degree of temperature. Even my energy returned, enabling me to function normally, once more. This same thing continued all week. I felt fine, except for that one degree of fever.

On Friday morning when I woke up, I knew immediately the fever had left. *That's strange. Lord, why did that fever linger those three days?*

The Spirit let me know: **That is how long all your symptoms would have continued, if you hadn't started praying and praising Me by faith, while you still felt sick that night.**

Oh wow! Thank you for my first lesson in training my spirit to take dominion over my flesh!

He would teach me much more about this as time went on.

ANOTHER BOUT WITH SICKNESS...

In fall of 2023, I wound up with a second run of Covid, after having one five-day bout back in 2020. Both were mild, thankfully, since I took heavy doses of my heavenly meds: the Word of God, praise and hope, in place of despair. Prior to this, He had been helping me understand **Galatians 3:13** on a deeper level than before. **"Christ redeemed us from the curse of the law by becoming a curse for us..."**

Despite the basic truth of this verse that we embrace, most of us as Christians, are still living under the curse. The curse for Adam and Eve's sin would be death. Since sickness and disease are part of the death camp, they both clearly came as a result of the fall. Since we are now born of the second Adam, not the first, we are in essence born-again, free of the curse. He is helping me to shift my mindset in order to walk in this light. It's called "good news!"

My symptoms this time were a mild cough, low fever and very low energy. On the second morning of this attack, I forced myself into the shower, though I felt too weak to actually stand up the whole time. I hoped it would help revive me. The Lord had more in mind. He employed **Genesis 50:20** and took what the enemy intended for evil and used it for good. While the water splashed some refreshment on my weakened flesh, the Lord gave me an assignment: ***While you are in this place of weakness, write a decree to rise up OUT of sickness!***

Oh!

As always, the Lord comes up with some great ideas I would never think of myself.

Yes, Lord, I will.

In a few minutes, I settled onto the couch with my Comforter and began to write whatever He gave me. Soon, with a new power-packed decree in hand, I began to speak it out over myself. I felt so weak however that I had to stop twice, to take a break and rest a few minutes, before even finishing that one page of verses. *Whew!*

I am very happy to report that by bedtime, my energy had returned to about 50 percent and the next day it was up to 90 percent. Despite my faith, He shocked me with such fast results! Wow, the power of the Word is incredible!

Please see the Decree on the following page.

Implement this Decree by reading it *out loud* over yourself the next time you are struggling with sickness or weakness.

A DECREE OUT OF SICKNESS:

UP, up, up, out of the pit of weakness and sickness, I will now ARISE, in Jesus Name.

Your Kingdom come! Your will be done in this earthen vessel, as it is in heaven!

I bless my spirit to dominate over my flesh in complete ALIGNMENT with heaven, according to your word in Philippians 3:20, that I am now a citizen of heaven.

Behold! You are doing a new thing in me today.

Today I am breaking agreement with old mindsets of weakness of the flesh and aligning fully with my complete RESTORATION, as in the beginning, before the fall of man.

Thank you for taking the curse of sickness and disease upon Yourself for me (Galatians 3:13). I now appropriate my freedom.

Thank you for being the lifter of my head.

The OLD must GO, and the NEW must COME!

I believe. I receive my blessings of grace, grace, grace.

No weapons of sickness formed against me shall prosper.

I am now free to rise UP on wings of eagles—to walk and not grow weary, to run and not faint, to soar high and higher in the power of Your Spirit.

I have fixed my eyes upon You, Lord Jesus, as my Deliverer.

This daughter/son has cried out and you have heard my plea and delivered me from all my troubles. (Psalm 34:6)

Prince of Peace, reign here in my body, soul, spirit.

The God of Peace shall now crush the enemy of LIFE underneath my feet.

Hallelujah! Victory is mine!

THANK YOU! As I decree a thing, it shall be established. (Job 22:28)

Anything else Lord?

Praise Me! Praise Me in the storm.
Let no unwholesome words proceed out of your mouth, only praise!
Rejoice always!

Thank you, Lord, the victory is won. IT IS FINISHED!

Let's rise up and walk in our God-give authority over sickness, starting with our own bodies! We can and we must! As we do so for ourselves, we will have even greater faith to do so for others.

A BLESSING

I bless you to hear the voice of the Lord leading and guiding you to release His power in new ways. I bless you with growing, bold, obedient faith to walk in the healing of minds, hearts, and bodies at home, or wherever you are. I bless you to *fight the good fight of faith, and win!* (1 Timothy 6:12)

He wanted to help them more than they could ever know.

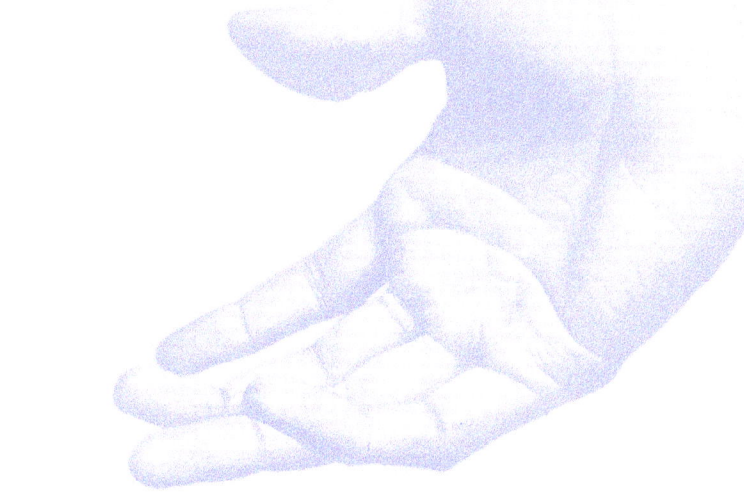

4
CITY SEEKS JESUS AT PETER'S HOUSE

Matthew 8:16-17, Mark 1:32-34, Luke 4:40-41

The whole city had gathered at Peter's door as He prayed for Peter's mother-in-law. They brought Him many to be healed. They witnessed demons being cast out with a word, crying, *"You are CHRIST, the Son of God!"* He did not permit them to speak any further.

He laid hands on the sick and healed them all!

Matthew 8:17 tells us, **"This was to fulfill what was spoken through the prophet Isaiah, He took our infirmities and bore our sicknesses."**

REVELATION, LORD?

I saw the Lord sitting in Peter's living room, near the old wooden door, with a gentle smile playing upon His face. His eyes twinkled and His head cocked to the side as He listened to the increasingly loud clamor of voices out in the dusty yard. He had walked amid humanity for so long, as an unknown man whose identity had been veiled. How it pleased Him to know the Father had brought them here to Him now, just outside the door.

Finally, the world had come! He wanted to help them more than they could ever know. Joy and compassion eagerly greeted them at the door. The disciples curiously followed Him out the door, where each cry was met with His power and love.

None who came left the same! Those same voices that had sounded so desperate now created a symphony of joy and praise as they celebrated each transforming touch by this Miracle Man.

The Lord gazed heavenward with glee and gratitude, mouthing His own words of praise to the Father above.

ALONG THE WAY

I stopped in my tracks one day, reading a passage that instantly convicted me.

"I pray that out of His glorious riches He may strengthen you with <u>power</u> through His Spirit in your inner being, so that Christ may <u>dwell in your hearts</u> through faith" (Ephesians 3:16-17 NIV).

The words emphasized sliced into my heart. I had a sermon note written in the margin of my Bible that said: Dwell means complete freedom to act. My piercing admission was *No Lord! Your power is NOT seen in my life, and I now see it's because You do not have complete freedom to act in me. Help me!*

That conviction plunged me into a nine-month Bible study for myself, looking up all the "power" verses in the Bible. This proved such a slow process in those years before online search engines had come into fruition. Finally at the end of my long deliberations, I heard someone quote an old pastor who said, "What we need is not greater power, but deeper death!"

Oh no! My nine months of seeking more power had been a set-up for that moment! It was time to die to my flesh and let Jesus take over.

I remembered that Jesus once said to his disciples, **"Whoever wants to be my disciple must deny themselves and take up their cross and follow me. For whoever wants to save their life will lose it, but whoever loses their life for me will find it"** (Matthew 16:24-25 NIV)

That's so simple, right?! Nevertheless, things began to shift for me as I took this new approach. I knew I must get out of the way and let Jesus do it! My new mindset became much more expectant about His power working in my life.

The next week, I attended a spiritual awakening conference in Gettysburg, Pennsylvania. From the first moment of the first prayer, the power of the Spirit noticeably permeated the air. I knew I would go home as a different person.

Each of the five speakers shared with incredible anointing. My heart clung to every word. One speaker especially gripped me: Dr. Henry Blackaby. He would later write the *Experiencing God* Bible study, which has awakened many lives around the world. He had been raised in Canada with pioneering parents who boldly planted churches where no one else would go. His filter for his entire life became radically entrenched at a very young age, for an unshakable faith, and a continual hunger for God.

That night, he led us through a powerful time together that I had never experienced before, a "solemn assembly" as mentioned in Joel 1:14. He walked us through a time of corporate confession and repentance. I remember confessing out loud, "I want to release all that hinders!"

Things in my heart shifted. I felt as if I had been sitting up in bed for about a year, rubbing my eyes, trying to wake up, while plowing through that study on "power." At the conference, the Lord took me by the shoulders, pulled me out of bed, stood me up on the floor, and said, ***There! You're awake!***

I have been awake and hungry ever since! On the way home, I reveled in all those overdue heart changes, in complete awe of what had happened. Suddenly, the Lord dropped a new bombshell in my lap. I can still see the scene before me on Interstate 78-E, between Harrisburg and Allentown, when I heard, **Start praying for revival in the Lehigh Valley!**

Me?

I had never prayed for a whole city before, much less a whole *region*. Our tri-city area at that time boasted a population of about 800,000, encompassing Allentown, Bethlehem, Easton and the surrounding 62 towns. As soon as He gave me that word about revival, however I knew it meant *revival was coming!* Hallelujah!

As a result, within about six weeks, the Lord led my husband Gordon and I to start a prayer movement to pray for revival in our area. The Lehigh Valley Coalition of Prayer Warriors drew many seasoned intercessors to us, like moths to the light! The Lord prompted us to enlist people to pray once a week together with a prayer partner and to also meet corporately once a month. Surprisingly so, the Lord creatively led me to a new prayer partner every month, as He had prompted us to suggest to everyone.

About three months later, I sat in our prayer room at church with a new intercessor friend, who happened to be a female truck driver. I relished the thought that there were countless prayers crisscrossing our state, strewn about by this hidden gem. About halfway through the hour of prayer, we heard an interrupting knock at the door by our church secretary. She apologized for interrupting but said an unusual phone call just came from a local prison minister, desperately seeking two ladies to help him. He needed them to meet him at the women's prison in about an hour! The two women he thought he had lined up had just cancelled, and his visiting evangelist from Texas didn't want to forego the meeting.

My startled friend and I looked at each other, totally caught off guard by the situation. "They want us to go to prison right now?"

We had never been in a prison or had any thoughts of going. My prayer partner quickly declined. I paused to contemplate the situation. We had just been praying for new doors to open for us to impact the city! Being called to pray for revival, doesn't that include the prison? I had my answer.

"I'll go," I offered. I already felt stretched, just saying that!

The secretary standing in the doorway matched me with, "I'll shut down the office and go with you!"

We bravely smiled at each other, trying to hide our true thoughts of *what are we doing?!*

Off we went. We had no idea what to expect. The pastor said he called us because ours was the closest church, only about a half mile away. The Lord had directed him to *us*—out of all the churches in the area.

The visiting evangelist with his strong Texas accent gave a stirring message and kept the women's hearts and eyes engaged. We saw many tears. He spoke with gentleness and compassion. God was moving. The eight ladies in our circle that day seemed hungry, hurt, and needing help. The Lord broke both of our hearts for those wounded and broken ones.

Afterwards, as we talked on the way home, we both decided we wanted to keep going in to meet with the ladies! Later that day, we made the call back to the pastor and asked if we could go in every week to lead a Bible study ourselves. He wasn't expecting that response!

"Are you sure? You might get burned out going every week. Why don't you go in once or twice a month?"

"No," we told him, "we wanted to build relationships with the women, so we knew what we needed to do." He was delighted and consented with a resounding, "Yes!"

Little did we know we had just started their women's prison ministry! He did not tell us that for several years.

In the 30 years since then, healings of all kinds happened among the women. One of my greatest blessings has been seeing light and hope being born on their faces. Some of their stories will unfold in this book. I have looked heavenward in thanksgiving many times.

It felt like the prison came knocking at my door that day long ago!

Over time, the Lord gave my husband and I many more directives to impact our tri-city region, such as prayer rallies, and other dedicated events, whether weekly, quarterly, or annually.

Ironically, in another twenty years He led us to initiate Adopt-A-Street in our region. My husband adopted I-78 in daily prayer, the very place where I first heard the mandate to pray for revival.

Early signs of revival have begun!

A BLESSING

I bless you with the courage to answer the wide-open door to the world, knowing you have what the world needs. I bless you with the willingness to die and let the power of God break forth freely to bless those He brings your way. I bless you to GO today where you have never been.

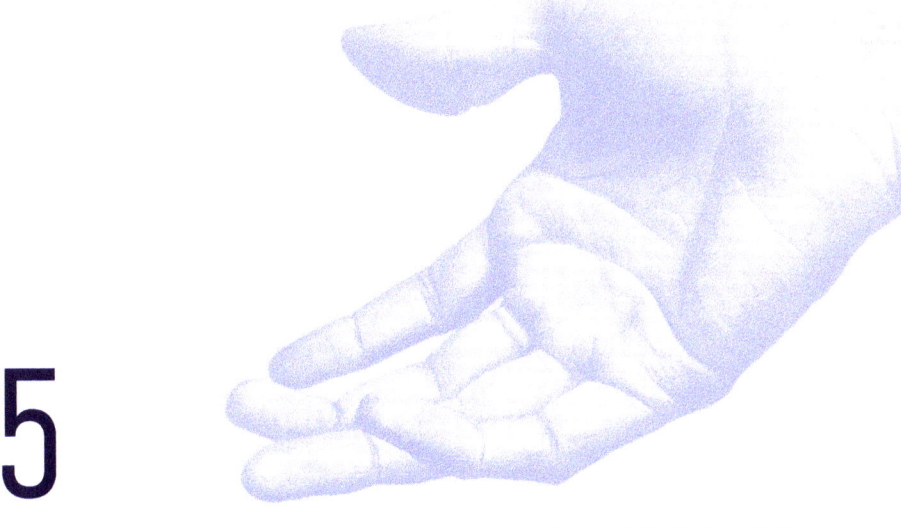

5
MIRACULOUS CATCH OF FISH
Luke 5:1-11

Multitudes pressed in eagerly around Jesus at the Lake of Gennesaret to hear Him expounding the Scriptures. While speaking, the Lord noticed two boats left there by some fishermen, now washing their nets. Soon, He decided to climb into one of the boats, asking its owner to put out a little way from the shore. Simon obliged, and the Lord sat down, teaching the multitude from the boat. When He had finished speaking, He said to Simon, **"Launch out into the deep and let down your nets for a catch."**

Simon objected, "We have toiled all night and caught nothing! Nevertheless, at Your word, I will (go out and) let down the net."

They caught such a vast number of fish that their net began to break! Excitedly they signaled to their partners, James and John, to come and help them. Both boats began to sink, being filled with so many fish! What an incredible catch!

When Simon saw it, he fell at Jesus' knees, pleading, "Depart from me, for I am a sinful man, O Lord!"

Jesus said to Simon, **"Do not be afraid. From now on you will catch men!"**

When they brought their boats to land, they forsook all and followed Him.

REVELATION, LORD?

I saw Simon sitting there in the boat, with his weathered complexion, clad in a weathered garment, waiting quietly as Jesus spoke to the multitude. The fisherman didn't care for such a trying interruption in his day, but the words pricked his interest. He cast a look of skepticism and veiled annoyance, as he soon heard the Lord's instruction to launch out into the deep. With unmasked weariness, he turned to dissuade this Man.

However, he surprised himself as he pondered the Man's words; his protest suddenly melted into acquiescence. How did that happen? he wondered, as they set sail once again. A few furtive looks from his brother Andrew marked his displeasure as well.

Those transparent looks gave me a deep glimpse into their hearts, which seemed to be what the Lord wanted to highlight. He said, **I'm showing you My measure of grace flowing from the beginning. No faith had stirred yet, but the Father had made a choice and a calling, for these ordinary, unqualified men to follow Me. They would soon become world changers.**

To this point, the two seasoned fishermen had no understanding of anything beyond the sea and the fish market. Their everyday lives and toilsome labors in Galilee had not prepared them to expect anything beyond the ordinary.

As Jesus stood before them, they barely managed to speak with curt politeness to accommodate Him. This unexpected intruder and His lofty words to the people on the beach would hopefully be on His way soon!

Nothing prepared them for the day that greatness and notoriety chose to call their names.

Grace had come to sit in the boat.
Grace summoned some fish.
Grace looked Simon, a "blind man,"
in the eyes and saw a mighty fisher of men.

The scales fell off some eyes that day, as skepticism changed to fear and awe, until finally the new light of surrender emerged!

And so, Simon and Andrew left it all.

ALONG THE WAY

Our entire family had been mesmerized by the book, *Is That Really You, God?*[2] The author, Loren Cunningham, began the book with an amazing vision from the Lord, which led to the birth of Youth With A Mission (YWAM), a powerful compassion and evangelism ministry, founded in the '60s. In fact, our three boys were so captivated by the remarkable stories of faith and miracles, that they hoped to all go together on their first ever mission trip that summer, in Texas and Mexico, led by YWAM. Our oldest son, however, had recently graduated from Liberty University, and surpassed their age limit. But, with our bold prayers and their unexpected favor, YWAM granted special permission for them to venture forth together as brothers.

They could not say enough about the trip! Three months later, we shipped the two oldest boys off together to a five-month Discipleship Training School (DTS). Our middle son just graduated from high school, so both boys found themselves at life's crossroads, at the same time. Their sense of adventure soared high aboard the Anastasis Mercy Ship, the flagship of their fleet. Their exotic itinerary underscored their interest in missions: Belgium, Canary Islands, and Africa!

---

[2] Cunningham, Loren. (2001). *Is that really you, God? Hearing the Voice of God*. YWAM Publishing.

One of the most amazing testimonies shared in the YWAM book happened on that very ship, a few years prior. At that time, Mercy Ships needed quite a large amount to complete the refurbishing of the Anastasis to become seaworthy again. Extra funds were also needed to equip the ship medically to serve the poor with free surgeries. After a few months of financial losses, their next financial deadline was fast approaching.

As volunteers were painstakingly doing some painting and various repairs that day, the locals on the beach suddenly began yelling something in their local dialect they couldn't understand. All the people on the beach where it was docked were excitedly jumping around and pointing to the waves. The ship volunteers quickly ran out to see what was happening. An unbelievable scene met their eyes!

Hundreds and hundreds of good-sized fish had started jumping out of the water and landing on the beach! Everyone in the entire area stopped what they were doing and ran to fill buckets and barrels with this incredible supernatural blessing from the Lord. The fish market paid everyone very well. The locals and the YWAM workers all received lavish rewards. God had the whole town abuzz with excitement!

The encouragement and joy to see God's mighty hand of favor was equally rewarding for some weary workers and crew on the old ship!

"Jesus Christ is the same yesterday, today, and forever." (Hebrews 13:8)

What He did long ago, He may choose to do again, anytime, and anywhere! Our boys loved going to grow and serve on the very ship that had received such an outpouring of love from the heart of our faithful God! After three months of training, they spent two months off the ship backpacking through Ghana, evangelizing, speaking, doing dramas, visiting orphans, and serving in various compassion ministries.

Working on the final edit for this book, the Lord reminded me of a childhood conversation I had with one of the boys who had gone on the ship. I believe it took place when he was about 10. As we drove home silently in our van that day, he unexpectedly asked, "Mom, what does it mean to be a 'fisher of men?'"

I explained it to him, and asked, "Why?"

"That's what the Lord just told me I would be!"

Little did we know that Mexico and Africa would become some significant places where he would begin casting his nets, on a ship called the *Anastasis*, Greek for "resurrection." What a fitting name for a vessel of personal and global transformation and restoration. On their return, they both said it was the best five months of their lives.

A BLESSING

I bless you with a willing heart to let the Lord climb into your boat, to listen and learn like Simon, and follow the Lord with great courage! I bless you with readiness to heed His every call, to go wherever He leads you, as a fisher of men! I bless you with grace to pull together with the body of Christ, so your nets will not break!

I was looking for him. . .

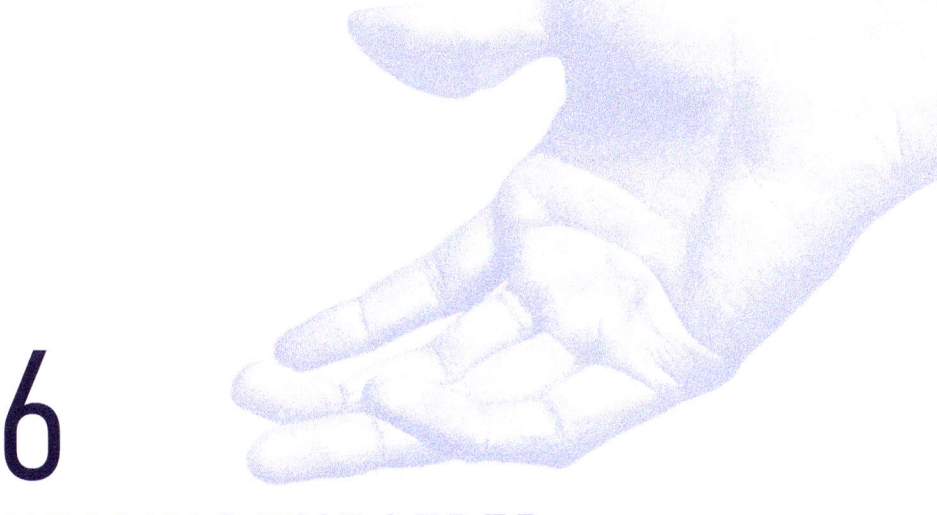

6
HEALING THE LEPER
Matthew 8:1- 4, Mark 1:40-45, Luke 5:12-14

The leper cried out to Jesus, **"Lord, if you are willing, you can make me clean!"**

He dropped to his knees, with his face to the ground. Filled with compassion, Jesus, reached out to touch him, saying, ***"I am willing! Be clean!"*** Immediately, the man's restoration came forth.

"Don't tell anyone but go show yourself to the priest," Jesus instructed him.

Instead, he went out and freely spread the news so that Jesus could no longer enter a town openly. He stayed outside in lonely places. Yet, the people still came to him from everywhere.

REVELATION, LORD?

I simply saw Jesus, with lots of brown curly hair, walking towards a crowd, turning his head from side to side.

Then He spoke to me about this scene: ***I was looking for him; the Father had shown him to me! I saw him, then he saw Me. We were ready. Faith came seeking its fulfillment in Me.***

I saw him clean; I touched him, and he became clean.

Wow! As I heard and saw this, I thought of Jesus' words later to His disciples, ***I only do what I see the Father do, and say what I hear the Father say*** (John 5:19 NIV). The King appeared upon the earth, largely unseen. But here, His subject had bowed low before Him, and His Kingdom manifested on the earth, for a moment, at that place. The power of God flowed freely in a most impossible situation.

ALONG THE WAY

Our intimate church of about sixty people felt the excitement of anticipation in the air, as an overflowing crowd showed up on a crisp, fall Wednesday night. A local pastor of a much larger congregation surprised us when he called to suggest a special speaker from India could come speak for us.

After listening to snatches of Pastor Harry Gomes' testimony, our pastor readily agreed. We eagerly awaited to hear this converted Hindu man share his heart.

A handful of our intercessors gathered early that night to join in prayer with our guest. As we watched him striding up our long sidewalk, someone remarked they hoped he would use the Bible, as he was carrying nothing. Cell phones and digital Bibles had not yet arrived on the scene.

As Pastor Gomes began sharing his story, we learned that he had been highly successful for many years in the business arena. However, at the peak of his flourishing business, something devastating happened that shut down all his business dealings. He contracted a serious skin disease that created large white blotches, marring his usual dark complexion. After consulting numerous doctors and expending his income to no avail, he gradually found himself isolated at home, in bed, depressed. He didn't know what to do; he had nowhere to turn.

Soon the barrage of calls started from creditors, as all his business ventures began to fail. He had never faced such losses, financially, physically, and emotionally. No laws in his country allowed for bankruptcy; they simply took you to jail for non-payment! His outlook couldn't have felt more hopeless.

One night in this deep dark pit, a bright light awakened him in his room. As he opened his eyes, he saw a shining man of pure light and love, walking into his room. *Is this really happening?*

He didn't know, and it didn't matter! He felt amazing love and power emanating from the Light. The Shining One spoke to him, **I am Jesus. I am here to help you!**

Those power-packed words took his breath away.

The Man had a message for him: **I want you to call all your creditors and ask them to give you six months to pay back what you owe.**

"How can I repay them?!" He was finally able to respond to the voice of the Light. "My businesses all failed, and I owe millions of dollars!"

The Voice continued to speak, **I am going to give you a new business.**

"What is it?" He ventured to ask.

Chemicals

"Chemicals?! I don't know anything about that."

I do! The voice of the calm, peaceful Shining One stated.

Our Hindu friend continued to object. "But I can't even work because I have this terrible skin disease!"

It's ok. I am going to heal you! With that, the Light of Love disappeared from his sight.

Peace remained however, and the man quickly fell into a deep sleep.

The next morning when he woke, he was overtaken again by the surreal emotions from his nighttime visitation. *Was it just a strange dream, or did it really happen?* He had no idea.

Just then, he looked down and couldn't believe what he saw. His skin looked totally healthy, once again! The white blotches had disappeared completely!

It was real! It was all real!

He didn't know what to do next but decided to obey the Voice that had healed him. He must make those calls.

As he began calling his creditors, he felt sure that none of them would give him any grace for the six-months request that the Voice had suggested. But, to his complete shock, every single one responded with favor! They agreed to let him pay the money back in six months! He hung up knowing he had just received a second miracle!

Now, he must open his heart to this man Jesus. And he did.

With that decision, came new boldness that this All Powerful One who healed his skin, and gave him favor with the creditors must also be able to guide him into his new business field. Various insights and downloads in dreams that began to come, along with contacts with notable chemists, and soon his new business began to soar. He founded a highly successful company, then another and another. In the first six months of these ventures, he paid off the millions he owed in credit, just as the Lord had said!

Jesus, his new friend, amazed him in every way! Now he knew without a doubt, He was the way, the only way to walk in victory and peace.

Soon, Dr. Gomes began to experience a great passion for his fellow Hindus to come to Jesus and be set free from darkness.

Of course, his new friend had a great plan for that. One day, He told him to rent a large meeting hall that would seat 500 people. The Lord told him to invite an evangelist and put posters for the event all around town. The promos invited people to come and learn how to live a successful life.

The Lord instructed him to print this on the signs:

NO CHRISTIANS ALLOWED!

The Lord didn't want any Christians to take up seats intended for the lost, in this evangelistic meeting! Only the lost would be allowed inside. Of course, the Hindus thought it would be a safe Hindu meeting.

He only knew of one speaker to invite. When he called him a few months ahead of time, the man eagerly agreed to come. However, the day before the great event, he called to say he had become very sick and must cancel his trip.

Oh no! Now Dr. Gomes feared that he would lose face in the whole city, cancelling the event at the last minute!

But the Lord had other ideas. **I didn't tell you to cancel it.**

"But I have no speaker coming!" He argued with the Lord.

Yes, you do. You are the speaker! You are the one I picked.

"Oh no!" He tried to enlighten the Lord on this impossible scenario. "I'm not a speaker, or an evangelist. I don't even know any Bible verses yet!"

I do! Just open your mouth and I will speak through you.

Countless verses he had never learned came pouring out of his mouth. How amazing!

He couldn't believe people filled the house to capacity! He couldn't believe everyone listened. He couldn't believe that God gave him all the right words to say.

He couldn't believe everyone there accepted Jesus!

A few months later, the Lord wanted him to repeat the whole plan, but this time with seating for 1,000. The Lord made it clear who would be the speaker again: Gomes! Once again, everyone there came to Jesus. This continued for several years until eventually they began to meet in stadiums.

A few years passed, and the Lord alerted him to yet another God-sized plan.

I want you to build an orphanage and bring in all the boys off the streets. You're going to provide a home for them and tell them you're going to always be their daddy. When they turn 18, tell them you will continue to train them. Then you will send them all to seminary, and they will all become pastors!

He never expected to do anything like that! Once again, he knew he must obey, and he did!

During his presentation to us at our church, Dr. Gomes showed us precious pictures of little boys dressed in blue and brown plaid school uniforms, sitting on marble floors with marble pillars in the background. They had built no ordinary orphanage! Abba and their new earthly daddy knew how to take care of their precious sons.

This testimony by our dear brother was one I would never forget. It all started with his horrible skin disease that put him in desperate need of a healer. In addition to these amazing events, I also noticed he sounded like a "walking Bible," as our pastor remarked. Verse after verse rolled out of his mouth, as he shared his incredible story.

When he had finished speaking, he walked around briefly and prayed over five people: our pastor and his wife, my husband and I, and a young college student. Dr. Gomes had no way of knowing that the young man had driven five hours to be there.

When he came to us, Dr. Gomes prayed one of my favorite verses over us, Jeremiah 33 (NIV), **"Call to me and I will answer you and show you great and mighty things you do not know."** He spoke several amazing things over us that are still coming to pass.

Towards the end of the evening, I began to reflect on all the amazing details that transpired in his life. But the Lord saved the best news for last for me that night.

As I stood at the back of the room when it was over, He spoke something startling: ***I'm letting you see, right here in this place, some fruit from your prayers for the 10-40 Window. I brought him here for*** *you to see a life who was changed by your prayers, in the same years you were praying for this!*

What a precious jewel He just handed me!

Yes, at the very time this man had come to Jesus, we had prayed often in our church, and in our Lehigh Valley prayer coalition for that very thing—that the Lord would walk into their rooms, if necessary, to bring Hindus, tribes, and other unreached people to salvation in that 10-40 Window.

"Now this is the confidence that we have in Him, that if we ask anything according to His will, He hears us. And if we know that He hears us, whatever we ask, we know that we have the petitions we have asked of Him." (1 John 5:14-15)

Twenty years later, as I happened to be editing this book, I had the opportunity to reconnect with him unexpectedly and heard his incredible updates! Eventually, the Lord had led him into full-time ministry of both evangelism *and miracles*, touching thousands at a time: healing the sick, giving sight to the blind, opening the ears of the deaf, and even raising the dead. His ministry has now seen over 15 million souls who confessed Jesus as Lord in over 350 different locations around the world!

A BLESSING

I bless you to see the world through the Lord's loving eyes, with the confidence that nothing is too difficult for Him. I bless you to be made whole and to quickly obey the Voice of the Lord. I bless you to see **"great and mighty things, which you do not know." (Jeremiah 33:3)**

The blessing went beyond the request. . .

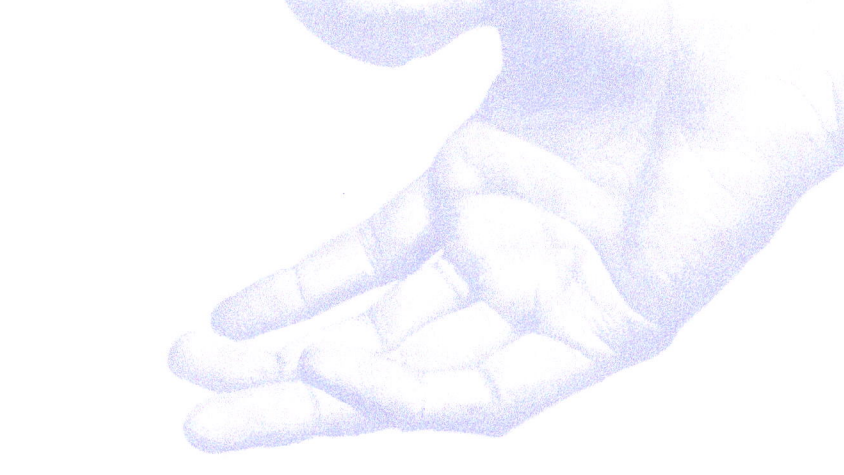

7
PARALYTIC LOWERED THROUGH THE ROOF
Matthew 9:1-8, Mark 2:1-12, Luke 5:17-26

Jesus returned to Capernaum and entered someone's house. The room quickly filled, so that no one else could enter. As He preached the Word to them, four desperate and compassionate men carried their paralytic friend up to the roof and uncovered the roof tiles to lower him into the room on a mat. Jesus stopped speaking, and turned to him saying, **"Son, your sins are forgiven."**

The scribes called it blasphemy, so He reworded it to prove his authority to both heal and forgive. **"Arise, take up your bed, and walk!"**

The crippled man stood up immediately! The multitude glorified God and exclaimed, "We have seen remarkable things today."

REVELATION, LORD?

I saw the same gentle smile upon Jesus' face, hearing the commotion on the roof, as when He had previously heard the commotion outside

Peter's door (see Chapter 3). Now I saw the Lord standing tall in a shaft of sunlight, arms extended, to receive this man being lowered down through the roof. Faith came again in zealous pursuit of His Blessing. He received the paralytic eagerly, not as an intrusion, but happily and compassionately.

The blessing went beyond the request, not just physical healing, but a healing of the heart. Despite the furor it would cause, Jesus carefully made known the greater need: forgiveness!

The four men captured my attention, like four pillars of faith, laboring together in the Kingdom. Boldly they took this risk of foolishness for their friend, in hope of a drastic breakthrough, not just in the roof.

But then, a new thought emerged. It seemed the four men also represented the four writers of the Gospel—those who carried the weight of the life story of their Friend—breaking through the darkest barrier of silence of 400 years. Suddenly new Light from above opened the minds of men on earth, to release the new revelation coming in the form of the God-Man, Christ Jesus!

Then the Lord overlaid these thoughts with yet another—the picture of God the Father releasing His own Son into the hands of men, who loved Him, but eventually carried Him to his death, as He became sin for us. Thus, He had been lowered down briefly into the earth in His burial and death. God the Father administered the payment of grace through His Son's death, and spoke to the world, **"Your sins are forgiven!"** Just as the paralytic took up his mat and walked, so Christ arose from the grave, breaking the chains of our sin off His own body, and making a way for us to walk a new walk of freedom! *Hallelujah!*

ALONG THE WAY

For years, in praying for revival in the Lehigh Valley, I knew the Lord wanted to raise up a House of Prayer sometime. Many of us weighed the need, but the task seemed daunting. We all wondered who the

Lord would call to start it. Surprisingly, the Lord brought in a person from across the country to do so. What a blessing!

We also knew the Lord would use the Mosaic House of Prayer (MHOP), to help re-dig the "old wells" of intercession that saturated our history, due to the on-fire Moravians who founded Bethlehem. They came in the 14th year of their famed 100-year prayer meeting, fueled by their burden to evangelize the native Americans in the region between New York and Philadelphia.

My involvement began during the second or third month of MHOP. Once I heard about it, I eagerly dove in, taking prayer sets of praise and intercession at the keyboard, and serving on the Board. How rewarding to see intercession and unity growing in the Lehigh Valley! After a few years, a new branch sprouted forth, The Bethlehem Healing Rooms. We began to see many more healing requests than before, both physical and emotional healings.

During one of our weekly MHOP praise and prayer sessions, we heard some noise at the back of the sanctuary. A young father from our church who had never come to MHOP before came through the door. Immediately, we noticed his face was white as he staggered into the room, holding onto the backs of the teal sanctuary chairs.

We rushed back to help. "What's wrong?"

He had just dropped off his two young children at a friend's house, on the way to the Emergency Room nearby. He managed to tell us he had been having unbearable pain, possibly from kidney stones. His friend had suggested he stop by the house of prayer to see what God might do for him.

"Maybe you won't even have to go to the ER," she encouraged him boldly.

I might as well stop by, he thought.

There were only five or six of us there at the time, but we immediately stepped into action. Compassion and urgency filled the atmosphere.

We marveled at the faith of his friend who urged him to come to us. None of us had ever prayed for healing for kidney stones before, but the Lord impressed us that He had brought him to us for a reason.

Okay, Lord!

We had him lie down and began praying for both comfort and healing. Soon he drifted in and out of sleep, as we kept interceding. Whenever he stirred, we helped him agree in prayer for things to shift in his body. The pain remained, but he knew he had come to the right place.

After a while, his concerned uncle showed up to check on him. Soon he seemed reassured that God was at work, so he began agreeing in prayer with us. After about two hours, our friend sat up, and felt he needed to visit the restroom. We noticed he walked without staggering now! The Lord encouraged us with his progress.

When he came back out, he felt a bit better. We continued praying for him in a different room then, as more people began to arrive for an evening service. Just as the worship time began, we shared the request with the larger group, so they too could pray for him.

He lay down again, then, in our small prayer room, but only for about 20 minutes, as we continued praying over him. Suddenly he sat up again rather quickly and asked, "Did I pass out?"

"No, you seemed to just be resting," we responded.

"Oh, something just happened! In fact, all my pain is gone!"

As he smiled for the first time, we noticed the normal color had returned to his face. Only some tightness remained where the severe pain had been!

He didn't remember much from his time with us. But the healing hand of the Lord had accomplished a great work. His ER trip was replaced by a JR trip—with Jehovah Rapha—God, our Healer!

We all rejoiced greatly that our brother could now walk freely and return home, no longer suffering from pain.

He had a very good night!

Two years later, my husband and I had flown coast-to-coast, starting at 4:30 am in Pennsylvania, arriving in San Jose, California, just in time to check in, get changed and go downstairs for supper. We looked forward to reconnecting with many friends from around the globe, at the welcome banquet for the Transform Our World Annual Leadership Summit.

Halfway through my delicious salad, one of the leaders hurried over to ask two of us to consider going to pray over a man suffering dire pain from kidney stones. He too had just flown in from several states away. The two of us left and found him resting upstairs, unable to walk, due to this painful attack.

This time I had great confidence the Lord would intervene. I shared our previous testimony with my church friend healed of such pain. Since the word "testimony" means "do it again," it's helpful to share a victory story before praying for healing, to build faith.

As we began to pray, I immediately heard, **This too shall pass!** The Lord has a way with words, even in prayer sometimes. We each took about ten minutes to pray over him, until we felt we had done all we needed to do. As we left, our friend sat up cautiously, then stood up with no discomfort and even took two or three steps!

"I feel much better," he said as he lay back down to rest.

We suggested he keep some praise music playing to stay mentally focused on the Lord. He agreed. A couple hours later, however, we found out his pain had gotten worse again, so this time he simply headed to the ER. We kept praying for his breakthrough.

The next report, however, was great! Before the doctor even made it in to see him at the ER, he passed the stone and was able to leave. Our prayers had been answered!

This too shall pass, the Lord had said.

The next day our friend was able to stand and keep his speaking engagement on the program. Hallelujah!

We knew once again, it had clearly been His hands, and our feet!

A BLESSING

I bless you with courage to face every pain in your body or in your heart, with the ever-present HELP of the Lord! I also bless you to boldly take your friends to Jesus when they feel helpless and watch Him raise them up to walk again. I bless you to do whatever it takes to discover new victories in ways you formerly thought unimaginable.

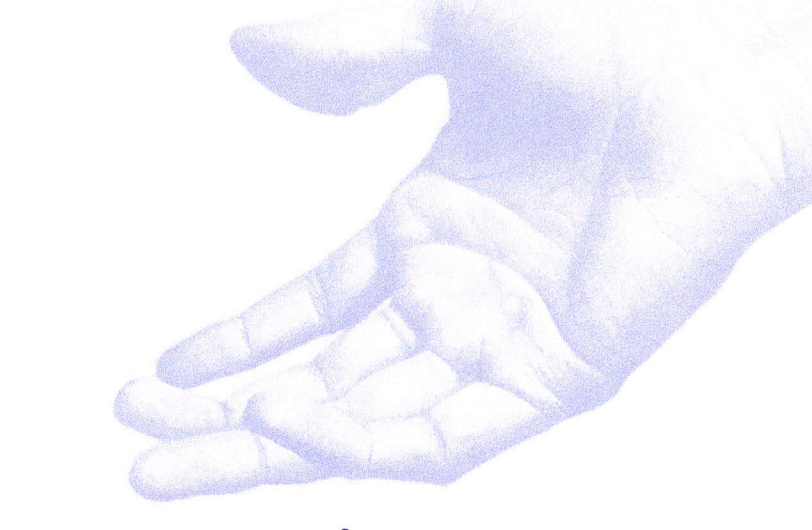

8
HEALING A MAN'S HAND ON THE SABBATH

Matthew 12:8-14, Mark 2:27–3:6, Luke 6:5-11

Jesus' disciples were hungry. As they walked through some grainfields they picked and ate some corn on the Sabbath. The Pharisees were appalled. Jesus replied, "The Son of Man is Lord of the Sabbath." Next, they entered the synagogue, where they saw a man with a withered hand.

"Step forward," the Lord immediately engaged the disabled man.

Jesus asked the Pharisees, *"Is it lawful on the Sabbath to do good or to do evil, to save life or to kill?"*

They didn't know what to say. He looked around in anger, being grieved by the hardness of their hearts, and said to the man, *"Stretch out your hand."* All those present saw his hand fully restored!

The Pharisees plotted how to kill Jesus.

REVELATION, LORD?

I saw the Lord walking up the steps of the synagogue in a brown and tan striped garment, with resolve and deep contemplation, knowing what was about to transpire, as the Father had shown Him.

I heard Him say, ***How oppressive to spend time in the synagogue where Truth should be best received, yet it escaped them. The enemy of Truth slithered pride and arrogance all through the atmosphere there, so that humility and wisdom could rarely be found.***

Openness to learn from the heavenly Father had been replaced by the rigid rules and expectations of men, entombing the original laws intended to bless and protect.

The singular healing of just one man's hand forced Jesus to vacate the synagogue, with the threat of death in the air. How tragic He had to look elsewhere to extend His own hand of blessing!

ALONG THE WAY

Little did I know when I first walked through the clanging doors of the women's prison in Allentown, that I would minister there for twenty-nine years until the 2020 pandemic closed the doors to volunteers. Twice, I had gone into the old run-down facilities, before the new Lehigh County Jail opened in 1992, so I could certainly appreciate the upgrades!

Due to its four imposing stories of the red granite façade, the $51 million structure earned its nickname as the "Taj Mahal." Every week as I began walking through about five or six sets of steel doors slamming behind me, the oppressive atmosphere of incarceration gripped me.

The 10-20 women who came to the Bible study each week especially loved it when I brought in my portable keyboard to use in worship. I had to allow extra time, as I waited for the guard to search through the bulky case with all its deep pockets. Ironically, the tag on my case said,

"World Tour." I laughed to think of my incredible world tour each week to the county jail.

The women always shared their favorite song requests, from old to new. They blew me away at times with some of their solo-caliber voices. The first few years, we spent the Bible study time covering practical teachings on overcoming anxiety, worry, fear, shame, etc. Over time, the Lord pressed me into praying for their many physical needs also. These ladies had been put down or ignored for most of their lives. The Lord wanted them to discover His unique love for their precious hearts.

So! When I began to pray for healing, I really needed results! Sitting there in such bleak rooms with those desperate ladies seemed to be the Lord's set up for testing my faith. That's exactly where my faith for miracles first began to blossom.

He amazed us all with His sweet miracles, week after week! As the results increased over time, the ladies grew very expectant and invited new ladies to come just for the purpose of being healed! One day a girl asked me to pray for her friend she had brought for the first time, who was too shy to ask.

"She has pain in her arm all the time," she explained on behalf of her friend.

"What's causing the pain?" I prodded.

Now she decided to speak for herself. "Oh, I was in a car wreck last year and I can't straighten out this arm anymore." She held out her left arm for all to see.

Her elbow now had a permanent bend in it, so that she had lost about twenty-five percent of her extension. By then, doubts began to assault me, looking at this disabled arm. *Oh dear,* I had never prayed for straightening a crooked limb before!

"Well," I said, trying to sound confident, **"Nothing is too hard for the Lord!"** (Jeremiah 32:17b)

The eyes of fifteen women stayed glued on that crooked arm.

Here goes!

"Lord, straighten this arm fully NOW! All pain must go!" Our eyes grew wide to see her arm straighten out fully, within about five seconds. And the pain? Gone!

Now she didn't even know what to think. It seemed to be her first introduction to this man, "Jesus."

The next week, she came back. The Lord had her attention. I saw her weekly over the next two or three months, while her arm remained beautifully straight and pain free. She kept surprising me over the next two to three weeks, requesting healing for other parts of her body, all from the same accident. Every time the Lord touched her with another awesome miracle: her shoulders, her foot, and one of her legs. God chose to use an unbeliever to help train this Bible teacher in healing!

Finally, she put her trust in Him and received what was missing in her heart. Eventually, she brought another person for healing.

"Jesus Christ is the same yesterday and today and forever" (Hebrews 13:8). Our Healer has never stopped healing!

A BLESSING

I bless you to continually take your faith in new places, and to fear not! I bless you to let the Lord stretch your faith this week in unexpected ways. I bless you to faint not at the next set up by the Holy Spirit, for what He *wants* to do through you!

9
HEALING A GREAT MULTITUDE
Matthew 12:15-16, Mark 3:7-12, Luke 6:17-19

As Jesus left the temple, a great multitude followed Him and His disciples, coming from five or six surrounding regions! He healed them all—including various afflictions and plagues, as well as unclean spirits who fell down before Him crying, *"You are the Son of God!"*

Power went out from Him.

The crowd pressed upon Him so much that He told the disciples to keep a boat ready, if need be, so He would not be crushed by the crowd pursuing Him.

REVELATION, LORD?

I saw a joyful Jesus reaching out to touch many outstretched hands. I heard the fervor of the crowd! "He's here! He's over there! Let's go!" Everywhere He turned, He saw people pursuing Him. He loved their searching eyes and their seeking hearts! He loved the cries, "Yeshua! Help me!"

The healing power of His loving heart flowed freely, with just a touch. Nothing hindered Him outside the synagogue. He had come to love, to bless, to teach, to train, to restore. Heaven had come down to earth. No one was turned away. Love had come and had come for a great purpose.

ALONG THE WAY

About ten years ago, my husband and I enjoyed our first ever snow tubing at a ski resort in New York state, while our son and his friend went out on the slopes snowboarding. We all enjoyed the anticipation of a new snowy adventure coursing through our veins.

When our snow tube attendant asked us if we wanted a spin, neither of us hesitated. As we flew down the hill, I bounced off the tube and onto a three-foot peak of ice between the snowy lanes. When I landed, my tailbone took the brunt of the impact The experience no longer fit into that category called F-U-N.

When the pain decided to hang around for months, I found myself visiting the chiropractor's office, off and on for about two years. The ebb and flow of the pain proved to be totally unpredictable. Despite countless visits to three different chiropractors, my back continued to flare up.

One evening it came to a head, when I woke from a nap to find it completely immovable. I could not move enough to even get off the bed! I had to stay confined there for three hours, waiting for my husband to come home. Fortunately, when he came home, he was able to lift me off the bed, and get me onto a walker. Quite unexpectedly, the Lord impressed me to try doing a few stretches. With each one, He gave me more and more flexibility. This went on for twenty minutes. He gave me amazing results! About 80% of my pain left!

Then He had me do another twenty minutes of stretches on the floor. I could hardly believe it: this time *all* my pain had left! I could move completely normally again!

This scale of personal miracle had never happened to me before! It was as if a supernatural chiropractor just took care of me! My back felt great! When I walked out to show my husband my sudden flexibility, he grinned and shook his head in awe. We both had some praising to do!

All at once, I had no need for trips to the doctor.

That incident became the greatest catalyst of faith for me to pray against pain for others. If any pain ever tried to return in my back, the Lord taught me exactly what to do. The first time my lower back started to grab in pain, about three months later, I started to say, "Oh no, there goes my … (back again)."

He stopped me. I heard a sharp, **Don't say it!**

I abruptly stopped. *Okay, Lord, what do I say?*

Thank Me for healing your back and thank Me that you have a strong back!

Oh! So that's what I did, and the grab that I felt, totally left! That was the end of my recurring problem. It shocked me to learn I had the authority to shut down those attacks of the enemy on my body.

I continually stayed in awe of the difference my own words could make in situations regarding pain. Now I knew that my agreement with truth and light instead of agreement with pain would shut it all down. Throughout the ten years since it happened, I have marveled that He has enabled me to live pain free.

When most people have had back issues, they usually feel they must be extra careful trying to lift anything heavy and tend to "baby" their back. The first time I started to do that, the Lord reminded me, **You have a strong back!**

Oh yes!

Surprisingly, the Lord has proved to me, I can now lift heavier loads than I did in the past! This has always amazed my husband and I, as we continue to tackle strenuous projects together. For example, for a few years, we volunteered for Disaster Relief work, through our church. We trained to do "mud-outs" in flood torn areas and invariably carried heavy wet debris up from damaged basements.

The Lord taught me that pain needs to bow to the Name of Jesus! I also learned to view any type of piercing pain as fiery darts from the enemy. It clearly states in Ephesians 6:16 (NIV) that we are to **"take up our shield of faith, with which you can extinguish all the flaming arrows of the evil one."**

With my newfound confidence to see victory over pain, I began to pray boldly for others in pain, knowing there would certainly be immediate results. Sudden breakthroughs (miracles!) became the norm, especially in prison, where I saw such great needs.

Sometimes in the prison, I would forget to allow enough time for healing prayers after the Bible study. When that happened, I knew I needed to offer prayers of healing anyway, though I might only have five minutes to spare. The Lord showed me He can work faster than I thought!

One day, I prayed for a whole circle of 6-7 ladies all at once, against all types of pain. I stood in the middle of them all and they just quickly named the body part that had the pain. With just a brief one to two-minute prayer for the group, He did it all. Off they went, with miracles, grins, and hearts overflowing with His love, in one fell swoop!

The Lord let me know how deeply He desires to touch the multitudes, even through me! Once people have been touched by the healing power of His love, they are often ready to open their hurting hearts to Him, as well.

"Multitudes, multitudes in the valley of decision! For the day of the Lord is near in the valley of decision." (Joel 3:14)

A couple of years later, we were invited to Argentina with Ed Silvoso's ministry, called Transform Our World. What a whirlwind week we had, traversing several cities, from east to west. One Sunday morning, my husband and I spoke in an urban church in a local shopping center. Our interpreter picked us up and whisked us off to the service. When we got to the mall, the old building looked dingy and dark. We went up the old stone steps outside, through a nine-foot door inside, down the hall to a tiny doorway, then down another dark hallway to find some narrow dark stairs going down to the lower level. It felt like what I had always thought of when I had heard about the "underground church."

However, when we stepped through the folds of the dark velvety curtain, the Lord surprised us! Bright white paint covered the walls, and the room looked happy. The people had draped elaborate swags of brightly colored fabric artistically around the ceiling.

We smiled to be honored as their special guests. Our South American brothers and sisters warmly greeted us with happy hugs and smiles. The pastor's wife offered me a sip of the pastor's special mate tea, a caffein-rich herbal drink. Fortunately. I knew to say "Yes!" (with honey please).

After the worship time, when the interpreter announced I would be the first to speak, the Lord reminded me of an assignment He had given me first thing that morning. I had told Gordon back at the hotel that before I could speak that morning, I needed to ask if anyone there had back pain. We prayed together about it at the hotel and believed there would be breakthroughs.

As my interpreter relayed my offer for the back pain prayer, about 5-6 people stood. I knew God had a healing plan for all of them. After praying, I asked them to wave if the pain had improved by at least 80%. All but one waved happily! I prayed again for the one, and she too began to nod and wave, with a look of sheepish surprise.

"And the whole multitude sought to touch Him, for the power [Greek: *dunamis*] **went out from Him and healed them all."** (Luke 6:19)

A BLESSING

I bless you to rise and shine earlier in the morning, to make extra time for people in your day, along the way, for miracles! I also bless you to go for it, even if time is short. I bless you to pray with growing confidence that Jesus is more than ready to bless your world through you, wherever you go. Be blessed and pass on your blessing.

10
CENTURION'S SERVANT NEAR DEATH
(Matthew 8:5-13), Luke 7:1-10

Jesus landed back in Capernaum where He had turned water into wine. Some elders came to Him, sent by a Roman centurion saying, "Lord, this dear servant lies at home paralyzed, suffering terribly, and is about to die."

Jesus readily offered to go and heal him. But the official sent word, "I do not deserve to have you come under my roof; just say the word, and he will be healed."

Jesus was amazed, *I have not found anyone in Israel with such great faith!*

Healing came to his dying servant at that very hour.

REVELATION, LORD?

The humble faith of this centurion brought about this blessing. This man humbled himself and took the attitude of being a servant for his servant. He became a "least of these." His own servant heart of love and compassion collided with Jesus' servant heart of love and compassion and completed the healing transaction.

I did not see the Lord in this miracle, but rather I saw the dying servant suddenly sit straight up in his bed, seeing the face of Jesus before him.

"Am I dying? Is He taking me home? No! I'm healed!"

*Though Jesus did not need to go there physically, I saw Him there, clearly facing this man—as his **"ever present HELP in time of trouble!"** (Psalm 46:1).*

No weapon formed against him would prosper! (See Isaiah 54:17.)

ALONG THE WAY

When a new family of seven started attending our fellowship, they brought us great joy and delight, as they quickly became heavily involved. This family functioned powerfully in prayer, so we linked arms readily, on a deep level.

Their roots had started back at a church camp, where the mom and dad had met in high school. It seemed he had been sent there to get away from the wrong crowd; it worked! That began a long-distance relationship that endured over three years, while he served in the military, before they married.

About seven years after the Lord brought them to our place of worship, things suddenly went awry. He had been suffering a bad headache for a few days, and finally took some stronger medications on Saturday afternoon. He began to feel worse that evening but slept soundly through the night. She felt a good nights' rest would aid his recovery.

She decided to let him sleep in on Sunday morning, so she didn't disturb him before going to church. When she returned home, it looked like he had been up, but had fallen back asleep. However, a couple hours later she discovered she couldn't wake him.

After calling 911, she quickly called the church prayer team. With her permission, many of their close friends and family flocked to the hospital to pray on site together. The news came soon from the CAT scan: it revealed two masses on the brain. The doctors suspected cancer.

Further reports revealed he seemed to be in the sixth level of coma. (When people are in the seventh level, apparently the patient cannot be revived.) We could hardly believe it. His life hung in the balance, at age 49! We all clung to many promises, such as **"No weapon formed against you shall prosper"** (Isaiah 54:17).

The doctors decided to use steroids for two to three days to bring the swelling of the brain down in preparation for surgery. An early answer to prayer came when he woke up from that deep comatose state on Wednesday and could even speak! No brain damage seemed evident from the coma he had been in those 3-4 days! Encouragement and gratitude filled the room and our hearts. The couple happily exchanged some much needed "I love yous" before he headed into surgery.

The next news, however, proved hard to digest. The neurosurgeon told her that because of how much tissue they would need to remove, her husband could possibly lose a lot of functionality, and could even be non-verbal. Additionally, he might need to learn how to walk again. Other motor skills such as feeding himself could also be curtailed.

The surgery went long but well. The staff told his wife to go home for some rest because the next day would be very trying when he would awaken. She needed to be at her best, to start helping him in new ways, and to be emotionally strong. The church prayed as much for her as for him. The outlook began to sound formidable.

But God!

Our faithful Comforter kept the patient's wife in perfect peace throughout the long night. She could literally feel His peace wrapping around her heart, so that no fear was able to pierce through that supernatural covering.

The next day, as she walked down the pale sterile hall of the ICU, she braced herself to face whatever the conditions may be. She noticed, however, that peace and grace carried her powerfully down the hushed walkway. As she *got near his door, she heard a familiar voice calling out her name. It was her husband!*

She couldn't believe her eyes or ears! There he sat, feeding himself, all alone in his bed. Overwhelming joy exploded in that unforgettable moment!

Glowing with excitement, she recounted her praise to us that morning. A true miracle had happened! He had entered the hospital at one level below "brain-death," but walked out with full function, six days later!

Though none of us could be there with him in the hospital, his Healer had taken care of him throughout the surgery, and through all the long nights. Though the doctors had no answers for his stellar recovery, we did! Our incredibly faithful God had done what only He could do.

"God is our ever-present Help in time of trouble" (Psalm 46:1).

The Lord gave our dear brother 18 more months of life to enjoy with his sweet family of seven. A year later, his face shone with great joy and gratitude as he walked his youngest daughter down the aisle in her lacey gown, to unite with her high school sweetheart in marriage.

Things had come full circle! It was a wonder to behold, with their forest of Christmas trees and white sparkling lights all through the reception hall. But I noticed that those daughter-daddy eyes sparkled even more. It would be a December to remember.

Only 54 days later, his heavenly Father decided to call him home. Once his wife realized God's time for him had come, God's grace covered her bountifully to release her loving husband of 28 years.

His heart must have been relieved to hear her last words of loving encouragement, "Run to Jesus!"

A BLESSING

I bless you with the bold confidence that the power of your faith in Jesus will accomplish much, regardless of the circumstances or the distance. I bless you to readily follow the lead of His Holy Spirit to serve others in their trials. I bless you to stand tall in the darkest times and see the light breaking through your own heart first, then freely to others around you.

Death could not have this son. . .

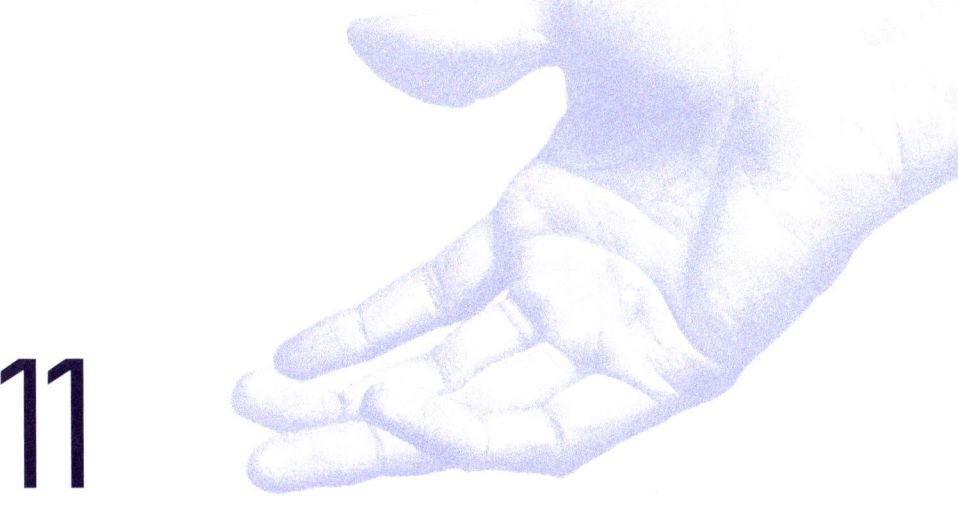

11

RESURRECTION: A WIDOW'S SON

Luke 7:11-17

The next day, in the city of Nain, Jesus and His disciples walked amidst a large crowd. Near the gate of the city, He had great compassion on a widow whose dead son passed by, being carried out in an open coffin. **"Do not weep,"** He said to her. They all stood still.

Touching the coffin, He said, **"Young man, I say to you, arise."** He sat up and began to speak.

Fear came upon all, and they glorified God saying, "A great prophet has risen among us! God has visited His people!"

REVELATION, LORD?

I began to hear, "Pass through, pass through the gates. Prepare the way for the people. Build up, build up the highway! Remove the stones. Raise a banner for the nations. The Lord has made a proclamation to the ends of the earth:

"Say to the Daughter of Zion, 'See, your Savior comes! See, His reward is with Him, and His recompense accompanies Him.'"
(Isaiah 62: 10-11)

The Savior had come! He lovingly intercepted the boy before he left the gates of the city to be buried. Death could not have this son; the time had come for this son to pass through a different gate. **"I am the gate: whoever enters through Me will be saved."** *(John 10:9)* **"Pass through, pass through the gate!"**

I saw a humble, compassionate Jesus, standing quietly beside the boy's coffin as the powerful Gate of Life, while the gaping mouth of the city gate loomed large behind Him. **"Where, O death, is your victory?! Where, O death, is your sting?"** (1 Corinthians 15:55)

ALONG THE WAY

My times going into the prison looked like this: In the morning, I would do the Bible studies with the women, leaving right before they had lunch. Then a couple hours later, I would return to do some one-on-one counseling, if they requested my name as their "spiritual advisor." In between, I would usually run errands and grab a quick lunch.

After a few years, the Lord instructed me to change my routine. He spoke to me one week about going to the nearby Jordan Creek, to sit there by the water, and spend extra time with Him. *Okay, Lord, that sounds like a better plan on my prison ministry days, instead of doing errands.* So, with journal and Bible in hand, and a beach towel to sit on, I began my new routine.

The first day, I took off my sandals, and waded into the water, since it happened to be a hot day. Being an avid water person, I found it very refreshing!

After awhile, I meandered over to my towel and sat down to read, listen, and journal. *Why am I here Lord, at this creek? What do you want to say to me about this?*

His answer came quickly but startled me: **Pray that the Holy Spirit will hover over this water, so that whoever steps foot in this water will be touched by Him!**

What? I had never prayed anything like that before. It seemed so foreign to my normal way of praying.

Lord, I'm not sure about this. Is there anything in the Bible you can show me like this?

Immediately I heard **"In the beginning, God created the heavens and the earth. And the Spirit was hovering over the waters."** (Genesis 1:1)

I had to laugh.

Okay, Lord, then I guess I can pray for that. I was still feeling uncomfortable, but remembered how much He loves to take us WAY outside our comfort zones. So, I began to pray the Holy Spirit would *hover over the waters.* I realized that all the years I had been praying for revival in our Lehigh Valley, that He may want to do it in a completely different way than I had ever dreamed.

Yes, Lord!

He kept me going there, week after week, month after month, as long as the weather permitted. In the winter, I sat in the car, close enough to still see the water, and prayed my special spirit-hovering prayers.

Soon, this Jordan Creek became my "Jordan River!" *Why not?*

A heavy rainy spell in the spring caused my river to overflow its banks one time. I had to delay going there at least a week. When I went back the first time, it gave me an eerie feeling, seeing the mud and debris everywhere. *Lord don't let me miss anything you want me to see.* At that moment, I casually glanced down to see my next step, and saw a beige rock the size of my fist, right in front of my foot, with a perfectly formed brown layer inlaid like a cross. *Oh, wow! The Lord knows I have always collected rocks of all sizes!* I picked it up and turned it over. It had an identical design on both sides! *Well, this is mine now,* I told the Lord with a crazy smile. *I'm glad you didn't let me miss that.*

Just then, I looked back up as I continued my walk, but again stopped in my tracks! There in front of me, about 15 feet away, I gazed at a tree that had two protruding branches, on the left and right, that made it resemble a cross. A large purple cloth hung eerily around the center, literally like a cross draped at Eastertime!

Lord! What am I seeing? What are you doing?

I walked over to it, to examine this strange sight. *Aha!* A fluffy comforter had been swept away by the floodwaters and had become tangled in the tree. *A "comforter?" Lord, You are too much!*

What an unforgettable day. He let me know he had me in the right place at the right time, and I felt His sweet smile.

Thank you, Lord.

Sometimes, I ventured further downstream, where a refreshing four-foot spillway ran across to the other side. I sat on the cool rock wall to journal, while listening to the rushing waters. That refreshing spot drew me back often.

One sunny day, as I sat there alone, I saw something unusual moving in the spillway, out of the corner of my eye; there were numerous fish jumping UP out of the creek below, attempting to get over the spillway! I thought only salmon did that!

I had to make some quick calls to tell others about the astonishing sight. That was my first cell phone, and it had no camera function. In about one minute while I was on the phone with a friend, I counted 30 fish that jumped up that spillway!

They appeared to be slender, greenish black fish, about eight inches long.

The Lord spoke to my heart, as I journaled this unusual sight, that He was giving me a preview of fish that would be jumping out of the water for salvation, when He would fill our revival nets full!

A couple of years later, we read an incredible article in *The Morning Call* newspaper. A six-year-old boy had been playing in the Jordan Creek with his family, when he went underwater, and became trapped in the large culvert there. No one had realized the danger it posed. His father tried to rescue him but almost got swept too far into the culvert, too. He had to fight extremely hard to get back out. Another adult had to hold his legs, so he could go back under to find his son.

Finally, after the boy had been submerged for about ten minutes, the distraught daddy pulled his son out of the water. He laid his lifeless body carefully onto the ground, as the family stood around helplessly weeping over his death.

About ten more minutes passed when an off-duty policeman drove up. "What's going on?"

When they told him, he hurried over to see the little boy. Seeing him lying there so helpless, he thought immediately of his own child at home, the same age. He felt he had to do something! Suddenly, he began trying mouth to mouth resuscitation, even though the boy had now been lifeless for about 20 minutes. The situation felt completely hopeless to everyone.

Miraculously, the boy soon began to gasp and spurt out water! No one could believe it! He had been revived! Suddenly they all went into action, and whisked him off to the hospital, where they pumped out several quarts of water. Amazingly, he spent less than 24 hours in the hospital, and suffered NO brain damage!

"With God, all things are possible!" (Matthew 19:26)

The Lord of Life snatched another dear son from the clutches of death!

This incident all happened at the spillway, where the fish were jumping out of the water! I knew it had been a special sign.

About a decade rolled by. A travelling evangelist arrived from Pittsburgh to preach in a church in Bethlehem a few times. However, he felt that the next time he would come it should be set as an outdoor crusade. They secured permission for a week at the Jordan Park!

My husband and I attended training to be counselors. Hundreds came forth every night for salvation. By the end of the week, there had been 1800 documented salvations.

The stage had been set up in a very special place—exactly where the spillway had once been! It had been taken out after the boy's drowning scene, to alleviate further incidents. But at the exact place where I saw those amazing fish jumping out of the water, I got to see the souls of men jumping into the nets of the Lord!

Thank you, Lord, for sending me to my Jordan River to pray for the Spirit to hover over the waters.

Hallelujah for all this new LIFE!

A BLESSING

I bless you with ears to hear Him boldly leading you every day. I bless you with new desire and courage to go forth in His Name with zealous faith and love, to obey His unpredictable voice. I bless you to see new life come forth from death, in the Name of Jesus!

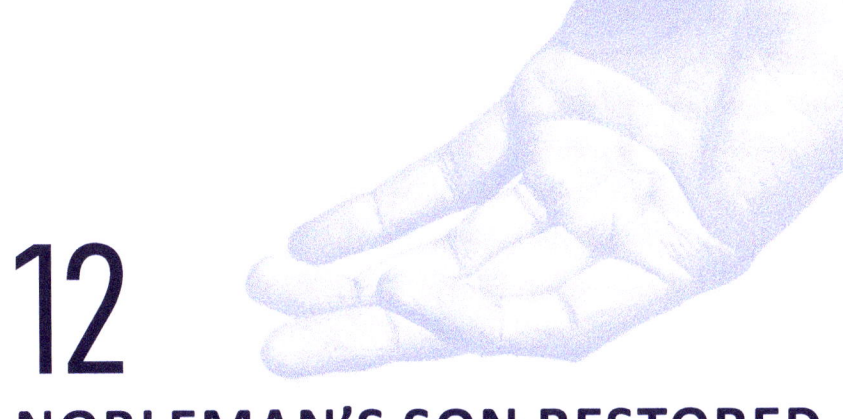

12
NOBLEMAN'S SON RESTORED
John 4:46-54

Once more Jesus visited Cana in Galilee, where He had turned the water into wine. The son of a royal official lay sick in Capernaum, and came begging Jesus to come heal his son, lingering close to death. **"Unless you people see signs and wonders, you will never believe,"** Jesus told him.

"Sir, come down before my child dies," the man pleaded.

"Go, your son will live!"

The man believed the word Jesus spoke to him and went his way. His servants met Him on the way, "Yesterday at one in the afternoon, the fever left!"

They marveled that Jesus had said, **"Your son will live,"** at that exact time! The whole household believed!

REVELATION, LORD?

The father of the son walked for a full day in hopes of bringing the Healer home. Instead, the Father of the Son, released a simple Word of healing through His Son, for the desperate man to take home.

I saw the Lord and this darkly tanned man from the side, their gazes locked intently, once the word was given. Grace, faith, and love were being imparted. The steps of the father were lighter, as he turned to go, leaving footprints of faith on the dusty road home.

Tomorrow the sun would be shining brighter in that household.

"And the Word became flesh and dwelled among us." (John 1:14)

ALONG THE WAY

Due to the arrival of a blustery Pennsylvania blizzard, all church services had been cancelled in our area. Gordon, our three sons and I all decided we should "have church" at home. Though our electricity was out, we had gotten prepared the day before, so the pass-through wood box was full. Soon, my husband had a roaring fire going in the fireplace, and we began.

After our time of worship, Bible readings and sharing from Mom and Dad, our oldest son said, *"We need to have an invitation!"* So, we did. We let him ask if anyone wanted to receive Jesus into their hearts.

Our eight-year-old said, *"Yes!"*

Soon two very blessed parents watched one brother pray with the other, with the help of *The Bridge to Life* tract (by NavPress) that he had a habit of placing in stores, "along the way," hoping the right person would find them. That day, our oldest son's evangelistic heart had some very rich fruit—saving the soul of his own brother.

"Whoever hears my word and believes him who sent me has eternal life and will not be judged but has crossed over from death to life." (John 5:24 NIV)

The next day, the sun would be shining brighter in this household.

But there's more …

Many years later, this same son would meet and marry a young lady who literally saw her life hanging in the balance, in her mid-twenties.

Before they met, she had been training for a half marathon; she loved running! Through the years, she had always been in perfect health. Suddenly some very disturbing health issues began to transpire in her body. Her hair started falling out, her fingernails were coming off and her energy took a dive. *What was happening?* She had no idea and desperately needed some answers.

The doctors could not find the cause right away. At first, they mistakenly thought her symptoms pointed to leukemia. Soon, however, they became alarmed to discover she was suffering from a rare blood disease, causing large clots to form. Tests revealed that five of her organs were shutting down, due to several large clots blocking healthy passageways.

She would need multiple organ transplants to survive. This multi-visceral transplant would all need to be done in one operation. They put her on the donor list and needed to locate that one donor very quickly. She had only a few weeks on the new time clock that was ticking quickly inside her body.

Not all hospitals perform this complex procedure. Fortunately, and not coincidentally, the city where she lived had the best reputation in the nation for this procedure! Within a very short time, a donor surfaced within about an hour of her location.

Her family grieved the fact that the organs coming that could possibly save her life, meant another life had been lost. What an unsettling time they faced, from every angle. Through this sobering situation, her heart grew exponentially in gratitude for the Lord laying down His life for us.

Once the organs became available, the doctors scheduled the surgery right away, with no time to spare. They told her parents the procedure would take about 12-16 hours, with lots of bleeding. However, as the doctors performed this intricate operation, they couldn't believe that as they took out her organs and replaced them, it seemed as though they were "putting her own [organs] back in," in the surgeon's words! They appeared to be identical in size and fit perfectly. Incredibly, it only took six hours and there had been very little bleed-out. God gave them an amazing miracle of new life for their daughter who had only weeks to live!

Nevertheless, she needed to stay hospitalized for several months. In fact, most of the first year, she had been in and out of the hospital, due to various complications. During those first twelve months, only about 50 percent of recipients normally survived. Despite all the complications, wires and tubes, monotony of the four walls, and unexpected return trips, she grew much closer to the Lord during that time. Though at first, she experienced anger about contracting this rare disease, over time she realized the devil had tried to take her out, but God had intervened. Her gratitude grew steadily, as He made His presence very real to her in various ways.

Eventually, she established contact with the donor's mother and daughter. They were happy to hear from her and to know that her life had been spared by their loved one. Fairly quickly, the donor's mother became an avid spokeswoman for donors to come forth, to help save other lives. The Redeemer's hand worked tirelessly.

About three years later, our son met this amazing survivor and overcomer. At that time, she could only consume six different foods! Plus, she had a daily regimen of numerous meds to take at various times. However, the first week they began speaking on the phone (in this long-distance friendship), he told me, "Mom, you know if we have a future together that she will be completely healed and will be able to eat anything she wants."

"Yes!"

Our son had gained a strong measure of faith over the years, from his own personal trials. After the two of them dated a year and got married, they had a pleasant surprise about a month later. *The Today Show* wanted her to appear on TV! The hospital had told her many times that her story far surpassed their normal outcomes in cases like hers. They considered her to be their "poster child."

In speaking further with *The Today Show* staff, they probed further. Would she be willing to meet the donor family for the first time in person on the show? Everyone agreed.

Compassion, awe, and gratitude flowed freely between hearts on the show that day. We watched an immediate bond unfold between them, at that incredible moment of meeting each other. Afterwards we all had lunch together. So uncanny is the fact that our daughter-in-law looks almost identical to the young mother who passed away. The donors' young daughter couldn't take her eyes off our sweet daughter-in-law.

Three years later, we received the *best news ever*. After undergoing new tests that they had never run before, her bloodwork showed that she no longer even has that disease in her bloodstream! It was the first time the lab had ever seen those results, as it is considered an incurable disease.

Just to be sure, they ran the same test again a few weeks later, to confirm it. Weeks later, our son called excitedly to say, "Yes, it's confirmed!"

Thank you, Lord, for this incredible miracle!

I knew our son had prayed for healing from the first week they met. Her parents had also been praying boldly for this miracle since the beginning of her whole ordeal. We were quick to add our prayers into the mix and *hallelujah!*

God cleansed her body totally of all those pathogens. He works in many various ways at various times, but He is always **"our refuge and strength, an ever-present HELP in trouble"** (Psalms 46:1).

My usual paraphrase of John 10:10 says, **"The thief (devil) comes to rob, kill, and destroy, but I come to give LIFE, and give it more abundantly!"**

Oh, and her diet includes almost everything now!

A BLESSING

I bless you to pursue God relentlessly in the most desperate situations, for yourself, your family, and strangers along the way. I bless you to settle for nothing less than LIFE ABUNDANT! I also bless your family with household salvation, in Jesus' Name!

13
CASTING OUT A BLIND MUTE DEMON
Matthew 12:22-30, (Mark 3:20-27), Luke 11:14-20

The man brought to Jesus that day had suffered a desperate existence for many years, being demon-possessed, blind and mute. Immediately, Jesus intervened with compassion and healed him, so that the man spoke and saw! The multitudes were amazed. "Could this be the Son of David?"

But the Pharisees said, "He casts out demons by Beelzebub, the ruler of the demons."

According to Luke, Jesus replied,

Every kingdom divided against itself is brought to desolation, and every city or house divided against itself will not stand. If Satan casts out Satan, he is divided against himself. How then will his kingdom stand? ... But if I cast out demons by the Spirit of God, surely the kingdom of God has come upon you. Or how can one enter a strong man's house and plunder his goods, unless he first binds the strong man? And then he will plunder his house. He who is not with Me is against Me....

REVELATION, LORD?

Countless blind and needy people came to pursue their miracle. The numbers surprised everyone. Yet, seeing eyes could not see the reality (of Jesus) appearing before their very eyes, and their accusing words needed to be silenced.

The Lord then opened my eyes to see His in this scene. Amazingly, I saw eyes of great mercy, looking first upon the physically blind, then upon the spiritually blind. Though He spoke sharply to silence the foe, His heart of love and mercy shone through His eyes to all who surrounded Him in such great need of a Savior. I saw hope that persisted despite the words of accusation hurled His way.

Perhaps one day. . .

Bright Light shone in the vast darkness to penetrate eyes, ears, and hearts to hopefully receive new power and wisdom.

ALONG THE WAY

Jesus had stated, **"every city or house divided against itself will not stand."** Sadly, our own marriage suffered division for many years. I was only 18 when I met Gordon on my first day of college. He and his friends invited me and my girlfriend to cut in the long line at supper, as our dorms shared the same cafeteria. Of course, I didn't mind cutting in with this handsome smiling guy. The guys all grinned from ear to ear as the two of us obliged.

Our one year of dating felt like over-the-top excitement for both of us since shyness had prevented us both from dating others. But we happily discovered that with each other our shyness had immediately disappeared! Our fun friendship blossomed beautifully. On our fourth date, the words, "I love you," slipped out unexpectedly. We enjoyed a whirlwind year of dating, meeting the families, and making plans for our future.

We married the weekend before my sophomore year, the day after I turned 19. I can't say I felt at all prepared for the serious trials that marriage hurled upon us. Stress arrived on the scene like an uninvited guest as we drove away from our wedding reception. I quickly became devastated that Gordon had not realized the need to plan our honeymoon! That weekend away ranks only about one star in our memory banks! It literally went from bad to worse. When we arrived at our hopeful (but unplanned) destination at 2 a.m.—"there was no room at the inn"—or any other inn in Eureka Springs, Arkansas. Need I say more?

The next morning, I woke up nauseated (having forgotten to eat the day before). Our next unplanned stop took us up to Noel, Missouri, where the wise Hubbie thought the name sounded "so interesting." Alas, the place had nothing to offer. The "pool" in Noel had a bonus of green slime on the top. "Plan C" put us on the road back home—a day early on our three-day "honeymoon!"

Back at school, our heavy college workloads, part-time jobs, and financial strain kept us both stressed and quick to point the accusing finger at one another during our remaining college days. The fun and exhilarating times we had while dating had evaporated into thin air.

After graduation, our parenting years began as the Lord blessed us with three adventurous and fun-loving boys. Each arrived on planet earth in various states, as new jobs meant new locations. We welcomed our first son in Texas in 1976, our second son in Virginia in 1980, and our last son in Minnesota, in 1982.

We learned to make the most of our moves, playing tourist and exploring the sights and sounds of our new surroundings. Yet the how-to of parenting seemed to further amplify our areas of disagreement. Unfortunately, our eyes seemed blind to the fact that the enemy's primary scheme kept pitting us against each other.

Fortunately, we at least knew we must stand upon *The Rock*, but we hadn't learned how to *stand together* very well.

We felt very grateful that our parents' homes displayed commendable longevity. Over time we observed both couples weather many storms, and both would eventually celebrate over 60 years of marriage. Our own home, however, barely survived our turbulent times. We longed for peace, but its evasiveness constantly shook our faith.

One day, the Lord gave me a very welcome glimpse into a new strategy to help us! I saw my husband and I standing with elbows bent and arms linked together like a chain. We looked ready to withstand anything! That picture gave me new hope.

The Lord gave me new eyes to see the way it could be that day. He impressed me that when things started to go wrong, we needed to do exactly that: link arms and get on our knees together to pray. Together we could face the enemy who schemed to divide us. Our marriage enjoyed a huge turning point, as we yielded to this insight. We faced the enemy together and discovered the enemy was not us! We began gaining ground at once, as we united to fight the enemy of our marriage together, instead of fighting each other.

One beautiful spring day, decades later, we found ourselves enjoying clear skies and budding trees, as we tackled some yard work together. As I pulled some weeds out by some stone stairs we had built, I found a perfectly shaped triangular rock about four inches long. Since my childhood, I had enjoyed collecting rocks, usually with my mother. I smiled at the memories and slipped the find right into my pocket. Back inside the house, I ran my fingers over the smooth steely gray rock as I set it on the old pine bookshelf my daddy had built.

As I paused there for a moment, the rock's shape reminded me of a teaching I had heard on marriage a few years prior. The teacher had drawn a diagram of a triangle, and had written "God" at the top, with the husband and wife at the two lower points, on opposite sides. He had explained, "The closer each one draws to God, the closer they will be drawn to each other."

It made sense, but felt somewhat discouraging, since it depended on both of us choosing to grow.

I sighed.

The Lord's gentle voice quietly intercepted my thoughts with an interesting response: **Except it's not right**, I heard. He has a way with words! I knew He meant the triangle teaching.

It's not? Why not? He had my full attention.

He continued. **When you enter into "holy matrimony," you both agree to a new relationship with Me. I unite you together in a covenant love relationship as one. Your marriage vows place you both together at the top of the triangle. You are in a new sanctified place I have created. The two have become one.**

From that point on, the enemy of your marriage tries to come and divide you, pushing you down and tearing you apart from each other, if you listen to him.

I marveled at the wisdom of the Rock about the rock I now held once again. *Thank you, Lord!*

How incredible to understand for the first time, that the reality of our "Holy Matrimony" apparently stood in direct contrast to the wisdom of the world I had heard. God had already positioned us for supernatural unity in the beginning! I had been robbed again, wasting time questioning if we could ever attain it. He blessed me with brand new confidence that day, that we could live in unity starting right then, if we would truly believe He had already accomplished this for us!

Later that night, as I shared the insight with Gordon, he too felt awed by the Lord's gentle correction. We gained much more ground that night, standing together with thankful hearts.

Fast forward a few more years, and He had another piece of the unity puzzle to unveil.

I had just finished my morning quiet time, closed my Bible, and started out the door to go teach my class at the jail. In the dark hallway to the garage, He spoke six little words: ***I have made the two one.***

Ok, thanks! I started the car and planned to look it up later. I found it in Ephesians 2:14-16 (NIV):

"For He himself is our peace, who has made the two ... one and has destroyed the barrier, the dividing wall of hostility ... His purpose was to create in himself one new humanity out of the two, thus making PEACE, and in one body to reconcile both of them to God through the CROSS, by which He put to death their hostility."

As I wrote down the verses, I noticed it was all past tense when He spoke to me again:

I answered My own prayer of unity ON THE CROSS!

WOW! He knew I always prayed from John 17 that we would someday fulfil His heart cry for unity there!

I suddenly realized UNITY is part of the finished work of the cross, along with salvation! It is DONE!

Then He quickly gave me these 4 Steps.

HOW TO PRAY FOR UNITY

1. **THANK ME for accomplishing UNITY on the CROSS!**
2. **RECEIVE this finished work by FAITH, just as we did salvation!**
3. **CONFESS and REPENT of your own REBELLION in HOSTILITY against His finished work on the cross!**
4. **NOW, YOU CAN STEP INTO THIS UNITY!**

Good news! What a paradigm shift this has been.

Now we would be on high alert, not to walk and talk in rebellion against the cross. Thank you, Lord, for this finished work, which we choose to agree with.

"The God of peace will soon crush satan under your feet" (Romans 16:20).

The Lord replaced our painful division with great unity! For the last 20 years we have operated under a new "life motto" for our marriage: ***The Best is Yet to Be!***

Though Emily Dickinson penned those words in the 1800s, the Lord clearly spoke those words to me one day. They have been life changing, as we have spoken them almost every day over ourselves and have seen it come to pass.

We have also seen this blessing of reconciliation come to pass: **"All this is from God, who reconciled us to Himself through Christ and gave us the ministry of reconciliation"** (2 Corinthians 5:18 NIV).

For the last twenty years, we have found ourselves in a glorious season of life, with our marriage transformed and some new ministries unfolding. At the same time, we wisely decided to start keeping a convertible in the family, for one of our daily drives.

That means, several times a week, we must take a fun drive somewhere and explore God's great creation. We are in love with our God and His beautiful handiwork, whether mountains, beaches, flowers, animals, birds, skies, tree-lined back country roads, or the next new adventure around the bend. We grin our silly grins and simply enjoy the ride!

We are one. Oh, did I mention Gordon loves to buy me flowers all the time? He often advises husbands: "Never stop dating your wife!"

"Your wish is my command!" He loves to announce with a twinkle in his eyes. Our love grows deeper, daily.

A BLESSING

I bless you with eyes to see your breakthrough! I bless you to walk in the fear of the Lord, not the fear of the devil. I bless you to walk in greater unity and harmony with your family, defeating division together, in the Name of Jesus.

I bless you to believe in your heart: **The BEST is yet to BE!**

14
WIND AND WAVES OBEY
Matthew 8:23-27, Mark 4:35-41, Luke 8:22-25

In a boat with His disciples, Jesus fell asleep on a cushion, when suddenly a great tempest arose on the sea. Massive waves crashed over the sides, placing everyone in great jeopardy. Frantically the fearful disciples woke Him.

"Lord, save us! We are perishing! "

He sat up and questioned them, **"Why are you afraid, O you of little faith?"** Then He arose and rebuked the winds and the waves with three simple words, **"Peace, be still!"**

A great calm pervaded the stormy sea.

Some astonished disciples were beside themselves with wonder, **"Who can this be that even the winds and the sea obey Him?"**

REVELATION, LORD?

I saw Jesus standing on the shore ready to get into the boat as they set out that day, gazing out to sea. I then saw something He must have seen—a swirl of very high waves in the center of the lake, about 10-feet high, as if the storm had already begun to rage! He said nothing, but the Father had revealed they would soon undergo a furious encounter, physically and spiritually.

Later, as He stretched out in the boat to pray, the Father granted Him a peaceful sleep. Even though the disciples came to Him for help, they came in desperation, not faith. He not only had to rebuke the enemy's power in the wind and waves, but He also had to rebuke the enemy's awful waves of fear in His own disciples.

Turbulent waters needed to cease, inside and out!

"Peace, be still!"

ALONG THE WAY

On several occasions, my husband and I have seen great storms averted as our faith arose against ominous weather forecasts or darkening Pennsylvania skies: "We rebuke this storm in the Name of Jesus! This storm in the heavenlies is not allowed to come forth or cause any damage in this place!"

We have found Him faithful to answer those cries.

One of those times, a violent hailstorm clearly lifted, with zero damage in our county, but unleashed great devastation in nearby counties. The news showed unbelievable pictures of such heavy accumulations of hail, that it resembled piles of snow. That all commenced just as we gathered for our inner-city prayer walking group in downtown Allentown. The sky swiftly turned dark and foreboding, but as we prayed, it totally bypassed us!

He has led us to exercise our authority over the weather numerous times since then.

In America's past, there is a little-known historical account of Christopher Columbus rebuking a storm in the Atlantic, in Jesus' Name, which caused it to cease. Otherwise, they would have been shipwrecked, and the fleet would never have reached the shores of the New World.

In 1998, Gordon and I eagerly planned a three-day getaway for Valentine's weekend. Our flight path took us from Newark, New Jersey, to Houston, Texas, to Corpus Christie, Texas, where we had hotel reservations right on the beach. As we drove over to Newark, the skies began to dust the earth with a thin blanket of snow. Everything became surreal when we suddenly noticed a rainbow glistening through the snowflakes. We had never seen that phenomenon before! "That's odd," we remarked. We smiled and took it as a sweet, unexpected God-hug of love on our fun Valentine escape.

We breathed a sigh of relief as we settled into our gate area, with plenty of time to spare for our first flight. Soon, however, all our best laid plans received a huge jolt. The ticket agent's voice came over the intercom saying, "Sorry to inform you that this flight will be delayed, due to mechanical failure. You will need to rebook on a later flight." Now we clung to that rainbow blessing as a sign that all would still work out with His hand of intervention. We refused to be clobbered with disappointment.

Sadly, the next flight we could take would cause us to miss the last flight out of Houston that night, so we would have to fly out to Corpus Christi the next morning instead. Trying to soothe all their unhappy passengers, the airlines provided us all with ample vouchers for hotel, supper, and breakfast. Although one of our nights at the beach had just disappeared, we kept clinging to our rainbow image and trusted His hand in everything.

Fortunately, when we finally went out for supper at about 10:00 in Houston, we found a 24-hour diner that enabled us to treat ourselves to some juicy T-bones with our vouchers. To our delight, we realized we could have a second T-bone in the morning, "medium well, please!"

In the middle of the night, however, we had another jolt. Gordon awoke with extreme discomfort in his chest. We prayed and waited a few minutes, but it worsened. After calling 911, we prayed and waited some more. Since they didn't arrive too promptly, by the time they arrived, all the pain had subsided. They took his vitals, and everything looked normal. They indicated it could have been muscle spasms, not the heart. They gave him the option to go to the ER or not, knowing we would miss our next flight if we went. Gordon felt peace that our prayers had been answered and went back to bed.

We enjoyed "Round 2" of our T-bone steaks for breakfast, happy that today we would make it to the beach! As we prepared for landing in Corpus Christie later, we noticed a heavy fog blanketing the area. Incoming flights all began to circle numerous times, stalling for an opening. Our pilot finally told us we had one last time to circle and land or we would need to return to Houston, due to lack of fuel. Great. We all sighed with relief when he came back on the intercom and said they had cleared us for landing. As we began our final descent, the pilot suddenly jerked the plane straight up in practically a 90 degrees ascent! *What was happening?* Tension filled the cabin, as everyone questioned the abrupt shift.

The pilot only said, "The fog was too thick." Fortunately, he set the plane down safely after circling once more. We all sighed with relief. When we deplaned, Gordon checked the arrivals and confirmed his suspicions. A larger aircraft had just landed at the time we had first descended; thankfully, a collision had been averted! God spared us all. We are not ones to get fearful for the next flight, however, as we fully entrust our lives into His capable hands.

As we drove across the bridge to South Padre Island, radiant oranges and reds began to streak across the sky in a breathtaking display. We agreed we must quickly get our bags in our room and get down to the beach to catch some stunning sunset photos.

More surprises awaited us. Gordon failed to tell me that our resort boasted a unique décor, inside and out. The builders had secured the famed Robert Wyland of Hawaii, to paint murals of whales and other fish on almost every wall. His famous technique showed both underwater and above water scenes together in most of his paintings.

As we exited the elevator, we saw our room number on the first door facing us to the left. Directly in front of us Wyland had painted the three sailing ships of Christopher Columbus' fleet, extending from floor to ceiling. Despite our hurry, we simply stood staring for a few moments at the magnificent renderings.

Gordon informed me that Columbus had in fact landed there at Corpus Christie on one of his journeys. In fact, he informed me that life-sized replicas of the Nina, Pinta and Santa Maria had been built in Spain in 1992 for the 500th anniversary of Columbus' first journey and had been donated to Corpus Christie for permanent docking. Hence, the reason for the three ships painted on "our" wall.

"Oh, the beach!" One of us exclaimed. Our minds had been spinning through 500 years of history. As we stepped through the door of our back-to-reality room, a blazing crimson and coral sky that married east with west sizzled its neon lights through our giant window. We abandoned our bags and rushed over to shoot, shoot, shoot!

Throwing our winter coats on the bed, we scurried off to the beach with my batik wrap in tow. We could hear the beach calling our names. As we stepped foot onto the white sand, we felt the wind picking up a bit. We knew we had some incredible photos that needed to happen, so we tried to ignore the wind. In just a couple of minutes though, the wind abruptly changed direction, swirling the sand around and stinging our arms. I tried to wrap my batik throw around me, but it caught the wind and blew straight out horizontally.

Gordon laughed and tried to take a picture. Just as he clicked, I saw him looking startled behind me.

"What?" I yelled over the wind. I turned to see an air conditioner blowing across the beach. *Oh!* Then I noticed the metal beach signs were whipping dangerously.

"Let's get out of here!" Gordon yelled back. Dark clouds billowed in to thwart our glorious exhibit overhead. We had a mere five minutes outside, before needing to run back for shelter.

"Lord, protect us!" We prayed as we scurried away.

Once safely back upstairs, we headed to the window to observe the changing sky. Gordon noticed some sparks flying everywhere as electrical lines on the bridge began to arc in the wind, amidst the steady stream of traffic. It looked so dangerous! Gordon remarked, "We're going to lose power. We better pray for safety for everyone."

We tried to pray, but the howling winds and metal pieces flying by our window punctuated our thoughts and interrupted our prayers. Gordon stood up, seemingly agitated, and left to check on the restaurant situation while we still had power. He wondered if we should try to leave.

I knew I would not be crossing that bridge tonight. I opted to stay put and keep praying while he went to check on things downstairs. I expected him back in about five minutes, to let me know about supper. However, he stayed gone for about an hour, so I kept storming the heavens.

When he finally returned, he had a big smile and looked quite happy and peaceful, though the winds continued to howl. "Well, you look a lot different than when you left!" I blurted out. "What happened?"

Excitedly he recounted what he had been doing. "As I walked down the hall to the front desk, I heard a lot of angry, fearful guests complaining to the agent. He looked overwhelmed and I realized he needed help. So, I asked him what I could do for him. He looked so relieved. Immediately, he handed me a box of light sticks to put out on all the floors. By then, the power had gone out. That's what took so long!"

It was my turn to laugh. I pictured Gordon putting out all those light sticks in the dark hallways, and was hearing the old song, *"This little light of mine; I'm gonna let it shine!"*

He laughed too. Then he sat on the bed and said matter-of-factly, "We will just have to fast tonight since the restaurant is closed. We really need to pray tonight anyway!" Yes, we did. I failed to mention one of our purposes for booking the trip had been to seek the Lord for Gordon's career path.

He had been in insurance sales for 22 years. Things had become hard and monotonous. He wondered about resigning to do full-time mission work. The Mercy Ships compassion ministry had our attention, a powerful branch of YWAM, Youth With A Mission. Their story in *Is That Really You God?* by Loren Cunningham had captured the hearts of our entire family.

We stood at our stormy crossroads together that night in the hotel room. Not long into our prayer time, Gordon heard his answer: **three ships, three boys!**

Oh! We would not go. We would send our three sons. The destinies of five people hung in those four words. Gordon would not resign, but would go on to eventually complete 29 years, before taking early retirement.

We marveled at His ways that night, reflecting on the events of that trip: the snow, the rainbow, the mechanical failure, the 911 incident, the fog and near miss, the difficulties arriving, the storm, and the three ships painted on the wall adjacent to our door. We had found peace in the storm, so we could hear Him speak, not in the wind, but in His still small voice! Gratitude filled our hearts. Imagine our surprise the next morning to learn that we had just weathered an "unforecasted" hurricane.

Later, I thought of Elijah's story in 1 Kings 19:11-12:

Then He said, "Go out, and stand on the mountain before the Lord." And behold, the Lord passed by, and a great and strong wind tore into the mountains and broke the rocks in pieces before the Lord, *but* **the Lord** *was* **not in the wind; and after the wind an earthquake,** *but*

the Lord *was* not in the earthquake; and after the earthquake a fire, *but* the Lord *was* not in the fire; and after the fire a still small voice.

YWAM had three mercy ships at that time that were situated in various parts of the world: Europe, the Caribbean, and the South Seas. Their amazing service of free medical care, along with evangelism and various special projects had stirred all our hearts.

Five months later in July, our three boys left for their first YWAM trip to Texas and Mexico. In the fall, our oldest two flew excitedly to the other side of the world, to live on the Anastasis Mercy Ship, docked in Belgium. Soon, they would travel down to the Canary Islands, then to the coast of Sierra Leonne, Africa. They had been accepted into their five-month Discipleship Training School: three months training on board, and two months trekking through Africa doing missions on foot.

Two years later, our youngest son would graduate from High School and head out west to another DTS, with his best friend. They studied in Kona, Hawaii at University of the Nations, before heading to the Philippines for their two months of boots on the ground mission work.

Each week during the three-month training, they drank deeply from teachings from world class speakers that arrived for a week at a time.

Ministry time meant a wide gamut of things they had never done. The two in Africa backpacked during their two months, visiting several refugee camps. They learned to eat lots of unusual things and be very thankful for what they received. They all had their turn to preach. On weekends, they took off to explore their surroundings, with many crazy tales. They came home with a world view that had forever changed their priorities and their hearts. All three returned home saying it was the best season of their lives, and they would never be the same.

The next year, it was our turn. We finally took some short-term mission trips that took us to Honduras. As we lived in our compact berth those weeks, we realized that we did not miss whatever stuff we had left behind.

Years later, the Lord would grow our understanding of our authority, in learning to rebuke stormy weather in the skies overhead. But on that night, our blessing came as He gave us His perfect peace in the storm.

"God is our refuge and strength, a very present HELP in trouble. Therefore we will not fear, even though the earth be removed, and though the mountains be carried into the midst of the sea; Though its waters roar and be troubled, Though the mountains shake with its swelling." (Psalms 46:1-3)

A BLESSING

Any storms swirling in your heart at this moment must cease! I bless you to turn your eyes and heart fully upon the Lord, the Prince of Peace, to overrule every stormy wave. Be blessed with His perfect peace! *Peace be still!*

Tell others what great things the Lord has done.

15
CASTING OUT THE LEGION
Matthew 8:28-34, Mark 5:1-20, Luke 8:26-39

As they came to the other side of the lake, after the storm, they arrived in the country of the Gadarenes. Immediately, a man consumed with unclean spirits ran to Jesus. He lived naked in the tombs, and could not be restrained with chains or shackles, but always broke them off. He cried out day and night, cutting himself with stones.

As he ran to Jesus from afar, he cried out loudly, **"What have I to do with You, Jesus, Son of the Most High God? I beg You not to torment me!"**

Jesus commanded the unclean spirits, **"Come out!"**

They begged Him not to send them into the abyss.

"Send us into the swine!"

Jesus gave them permission. The unclean spirits immediately left the man and ran into the herd of two-thousand swine which ran violently over a cliff into the sea and drowned. Deliverance had finally come to this tormented soul. Now, he could freely sit down in peace, clothed and in his right mind.

Everyone from the area voiced great fear of such power and begged Jesus to leave. As He was leaving in the boat, the delivered man pleaded to go with Him, but Jesus sent the man home with the instruction, **"Tell others what great things the Lord had done."**

That's exactly what the man did, sharing all through the region of the Decapolis (meaning, ten cities). Everyone marveled to see this life transformed!

REVELATION, LORD?

I saw the face of Jesus from the side, smiling with great peace and joy, as He peered closely into the face of this free man. **"Let me go with you,"** *the man begged his new Master and Friend. There was a longing to nurture him playing across Jesus' face, as He thoughtfully considered this request.*

The Father had other plans, however. The Lord could see visions of this man blessing countless others with the miracle of his new life. He would be a natural evangelist! With His hand on the man's shoulder, Jesus had to release this new son, and send him back to his own family.

His whole household would soon step into the Light of the Kingdom.

ALONG THE WAY

When I was first asked to start teaching at the women's prison each week, I never knew it would continue for a span of 29 years. Since I usually had between 10-20 women come, you can imagine my surprise one day when only one woman walked in for our Bible study. I never received an explanation for that. I knew in my heart that God had something special for this woman. I'll call her "Lil."

She seemed quiet and calm. I had no idea the severe troubles that crouched within her small frame. Soon I began to meet with her privately each week in the visitor's room, as her "spiritual advisor." She seemed to respond well to my Bible teachings, counselling, and prayer sessions. Slowly her story came out.

She lived alone, divorced from a pastor, and had suffered a long drug habit. Her wounded heart had been extremely battered early in sexual abuse, which continued many years by several different men. Eventually doctors diagnosed her with extreme DID, or dissociative identity disorder. (She had 22 multiple personalities that surfaced frequently.) She helped me understand that people in long-term abuse often dissociate from their pain and trauma by escaping into other personalities, as a survival mode to not feel so much pain. To the best of my understanding, many somehow choose to allow this to happen, rather than choosing suicide or possibly going insane.

At the time I met her, she had lost all friends, and felt no one cared. The Lord stirred His compassion deep within my gut; I cared. After about nine months more in jail, they sentenced her to Work Release. Since our church collected clothing for women, I offered to take her to find some things she needed. She appreciated the kindness and took delight in her new clothes. It was great to see her in colorful clothing after seeing her only in the prison khakis all year.

After we left the church, we had some extra time, so I thought we would find a place to pray. I pulled my white van under the shade of some tall oaks in the city park. She began sharing a major stronghold she hoped we could pray about. Unsuspecting that the stronghold had been fueled by a demon, I readily agreed. As I began praying over her, however, white foam soon started bubbling out of her mouth. Even more alarmingly, as the unclean spirit manifested, I noticed her facial features being distorted! Now she looked much older and even resembled a different nationality.

As I wondered what to do, Lil's body lunged toward me. Although the unclean spirit had caught me off guard, the Holy Spirit intervened on my behalf, as my **"very present help in trouble"** (Psalm 46:1). I heard myself boldly proclaiming: "The blood of Jesus is over you!" As I spoke those words, Lil's entire body froze, and her face jerked back as if I had physically struck her! She fell back in the passenger seat, as her body suddenly went limp.

Those dramatic results startled me more than her actions had. I quickly thanked the Holy Spirit for taking charge. Within another minute, however, the demon roused and made the same move a second time. This time I knew to speak the blood of Jesus over her again. The results were the same, as her head jerked away, and her body fell back in the seat, seeming completely exhausted. She dozed off in a slumber for a few minutes, and the distortion slowly left her face.

"And they overcame him [the accuser, the devil] **by the blood of the Lamb, and by the word of their testimony."** (Revelation 12:11)

I felt deep compassion for this weak and struggling sister. Despite all the turmoil, the Lord gave me supernatural peace ministering to her. My Prince of Peace proved Himself faithful in this storm. He impressed me that any demonic encounter I might face would not harm me. He had dramatically demonstrated to me the authority I had been given in His Name. I thanked Him for entrusting me with His power and authority to "set the captives free."

I realized we needed to end our session before anything else stirred itself. As we headed back to Work Release, Lil roused and seemed her normal self. She asked if I would continue to help her and pleaded with me not to give up on her. Somehow, she had been aware of the drama that had just transpired, though powerless to prevent it.

Later that evening, she called me from Work Release and requested some further prayer over the phone about the same stronghold. When I hesitated, she said she knew it would be okay. She felt close to her breakthrough and seemed desperate to press in again. The Holy Spirit gave me the words to pray, and wisdom that was not my own. His deliverance knows no bounds! She felt the demon leave her body, and abruptly ran to the bathroom, as she left the old phone receiver dangling for a few minutes. (There's often gagging that happens as demons leave.) When she returned, she sounded like a free woman. She knew one dark door had been shut and expressed deep gratitude. I heard some new joy sprinkling through her words as we hung up.

"For My thoughts are not your thoughts, nor are your ways My ways," says the Lord." (Isaiah 55:8)

In the months ahead I witnessed her operate in growing faith and peace. Eventually after her time at Work Release had been completed, she asked if I would be willing to supervise her weekly visits with her young son. I agreed. Month after month she gained more healing.

After about three years she moved across the state. I knew that our God would complete the good work He had begun in that broken vessel.

"Because of the Lord's great love, we are not consumed, for His compassions never fail. They are new every morning; great is Your faithfulness!" (Lamentations 3:22-23 NIV)

"The Lord is my rock, my fortress and my deliverer; My God is my rock, in whom I take refuge; my shield and the horn of my salvation, my stronghold." (Psalms 18:2 NIV)

A BLESSING

I bless you to stay ready for service—any service, any time! I pray you will not shrink back when the enemy amps up his game, rather that you will stand firm. I bless you with the understanding that the Lord will always lead you in triumph. I bless you with the freedom and courage to set the captives free.

Your faith has made you well.

16
TWELVE-YEAR INFIRMITY
Matthew 9: 20-22, Mark 5:25-34, Luke 8:40-48

A ruler had come to Jesus with a serious request. He hoped Jesus would raise his daughter back to life! Jesus began walking with the man through a crowd to go help the man's daughter. Suddenly, Jesus felt healing power leaving Him. He turned around and asked, "**Who touched my garments?**"

The disciples scoffed at the request, saying *many people* had pressed against Him! But Jesus knew an urgent pursuer of healing had touched the flow of His anointing.

Finally, a woman hesitantly spoke up as she trembled and fell down before Him. She had gone to many doctors for 12 long years about her flow of blood, and had spent all her means, but none could help her. She knew if she only touched the hem of his garment, she would be well!

Despite her trembling and shame, and her deep embarrassment of her long-term defilement, she submitted to her Master.

"**It was me,**" she replied in great humility.

"Daughter, be of good cheer! Your faith has made you well. Go in peace and be healed of your affliction," He reassured her.

REVELATION, LORD?

"God resists the proud but gives grace to the humble." (James 4:6)

I saw the Lord suddenly freeze in action, as He felt the power leave, and as He "saw" a hand reaching out behind him. Who had touched Him?

The Father did not reveal it. Jesus realized that faith needed to voice its private request openly that day, to fully glorify God before the world with Love's intervention. The desperate woman braved the scorn and spoke her need.

Faith had pursued. Faith had acted. Faith had been heard.

Now, this humble woman would forever walk a new walk, as a renowned vessel of honor. The years of her dishonor were over. Love had heard her desperate plea and set her feet on a new path.

(Next, some dry bones awaited His touch!)

ALONG THE WAY

There had been many times when I prayed for people with pain, who afterward told me that they had been in accidents many years prior, and they had suffered pain ever since.

One man simply told us he suffered horrible back pain every day. My friends and I prayed for him. and it all left immediately. He couldn't believe what God had done for him. He had never believed God loved him until that moment.

We found out the next week that about five or six years earlier, he had broken his neck in five places and his back in five places. Though the pain tried to return several times, we won the battle, praying once on the phone with him, and again the next two to three times we saw him.

The next week, in our prayer time, a woman had severe shoulder pain. We encouraged him to pray for her, so he laid hands on her, and God healed her instantly! Now, he was even more shocked that God would let him help someone else. We have observed that when one receives healing in a certain area, one can very readily see the same results in others if he or she will step out in faith to pray for them.

One memorable day at the women's prison proved to be a milestone in the healing breakthroughs. One girl came in saying how her back had been healed the week before, and she had never even believed in God before. "Now, I'm a believer!" she exclaimed.

She told other girls they needed to get prayer for any pain they had. So, with that recommendation, the requests began. One girl said she too had terrible back pain. I laid hands on her, prayed and it left. Then another girl said, "I have a horrible sore throat, and it even hurts just to swallow." The Lord took all her pain away immediately.

They all became wide-eyed as they watched His healing power flowing so freely! Another girl had a bad toothache with a swollen cheek. The pain stopped immediately in prayer, and by the time our session was over, the swelling was gone.

One girl had carpal tunnel syndrome in both hands. Gone! We saw seven miracles that day!

Another day, the Lord led me to pray for His healing in a very different manner. As I was halfway across the room to pray for the first person, the Lord impressed me to go back and sit down. Then He wanted me to ask the person who was healed the last week to go pray over her. She hesitated but willingly did so. God released His healing power under her hands!

Then as the next woman asked for prayer, I asked the one who had just received that healing to pray over the next person. She did and the next healing came forth. They each prayed very short and simple prayers, but it didn't matter. If they needed help with the words, I would help them from my seat.

Some shared that their pain had originated with accidents about 20 years prior. Much rejoicing filled the room that day.

God's sweet grace amazed us all!

That day as I left the prison, with a heart full of gratitude and praise, the Lord surprised me with yet another healing need. As I started to descend the long flight of stone steps outside the prison, a woman came hobbling up the stairs on a cane, moaning in pain with each step.

Ok, Lord, here we go again!

I knew I couldn't ignore her, after seeing Him heal seven or eight ladies upstairs. So, I offered prayer for this stranger in need.

"Absolutely!" She exclaimed.

I told her that the Lord had just healed a roomful of ladies upstairs, so I guess His plans that day also included her.

Now I really had her attention.

I usually ask people how bad the pain is on a scale of 1 to 10, with "10" being the worst. It's very helpful to measure their progress. I prayed for her hip pain, and it went from an "8" to a "4." We prayed again, and it went down to a "2." Joy beamed forth in her eyes! She couldn't have felt more blessed.

I watched her drop off some money at the window for her sister in prison, then saw her get in the car as a passenger. I felt I was to give her my card in case she wanted to call for more prayer. More joy!

"Yes, I will call you. Thank you so much!" She began to tell her driver all about it.

A few days later she called. We prayed on the phone and her pain improved once again. Her hip was still much better, but now it was in her back. The Lord's blessings continued.

The next week when I went back to the prison, one of the ladies who had been healed last time said, "That was my sister you prayed with on the steps!"

Oh wow! Only God can orchestrate all that. Then I remembered something else. "Didn't you ask prayer for her because she wasn't speaking to you?"

"Yes."

"And now she is?"

"Yes!" God had touched her heart, not just her hip!

"In fact, she is hoping you will come over and pray with her more in person."

So, I did.

Three months later when the incarcerated woman was released, her sister invited her to come stay with her awhile! Now they are great friends again. Thank you, Lord, for your amazing plans to use us to set the captives free, inside and outside the jail!

A BLESSING

I bless you to go forth each day in His peace, not needing to plan every minute of your day, but growing in flexibility and yielding to the supernatural work of the Spirit along the way. I bless you to see the "least of these" along the way and to shine His love, peace, and power to everyone the Spirit draws to you.

Do not be afraid. Only believe. . .

17
DAUGHTER'S RESURRECTION
Matthew 9:18-26, Mark 5:21-24, 35-43,
Luke 8:40-42, 50-56

When Jesus crossed the Sea of Galilee again after casting out the legion, a great throng was awaiting Him. Jairus, a ruler of the synagogue, came begging at His feet, **"My only daughter lies at the point of death! Come and lay your hands on her and she will live!"** As Jesus began to walk with him, the needy woman intercepted Him."

Meanwhile, friends came and said the girl had died, "So why bother the teacher any further?" But Jesus responded to the father, **"Do not be afraid. Only believe and she will be made well!"**

When they reached the house, they heard mourners wailing loudly and playing songs of mourning on the flutes.

He sent them all away saying, **"Go away! Do not weep; she is not dead; but sleeping."** They ridiculed Him because they knew she had died. Allowing only Peter, James, John and her parents inside the room, Jesus took the young girl by the hand and called, **"Talitha, cumi—Little girl, I say to you, arise!"** Immediately she arose and walked! He commanded that she be given food to eat. Astonishment filled the room. He then charged them to tell no one about it! Of course, the incredible news of this resurrection spread throughout the region.

REVELATION, LORD?

God had brought a lofty ruler from the synagogue to his knees in the dust. He had come to the end of himself and his powerless rules. Now faith and humility would not be denied.

As the delay took place for the desperate woman's healing along the way, the Father clearly allowed the time for the daughter's death to transpire, much like He would do later with Lazarus. God had in mind a greater miracle, a resurrection!

Again, Jesus only did what He saw the Father do.

The Holy Spirit gave me a glimpse into the room where death had come that day. I saw an arm in a flowing white sleeve, extended over the girl. It seemed likely it's what Jesus had seen as He approached the closed door where her deathly form lay. The arm of the Father of Life hovered there well ahead of Yeshua's presence.

Hence, **"She's not dead, only sleeping."**

She awoke. Shocked gasps and whispers replaced the wailing. Fear vanished. Holy awe swept through the atmosphere.

Life and light had trampled the darkness of death.

"O death, where is your sting?" (1 Corinthians 15:55)

ALONG THE WAY

In 2011, Pastor Larry Burd invited Gordon and I to appear on his television show, *Living Truth,* in Allentown, Pennsylvania. He wanted to interview us about our new start-up ministry, Pray for Lehigh Valley. After we finished our taping, he invited us to stay and watch the next interview. He knew we would be interested to hear some radical healing testimonies that would be shared. The program did not disappoint.

The stories of Tom and Kay Whipple of nearby Easton stirred our hearts, as we heard radical faith in operation. When we dialogued with them in the studio afterwards, the Lord connected our hearts in rich communion. They had also heard our taping and wanted to commit to joining our team of street adopters in the Lehigh Valley, to pray daily for His Kingdom to come, and shut down the darkness over the land.

Recently we reconnected as I wrote this chapter to refresh my mind with this story. Tom and Kay had left North Carolina, and come to our valley here, as "sent ones" by the Lord. They answered His call to be "missionaries to the Lehigh Valley." The Lord indeed had great plans for them here. They eventually opened their "Whipple's Works Upholstering" in Easton and began their "marketplace ministry." They would both serve there as Kingdom entrepreneurs, with hearts of compassion, a strong evangelistic lifestyle, and the anointing of the Lord to impact many lives.

To walk into their shop, one could immediately tell that they ran their place of business very differently than most. A special prayer room had been set up for praying with customers. On one wall they had written, "It's God's problem!" Tom and Kay encouraged customers to write their problems and prayer requests right on the walls. Over time, numerous requests, along with answers and dates soon blanketed three of the walls. The fourth one they designated for "Salvations."

People signed their names and dates once they had received Jesus as Savior. I saw these lists, and all are too numerous to count! Hallelujah!

Tom shared an amazing story during the television recording of a young man in their neighborhood. When Tom met him, Lloyd was in his mid-twenties, and suffered some mental challenges. He lived a sedentary lifestyle, and now resided in his grandfather's home. His loving mother suffered poor health and could no longer take care of him. His grandfather insisted on helping. Lloyd weighed about 250 pounds and loved to eat! At times, he would go knocking on the neighbors' doors for extra food, saying, "I'm hungry." All the neighbors knew his situation and kindly offered him a peanut butter sandwich or possibly a warm plate of food.

One fateful Tuesday, however, everything changed. Returning from a walk in the neighborhood, he blurted out to his grandfather, "I sick!" His grandfather didn't think much about it and sent him upstairs to lie down. A little later when he went up to check on him, he discovered that Lloyd's body weight had ballooned to twice its size, his face and lips had turned red and he seemed to be unconscious! Greatly alarmed, Grandfather immediately called the ambulance. It took six men to carry him down the narrow stairs. Lloyd's heart had gone into shock. With his weight now around 450-500 pounds, it took two beds to support him at the hospital, and five sheets to cover him. By the next day, he had no brainwaves and had to go on life-support.

That Saturday, Lloyd's mother desperately reached out to Tom and asked, "Will you go pray over Lloyd at the hospital? He's dying!" Tom had been praying at home every day for him, but despite the mother's request, he strangely felt no leading of the Lord to go to the hospital.

Driving home from church the next day, however, Tom heard the Lord speak two simple words: "Go pray."

Now he knew he must go to the hospital right away. When he reached Lloyd's room, Tom walked in to find the staff had already been shutting down Lloyd's life-support. They had removed the oxygen and all the electrodes and pronounced him dead. He hadn't had brain waves for four days and his body had transitioned from red to black and blue.

Tom walked over to the doctor and told him matter-of-factly, "I came to pray for him."

Exasperated, the doctor turned to him with a tone of ridicule, "What's with you Christians?! Can't you see there's no brain waves? Look! He's already turned black and blue!"

Tom stood his ground, and all the staff backed away as he moved close to Lloyd's bedside. Just then, the Lord reminded Tom of a verse from Jeremiah on their church bulletin that morning. "What's better than the Word of God to pray over him?" he thought.

He simply spoke the verse over Lloyd's lifeless shell:

"'For I know the plans I have for you,' declares the Lord, 'plans to prosper you and not to harm you, plans to give you hope and a future.'" (Jeremiah 29:11 NIV)

"Amen!" Tom ended his simple prayer and laid his hand on Lloyd's hard, blackened foot.

As Tom started to walk away the heart monitor beeped, brain waves reappeared on the monitor and Lloyd's finger started moving!

"Momma!" he suddenly heard the young man speak! Shock and astonishment flooded the room!

Momma wept for joy while Grandfather ran up to the bed with his cane. The doctors and nurses rapidly flew into action, despite their stunned disbelief. *"He's alive!"*

Tom stepped back from all the commotion and left the room. As Tom exited the corridor, Grandfather came hobbling down the hall and told the nurses: "Tom is next of kin, if he wants to come in again!" They all agreed.

As the Lord delayed Tom's visit to the hospital, our heavenly Father clearly allowed the time for the young son's death to transpire, much like with Jairus daughter. God had in mind a greater miracle, a resurrection!

The backstory of Lloyd's sickness and death is quite tragic.

One of his neighbors had become irate over Lloyd's persistent begging for food. That fateful day, the angry neighbor decided to slip some poison into his sandwich! After Lloyd's resurrection miracle, the neighbor grew remorseful and confessed.

Fortunately, there is a better ending to this story.

Genesis 50:20 (NIV) reveals the heart of the Redeemer, as Joseph spoke these words of grace to his brothers after their brutality and betrayal: **"You intended to harm me, but God intended it for good to accomplish what is now being done."**

Monday morning, our friend Tom asked his pastor from Nazareth, Pennsylvania, to go into the hospital with him to meet Lloyd. When Pastor Sean walked in, he couldn't believe Lloyd's incredible size! Nurses had to work hard to prop Lloyd up with some pillows and hold up his head to see his visitors.

"Hi, Tom!" Lloyd called to him.

"Hi, Lloyd."

"Who's this?" Lloyd asked.

"This is my pastor, Pastor Sean."

"No, you're the pastor!" he said to Tom.

"No, I'm just a member of the church."

"Are you going to pour oil on me?" Lloyd wondered what they had come for. A Catholic priest had ministered "last rites" over him the day before, so he seemed to be wondering what would happen next.

"No, Lloyd. We are wondering if you would like to receive Jesus as your Savior?" Tom stated.

"Yes!" so Tom prayed over Lloyd once again for new life.

Lloyd opened his heart to the love of Jesus! Hallelujah!

"Most assuredly, I say to you, he who hears My word and believes in Him who sent Me, has everlasting life, and... has passed from death into life." (John 5:24)

Lloyd had a lengthy hospital stay of about three months, but slowly, his weight dropped back to its normal level. When they finally released him to return home, he had a new start, a new heart and a new Friend!

Of course, the incredible news of this resurrection spread throughout the neighborhood. Many came to their house for a long-awaited "Welcome Home" party. In the beginning, neighbors had had a hard time believing he had come back to life. But the power of Jesus could not be argued. Lloyd had come home after being pronounced dead! Tom and Kay gave him some special hugs. Grandfather, once reserved, now beamed from ear to ear.

New life and light had trampled the darkness of death.

"O Death, where is your sting?" (1 Corinthians 15:55)

Over a decade later, Lloyd still resides here in the Lehigh Valley, and takes his solitary walks through the neighborhood. But today Lloyd is a new man, and he knows he has a very special friend in Jesus!

Recently, he found himself back in the hospital for kidney issues, with pending surgery to remove one. Tom led out in prayer for spiritual awakening at the National Day of Prayer in Bethlehem. He relayed this resurrection story and ended by praying for the healing of his kidneys. The next day they informed him that no surgery would be necessary!

Thank you, Lord, Your hand of blessing remains upon this son.

A BLESSING

I bless you with the faith of Abraham to exhibit a powerful wait of faith in your life journey. I bless you to have eyes to see as the Father sees, and to *fear not* when faced with dire circumstances. I bless you to see the resurrection power of Jesus through your growing acts of obedience and faith!

According to your faith let it be to you.

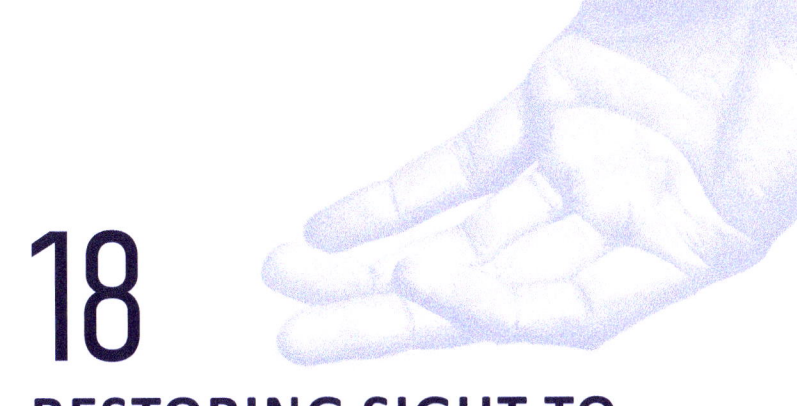

18
RESTORING SIGHT TO THE BLIND
Matthew 9:27-31

Two blind men began to follow Jesus, as He left the death-to-life scene of the ruler's daughter. They began crying out, **"Son of David, have mercy on us!"**

He replied, **"Do you believe that I am able to do this?"**

"Yes, Lord!"

He touched their eyes, **"According to your faith let it be to you."** They received their sight. He warned them [Greek: thundered, warned] not to tell anyone. However, they could not be silent. The news spread everywhere.

REVELATION, LORD?

Their spiritual eyes had already been opened, "Son of David!" They recognized His lineage as the Messiah and Lord. They already saw what many could not. Light had already penetrated their hearts.

The Lord has a way with words.

"Do you believe that I AM able to do this?"

*I saw Jesus standing face to face with these two godly men, His eyes filled with delight to do what He had come to earth to do: open the eyes of the blind! Yeshua said **"Yes"** to their "Yes," and in a flash, they now saw what they had only heard before—the Light of the world!*

By force of habit, their observant hands reached out to touch this Face of Grace. Shock, wonder, and joy overcame them! Love and Light embraced them as they squinted through years of tears. The Kingdom of heaven had come to shatter their darkness.

*The same powerful Voice had once spoken: **"Let there be light!"***

And there was light!

ALONG THE WAY

In the last two to three years, a newcomer, Gary Hale began to join us weekly at the Mosaic House of Prayer. Each session, we followed the lead of the Holy Spirit for our times of praise, prayer, prophecy, and personal ministry for one another. Gary proved to be a powerful addition to our crew. We came to know him as a passionate follower of Christ who expected the supernatural to happen every day. Soon, we learned that for the last 16 years, the Lord had opened some unusual doors for him in Africa, often travelling alone, preaching the Gospel and moving in miracles.

On his trip in 2022, Gary had just finished speaking when a desperate lady came to the platform seeking healing for her eyes. She could barely see two feet in front of her. With the aid of his interpreter, Pastor Gary declared full restoration of her eyesight. Despite the language barrier, Gary could clearly see wonder come over her face as she looked all around with caution giving way to joy. Blind eyes had been opened! Awe and gratitude swept through the onlookers.

The next night, she returned, happy eyes glistening with gratitude, asking to stand up and tell everyone what God had done. Glory hallelujah!

The next year as Gary returned to Tanzania, the pastor eagerly showed him the new platform they had built for him. It had been lovingly designed by two of the ladies in the church. Despite their neediness, they tried to anticipate his needs for the week. Such love!

The first Sunday morning, his eyes fell on a sweet little blind lady who had come. Her eyelids appeared to be closed so tightly that they almost seemed to be glued shut. The compassion of the Lord captured his heart immediately. He hoped those blind eyes would soon see!

On Tuesday morning of the seminar, he was excited to see her coming up to the platform to talk to him. She surprised him by sharing a testimony. "When you prayed over everyone about healing for pain, all the pain left in my feet and hands! I could not even go barefoot because it was too painful not to wear shoes." She could hardly contain her excitement. The leading to pray for her eyes still did not come that day.

Another day she came forward again, seeking healing, but this time for her knees. Gary had testified that God had healed his own knee pain. She said, "He healed your pain in your knees! Now, I need him to take away my knee pain!"

Gary prayed and all the pain left. She could hardly contain her relief! She unashamedly explained to him that the toilet in her house was just a bowl in the ground and her knee pain made it very difficult to squat down. Now there would be no more problems like that.

Eventually he was able to find out that she had lost her sight as a little girl when she was only one or two years old. Doctors told her parents she would never see again, so they enrolled her in a blind school. Gary had asked the Lord privately to tell him how to pray for her most effectively. The Lord impressed him that she had always carried that fear that she would never see again. Finally, he was able to tell her that she needed to break the power of those words off her. She agreed and they prayed to break them. Surprisingly, he still did not feel the leading of the Spirit to pray for her eyes.

The next day when he saw her, however, he was excited to see that her eyelids were almost halfway open! After he returned to America, Gary shared with me that she is still a work in progress, but he knows God will finish the work He began.

A few days later, his interpreter let him know that the blind lady had texted him that she now believes that God will heal her eyes soon!

With great expectation, we all look forward to hearing the end of this story!

Returning home to Pennsylvania, Gary always has opportunities to report on God's goodness in Africa. After one recent trip, as he shared the miracle accounts, bold faith began to spring up in hearts of listeners that God would do it again. Why not? Acts 10:34 clearly teaches that **"God is no respecter of persons."**

One Sunday morning at Word of Life Church in Allentown, a hopeful seeker came to Gary with his request. The seeker explained he had suffered compromised eyesight in one eye since his childhood. Immediately after the prayer of faith, he excitedly began to exclaim, "I can see! I can see!"

Later, he told his pastor, "I will never forget that man!" Gary gives all glory to Jehovah Jireh, our Healer! With each wondrous miracle, God underscores Gary's faith for multiplied miracles yet to come.

A BLESSING

I bless you to humble yourself and cry out for mercy! I bless you to step up to be the one to believe God for the new thing. I bless you to see SIGHT RESTORED in your own personal realm of influence.

19
THE MUTE SPEAKS
Matthew 9:32-34

An incredible chain of events unfolded that day. Immediately after Jesus healed the woman's issue of blood, raised the girl from the dead, and healed the two blind men, Jesus stood facing this man stricken with a mute demon. The disciples observed yet another incredulous miracle, as the Lord cast out the demon, and the man began to speak.

Despite the magnitude of this series of miracles, the day concluded in ridicule and false accusations from the religious leaders. **"He casts out demons by the ruler of the demons!"**

The crowd, however, fully acknowledge the supernatural being displayed in their midst, **"Nothing like this has ever been seen in all of Israel!"**

REVELATION, LORD?

I clearly heard: ***God is love. This is not a decision We make; this is who We are. When the Father's children are in step with His ways and have surrendered to His timing, as even I had to do*** *(waiting 30 years* to speak as the Messiah), **then the purified hearts are able to both carry and release purified love that will change the world.**

I learned obedience as a man through the sacrifice of suffering, waiting for the times of the Father, known and understood only by Him. He taught me to walk by faith as an Adam during those 30 long years of hiddenness and seeming powerlessness.

I saw Jesus agonizing alone in prayer, laboring on his knees before the Father, much as we have seen the renditions of Him in Gethsemane. He seemed to be crying out for strength to carry on in the face of deep ridicule, rejection, and painful attacks upon His kind and gentle Spirit.

ALONG THE WAY

Ever since I met Karoline, her deep hunger for the Lord has been evident. Hence, she has always believed that His supernatural power should flow out of her life, as a natural part of her day. She eagerly expects opportunities to pray for strangers "along the way," whether in the grocery store, or the doctor's office. There's no slowing her down. No one can believe she is 90! God has kept her beaming, spry and young at heart.

At times, Karoline has had opportunities to speak in various places. She told the Lord she was tired of not seeing much happen after the meetings, as she believed miracles should take place each time. Her next engagement would be at a Women's Aglow meeting. Seeking a breakthrough, she asked the Lord: *What do I need to do in order to see the miracles of the Bible?*

You must fast and pray! He instructed her. So, she did.

After speaking that night, a woman approached her seeking healing for a young man at her side. He had gotten electrocuted on his job as an electrician and as a result had lost his ability to speak. Sadly, he always needed to carry a doctor's note with him verifying that he could not speak.

Karoline agreed to pray and see what God would do. As soon as she turned toward the young man something unusual rose in her and she didn't even need to pray! Without even thinking about it, she simply pointed to him and declared to him: "You will speak today! In the name of Jesus, Say 'JESUS'!"

"JESUS!" he immediately spoke! The healing power of Jesus settled upon him, as he continued to speak to the people around him. Karoline moved on to pray for others.

Hallelujah Lord, for releasing the tongue of the mute and setting this captive free! Manifest your power in each of us Lord, as we go forth with Your heart of compassion.

ON ANOTHER NOTE

The Lord brought a different type of breakthrough to mind, to share in this chapter.

I had personally suffered great shyness during most of my school days, as my family had moved frequently for several years, due to Daddy's accounting job with the oil wells in several states: Texas, Oklahoma, New Mexico, and Mississippi. Because of the transient nature of Daddy's job, I attended four different elementary schools in first grade! Moving so much had left its mark. Even though my struggle lessened over time, the battle was not fully overcome until my college days. Finally, I no longer felt like an outsider.

My sister and I, along with our sweet daddy, all tended to be soft spoken. Through the years, people often said to me, "No one can hear you, Gail. You need to speak up!"

I must admit, it became rather annoying to hear that over and over. I believe it caused my voice to recoil even more. Years later, as an adult, the Lord had a surprise for me. He informed me, **You don't have a soft voice. You just have a habit of speaking softly!**

I welcomed that sweet insight from my Maker and chose to believe Him. Now I knew I could break that bad habit, which had become a stronghold.

Eventually I enjoyed freedom and grace to be loud, or quiet—my choice! Recently, the Lord revealed another aspect of training for my speech. This time, He spoke to me in a dream, with several brief nuggets of wisdom. One of them was just two words: **Be bold!**

I woke up and jotted down what I had heard. He continued to speak. **Your days of being reserved are over. Being reserved is confining yourself to yourself, not sharing yourself with the world. It is fear based and self-focused.**

To be bold is to know:

a. **Who you are.**
b. **Who I have made you to be.**
c. **What you have to bless others.**
d. **Caring enough to do it.**

It is being a good steward of YOU. Being bold must be balanced with love and humility. True boldness is not arrogance, but confidence in Me.

Thank you, Lord!

This ties in with yet another breakthrough He had for me one time. He had begun to give me prophetic words for people. I shared them quietly and privately. One day in prison, the Lord decided to help me walk in new freedom! I had been leading worship on my keyboard before the lesson, when I heard Him say: **Quit playing and give all the ladies a word.**

Are you kidding, Lord?

I had learned by then not to argue with the Lord. He was telling me to go way out on a long limb with those eight ladies, to be seen and heard in a new way. Faith suddenly began to surge inside my heart for this new thing, even though He had chosen to surprise me with some "on the job training" that day.

Okay, Lord.

I stood up and told them the Lord wanted me to pray over each of them and ask Him what He wanted to say to each of them. They were all as surprised as me. I reassured them, He would only have encouraging words for them. So, after one gal agreed to write all the words down for everyone, I began.

None of them saw that long shaky limb where I had to stand, so that helped. Somehow, I knew the Lord had the limb. And He did.

With the first seven women, He first gave me a picture of an object or a scene, pertaining to the person. I then would open my mouth to start describing the picture, and out came the rest! The meaning and the encouraging words all came from Him. He simply chose my mouth as a ready vessel. I felt like a mute speaking for the first time.

To my amazement, I felt the river flowing deep and wide! Refreshment washed over each unsuspecting heart. When I prayed over the last woman, instead of a picture, I heard one solitary word. Of course, the Lord chose to give me an unfamiliar word! So, I released the word and asked if anyone knew the meaning. The Lord loves to keep us humble. Fortunately, one young lady knew the meaning; after her definition, the Lord gave me the word of encouragement to follow.

Since that day, the ladies have asked me countless times for "that thing you do!" Each time the Lord has released unique words of life to them that shows how well He knows them and cares about their hearts. Few people had spoken life and hope over them before. Usually, a Bible verse is part of the affirmation and encouragement. They all keep their slips with those words jotted down and have told me weeks or years later how much it has helped them.

There are many stories I have from this. I'll share one brief example: one time as I listened, I saw the Lord drawing a word in the sand for a girl I hardly knew. The word was *stay*. There was more to it, but a couple weeks later she told me that part blew her away because she was picked up for escaping from Work Release. I had no idea what her charge had been!

She said all her life she had run from hard things.

Now she said, "No more running!"

The word of the Lord had changed another life.

A BLESSING

I bless you to see Him meet you powerfully at the point of your greatest need. I bless you to open your mouth wide, so He will fill it! I bless you to echo the greatest prayer in the Bible: **"Nevertheless, not My will, but Yours, be done."** (Luke 22:42b)

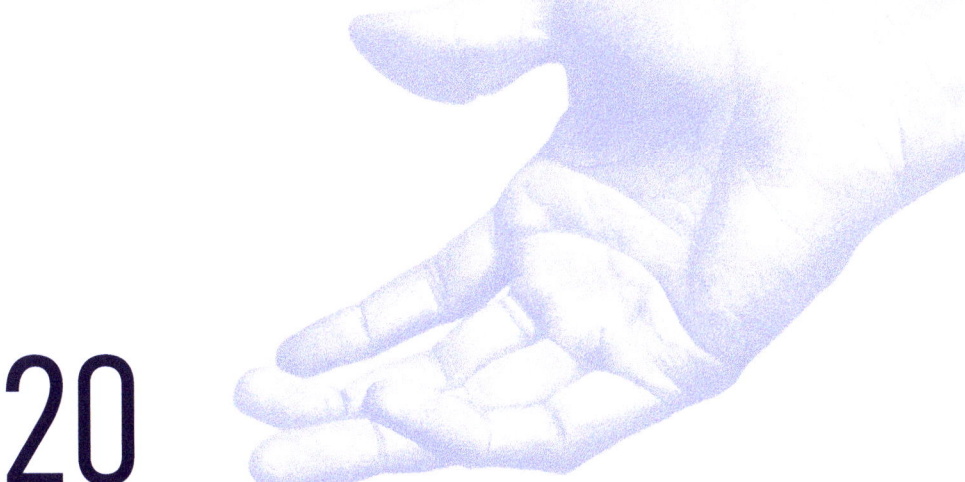

20
POOL OF BETHESDA ON THE SABBATH
John 5:1-21, 30

A man had been lying at this pool for many years, infirmed for 38 years. A great but weakened multitude was there (blind, lame, paralyzed) waiting for the angel to come down and stir the waters for healing. They all knew that only the first one into the water would be healed. Jesus saw the man and knew he had been there a long time, suffering paralysis. He asked him, **"Do you want to be made well?"**

He answered, "Sir, I have no man to put me into the pool, so that another person steps down before me."

Jesus said, **"Rise, take up your bed and walk!"** And he did.

The religious leaders rebuked the restored man for carrying his bed. When he told them about his miracle, he did not even know Jesus' name. Later in the temple, Jesus instructed him, **"See, you have been made well. Sin no more, lest a worse thing come upon you."** The Jews became angry and sought to kill Jesus for healing someone on the Sabbath.

Jesus responded, **"My Father has been working until now, and I have been working... The Son can do nothing of Himself, but what He SEES the Father do; for whatever He does, the Son also does in like manner. For the Father loves the Son and shows Him all things that He Himself does; He will show Him greater works than these, that you may marvel. For as the Father raises the dead and gives life to them, even so the Son gives life to whom He will... I can of myself do nothing... because I do not seek My own will, but the will of the Father who sent Me."**

REVELATION, LORD?

This blessing transported this unknown paralytic into the eternal pages of the Bible, not only with his healing, but also with a command to walk bravely in subjection to the Kingdom rather than unto men. To ***"rise up and walk"*** *had been music to his ears, but the instructions to* ***"Take up your bed"*** *on the Sabbath proved to be an immediate test. He passed! He walked! And he walked in brave obedience to the Lord on the Sabbath, despite the laws of the temple.*

The vision the Lord gave me came not from that day, but from our time, for us:

I saw Him peering down upon us from above, His large pool of Living Water waiting in our midst, fairly empty and waiting to be stepped into, with the multitudes lying paralyzed all around, afraid to believe, afraid to receive, afraid to look foolish and afraid of the ridicule of men.

The healing waters of the Lord are largely being ignored.

ALONG THE WAY

Early one blustery Tuesday morning, I picked up my friend who helped me teach the weekly Bible study at prison. She hopped in my car and rode downtown with me, since parking in center city Allentown can be quite challenging. We felt blessed as we found a spot right by the front steps of the prison. I shut the engine off and leaned back to hear the rest of a stirring God story she wanted to share. As she spoke, I noticed a man in his thirties across the street on crutches, wearing a full immobilizer leg brace. I silently wondered if the Lord had brought him here at this moment for a healing prayer from us.

Sure enough, as my friend continued telling her story, the man began to hobble across the street, straight toward us. I chuckled to myself, thinking today the Lord had taken the role of "Captain Obvious." I watched as the poor guy made several unsuccessful attempts to step up onto the curb, right in front of my car. My friend, however, still hadn't noticed him, engrossed in her story. I finally interrupted her saying, "Look, I think the Lord wants us to pray for this man."

When she saw him struggling, she said, "Oh, yes!"

"Just roll down your window and ask him if he'd like some prayer!"

She turned and gave me a strange look, like "really?" but rolled down her window and called to him.

He glanced our way with a surprised grin, "Sure!"

As we approached him, I asked him, "What's wrong with your leg?"

"Oh, it's not my leg. It's my foot." He explained that he had fallen off a roof and smashed all the bones in his heel. The surgeon told him he didn't have any fragments left large enough to heal. They scheduled him for surgery in two weeks to implant an artificial heel, after the swelling subsided.

Oh no!

My faith faltered, as I didn't feel ready to pray for that type of creative miracle. Then I thought about the likelihood of pain that I didn't mind praying for. Since the Lord healed my back pain years ago, I always have bold faith to believe He'll do the same for others.

"Do you have any pain right now?" I asked.

"Oh yes, constantly," he replied. On a scale of 1-10, with 10 being the worst, he said it was a 7 or 8 at the moment. So, I began to pray against the pain. Before I had finished, I heard myself also praying for a miracle, *that God would give him a new heel! What?*

Where did that prayer come from? Well, it just happened, and I tried not to wince in unbelief. Instead, I asked him what his pain level felt like now. He happily said it had gone down to just a 2! I gave him our "B-L-E-S-S-I-N-G-S" prayer card and asked him to call us with an update in a few weeks. By now we would be a little late for our Bible study, but we learned to be flexible and trust God with His ways, that are always quite different than ours.

Two weeks later, he called with some great news! "I just wanted to let you know, I went in for my surgical appointment, and the doctor said I don't need a new heel! He said my heel is 'healing nicely on its own!' So, I wanted to thank you for praying for me that day!"

Wow, even though the Lord knew I had NO faith for that heel to heal, He had performed the miracle anyway. I realized He always wanted me to *"go for it,"* even when my faith might be completely absent.

Thank you, Lord, for this great demonstration of your mercy and grace, not only for the man's miracle, but for the needs of a disciple in training!

How awesome is our God! I decided I would not falter in my faith any longer. He is more than able to accomplish whatever is needed!

"Jesus looked at them and said to them, 'With men, this is impossible, but with God, all things are possible.'" (Matthew 19:26)

The Lord told my friend Sharon one time: ***If it's not impossible, don't pray for it!***

Yes, Lord!

CHILDHOOD REFLECTION. . .

As I contemplated the vision from the Lord about His pool of Living Water, where people are paralyzed to pray, He brought to mind a boy from my childhood. For most of my elementary grades, I attended a small public school in our rural farming community in Northwest Arkansas.

This is the story of a boy I'll call Pete. When I arrived in Second Grade, my tender heart felt sad watching this little brown-haired boy walking with a horrible limp, which caused him to bear the brunt of frequent name-calling. I always thought he had a bad birth defect, because he walked only on the ball of his foot, with his heel way up in the air. With all his embarrassment and harassment, he mostly kept to himself.

A couple years later, I overheard teachers talking about his condition. It seemed he had broken his foot in a mishap as a young child. Being from a poor family, his parents did not have insurance, so they never took him to see a doctor! My heart broke even more for his dire circumstances. How could they totally neglect Pete's needs in such a horrendous way?

Despite his difficulty walking, I often saw him walking along the highway by himself. It just didn't seem right. Although I changed schools in the Seventh Grade, the tragic news travelled our way a few years later that he had committed suicide as a teen. Apparently, his pain and loneliness had been too much to bear any longer.

The Lord surprised me, bringing this deplorable story back to mind just now.

Let's not ignore those hurting around us.

Let's be the ones to care for those in our path who may be more desperate than we could know.

Let's let Pete's life, that was cut short, inspire us to love, to care, to pray and to risk looking foolish to help others along the way.

And Isaiah 63:9 prophesied, **"In all their affliction, He was afflicted."**

"...inasmuch as you did it to one of the least of these My brethren, you did it to Me," (Matthew 25:40)

Matthew 14:14 reminds us, **"He saw a large crowd and felt compassion for them and healed their sick."**

A BLESSING

I bless you with knowing you have been *chosen* to release miracles! You would not be taking this journey with me through His miracles otherwise. I bless you to pray boldly and say what you hear, even when it goes beyond your faith. I bless you with deeper compassion to stop for a stranger and see God's powerful touch happen through you, more and more and more.

21
MIRACLE OF IMPARTATION TO THE TWELVE

Matthew 10: 1-41, Mark 6:7-13, Luke 9:1-6

The disciples did not see this shift coming.

For the twelve disciples, the whole ministry of Jesus had revolved around two life changing words: "**Follow me.**" That had been *the plan* from start to finish. Today, He unfolded a new plan: imparting His own supernatural power to the Twelve and sending them out ahead of Him to do the same miracles!

In the days following, basically ALL of them would need to (in essence) get out of the boat and walk on water. This time, the Lord would be nowhere in sight. At least He told them to go two by two. Now it would be their turn to lay hands on the sick, cast out demons, and even raise the dead! There had to be some throbbing hearts as they left His side.

Coupled with the new mandates, they also carried His instructions to go forth blessing each place with peace.

Peace?

REVELATION, LORD?

I heard... **The disciples became my first miracle of multiplication! As I touched them and empowered them, they became my ready vessels to carry my bountiful Bread of Life to the hungry and needy. Freely you have received, freely give.** *(Matthew 10:8)*

I saw a joyful Jesus in solitude earlier that morning, pacing animated, grinning, and praising His Father! Jesus had gone up on the mountain once again to pray. (He looked like a proud parent on Christmas Eve who could hardly wait to share His special surprise!) Great anticipation filled His heart for the new era that would soon transpire upon the earth! His twelve followers would soon be going forth now as leaders, in His Name.

He continued; **They were entrusted because I knew the Father had chosen them. When the Father showed Me this time of anointing and releasing of My power and authority to them, it was my greatest joy! I knew much fruit would come forth upon the earth. Grace for My power and authority was about to be transferred, to bear and multiply fruit far and wide.**

ALONG THE WAY

Since 2011, Gordon and I have been actively involved with "Transform Our World," led by Dr. Ed Silvoso of San Jose, California. He introduced us to the powerful practice of impartation, which has been largely overlooked by the body of Christ. Clearly, the Lord Jesus set an amazing precedent as He sent out the Twelve, by releasing His own anointing unto His followers.

"Jesus called His twelve disciples to Him and gave them authority to drive out impure spirits and to heal every disease and sickness." (Matthew 10:1 NIV)

Ed teaches that as we minister, that we can and should be willing to impart the anointings that flow through us, to others. He never concludes a teaching without asking people to stand and receive as he prays a simple prayer of impartation to bless them with the power he is walking in, whether in wisdom or faith or miracles. We have received many impartations over the years in this way, at various conferences we have attended.

As Gordon and I began to teach our own transformation classes, we too have followed suit, to impart the grace we enjoy, along with faith, wisdom, power, and boldness. I would encourage you to do the same if you are an instructor or pastor.

Our friend Gary Hale excitedly embarked on his annual mission trip recently to Tanzania, Africa. After flying 15 hours Thursday and Friday, his host drove him 13 hours on Saturday, from the great city of Tabora to the small village of Kigwa. Sunday, he hit the ground running, preaching the Sunday morning service and a crusade that night. Both services concluded with many miracles. Monday morning began a five-day seminar the leaders had asked him to teach in the village. Despite the normal tendency for jetlag from all the travel, he felt energized by the Spirit for each new day, with great strength in his voice!

As Gary walked up to the platform to speak, the Lord said, **Don't start yet! I want you to pray over all the pastors first.** The Lord caught him completely off guard because he had never offered to pray over pastors until after they heard him speak. So, he paused and turned around with the Lord's offer, "Would any of the pastors like me to pray an impartation over you?"

All twenty responded eagerly, with hunger for more of the Spirit, even the overseer. As Gary laid his hand on each shoulder, the Lord also released an encouraging word to each pastor. One man, however, stood weeping under the power of the Spirit, so Gary chose not to interrupt what God had already begun his heart.

Later, Gary couldn't remember any of the words the Lord had given him. He knew the Lord had spoken words of life to impact each man uniquely, and he did not need to recall them.

Back in America, as he was sharing all the amazing testimonies of his three-week journey, he realized that his personal highlight had been this impartation to the pastors, to carry on the same Holy Spirit ministry of hope, light and healing from their own hands. His prayer would continue that their own miracles and breakthroughs would flourish and grow powerfully.

Mark 16:20 conveys the Lord's great plan to work among all His obedient servants who will work for the great harvest. **"Then the disciples went out and preached everywhere, and the Lord worked with them and confirmed His word by the signs that accompanied it."**

There is another way the Lord seems to impart his power: when I have the honor of praying over someone who receives a miracle, I explain, "Yes, this healing is a blessing for you from the Lord, but it is more than that! It is also His power being poured into your vessel, so that you, too, can flow in this same healing power to bless others in need."

For example, if someone's back pain just left, I encourage the person to not hesitate to pray for others with back pain. If they are a follower of Jesus, His power can flow through them just as powerfully as through me, as they boldly step out in new faith, praying in the Name of Jesus.

One noteworthy incident stands out. Two of my friends and I had just started teaching a Bible study at a men's Christian transition home. Right away, miracles began happening during our prayer times. About the third week, one of the men requested prayer for a friend he would be seeing the next day, who had a bad knee. He asked us to pray for her. I explained to him, that he had the same healing power from the Holy Spirit that we did. I asked him if we could pray over his knee for healing, standing in proxy for her. *Okay,* he said. We prayed for her healing, as we laid hands on his knee.

We told him what one of us had heard from the Lord: *Her knee will be healed tomorrow!* The next day, he laid hands on her knee, and it was healed! Thank you, Lord, for multiplication!

Thank you, Lord, for this *power of impartation* even today!

This coincides with some wisdom He gave me once when He spoke to me about **3 A's:**

Alignment + Activation = Acceleration.

- <u>Alignment</u> means to agree with Him/His word, not doubt.
- <u>Activation</u> means to be obedient to act on our faith.
- <u>Acceleration</u> means the results will happen more quickly!

A woman who I met in prison in 2011 and mentored several years, told me that she and two other ladies from a different prison enjoyed a great time at the Knoebel's Amusement Park recently. All have had some rocky roads but are choosing to follow Jesus today. After a while, they felt the nudge of the Lord to start offering prayer to other people at the park.

In years past, they had been with some of us on the streets of Allentown, doing prayer walks and blessing people. This would be their first time initiating prayers on their own, amidst their fun day. How awesome to see God's ripple effects going out from His body. For the next hour, they prayed for countless people from their own growing hearts of compassion.

Everyone needs a blessing. We don't merely need to pray for healing, we can also activate ourselves to carry blessings for other people, as Jesus instructed his disciples. Hallelujah for stirring these ladies' hearts that day at the amusement park. As I type this story, she just sent me a picture of a T-shirt she ordered for herself, her friends, and myself that says – "Godfidence." That is extra special because the Lord gave me that word about five years ago, and I had never heard it before that day. Last year, I saw it for the first time on a T-shirt and couldn't believe it.

THAT is how we go forth with great results—in Godfidence!

A BLESSING

I bless you as a follower of Jesus, to know you are empowered by our Lord, just as the Twelve were, because He dwells within you. I bless you to align yourself in His anointing and obediently respond to this task of advancing His Kingdom. I bless you to be fearless to go forth as He leads, in the Name of Jesus!

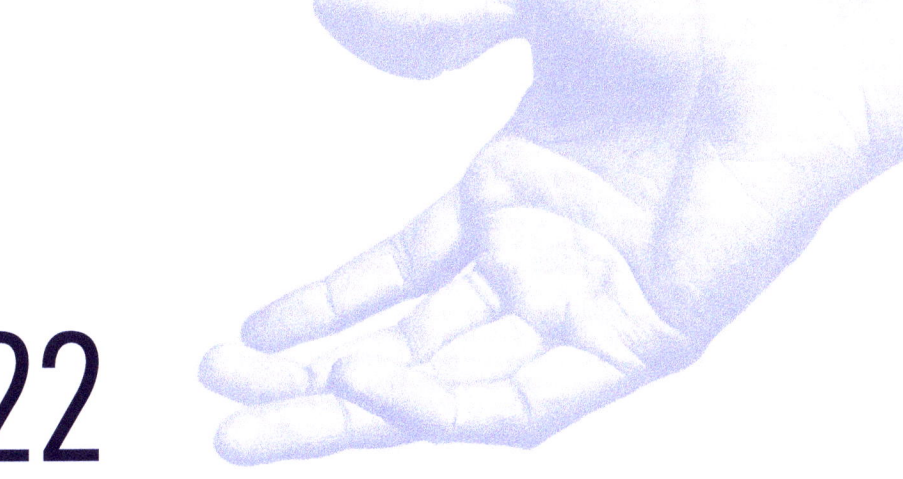

22
FEEDING THE MULTITUDE: 5000 MEN

Matthew 14:14-21, Mark 6:31-44, Luke 9:10-17, John 6:5-13

Jesus left in a boat with his disciples to go to a solitary place. He had just heard the shocking news that his cousin, John the Baptist, had been beheaded. He hoped to have time alone with His Father.

The crowd, however, arrived ahead of Him in Bethsaida. They wanted to be near Him. When He saw them, He disembarked with compassion, saying, **"They are like sheep without a shepherd."** Without hesitation, He began to minister to them, healing and teaching about the Kingdom. By evening, the disciples suggested sending them away to get some food.

Jesus asked Phillip, **"How much would it cost to buy enough bread for everyone?"**

Phillip replied, **"It would take eight months of wages!"**

Jesus only asked this to test him, as He already had in mind what He was going to do. He told them they didn't need to send the people away. "**You feed them,**" He told the disciples.

Andrew spoke up, **"Look! Here's a lad with five barley loaves and two small fish, but how far would that go?"** Apparently, the Father recognized a mustard seed of faith in Andrew's words.

Jesus told them to seat the people on the grass in groups of fifty. He lifted the fish and loaves up to heaven, blessed them, gave thanks, and broke the loaves. The disciples witnessed such an incredible miracle of multiplication! They had more than enough to fill their twelve baskets, with extra food leftover. Jesus told them to collect what was left, and to let nothing go to waste.

When everyone finished, 5,000 men, plus women and children, had eaten. They gathered twelve full baskets left over! Astonishment resounded in all their voices, "Surely, He is the One we have been expecting!" Knowing they intended to come make Him king by force, Jesus withdrew again to a mountain by Himself.

REVELATION, LORD

I saw Jesus in the boat, crossing the lake, head down, contemplating the death of John. Amidst His disciples, He had withdrawn to be alone with the Father in His thoughts. He knew the Isaiah 40 passage so well—that His cousin had come to "prepare the way" for Him. It seemed obvious that John's premature and violent death now **predicated His own.**

There was sorrow for both deaths, John's and His own to come. And yet, as He lifted His eyes to the crowd upon the shore, He knew that greater than His need to grieve, would be His privilege to deny the sting of death its victory this day.

Love could not cease to love! He gladly climbed out of His seat of sorrow. As He stepped out of the boat, into the rippling waters of the beach, Perfect Love flowed afresh, as steadily as the waves lapped from His feet to those in need.

The Living Waters of His teachings would sustain them throughout the day, until the next blessing came. Supernatural manna from heaven would soon be released by the Father, unto the Son, into the hands of the disciples—much like the Bread of Life they would serve long after Jesus would depart.

"You feed them!" The disciples were in a wonderful training session! Is it any wonder that God the Father chose to release this miracle of multiplication on this day to become the talk of all the towns, rather than the brutal death of a prophet?!

The Kingdom of God had come to Capernaum today!

ALONG THE WAY

The Lord amazed me with a most unusual dream several years ago. I seemed to be on a mission trip in a foreign land apparently, as all the people around me were of a different race. Holding a handful of dried beans, I walked into a small store where a friend worked. I soon realized however, that the beans kept falling out beside me on the floor, in a steady stream trailing all the way back to the front door. Somehow my hand stayed completely full.

As I found my friend in the back of the store, I told her what had happened. We both gazed in amazement at the trail of beans. As I opened my hand to show her my fistful of beans, they suddenly jumped out of my hand and covered the entire eight-by-ten wall beside us. Our eyes grew wide in disbelief! They had multiplied unbelievably in just one moment! My first thought was to share them with all the people in the village. I asked her if she had any small plastic bags to use.

"No, but I'll go get some!"

When she returned, I excitedly reached out to grab a handful of beans off the wall. As I did so, the whole wall of beans completely disappeared!

Oh no! We were stunned and dismayed.

What had happened to all our miracle beans?!

I woke up just then, still feeling stunned by it all!

What is the meaning of the multiplication of the beans, and their disappearance, Lord?

He immediately gave me the insight. **When these things take place, you must be sure to ask Me what action to take. Do nothing apart from Me.**

I was reminded that Jesus only did what He saw the Father do.

That made sense. Then He impressed me that He would have led me to bring people to the wall, to see the miraculous beans there, then have them get their own handful.

I could visualize the beans continuing to multiply! They would get to be a part of the miracle themselves, not only have to take our word for it.

Imagine the excitement of my getting to "see" this multiplication of food happening! His words to me afterwards though, brought the greatest joy: **WHEN these things take place ...**

Now I know I will be seeing multiplication miracles happen! The Lord works in mysterious ways!

IN REALITY...

About seven years later, the Lord had another surprise for me. I had been to the hairdresser for my annual jaunt for a haircut and noticed that her salon shampoo worked far better than mine, for sheen and texture. So, I splurged on an extra-large bottle. Surprisingly, it lasted almost a year.

When the level got down to about one inch at the bottom, I kept accidentally knocking it over in the shower. One day when I reached for it though, it felt heavy again. *That's strange,* I thought. *Who would add water to my shampoo?*

But, since we hadn't had any guests for a while, no one could have done that. As "empty nesters," Gordon and I had the blessing of having our own separate bathrooms to use. I took the lid off to see inside. *Oh! It's not water; it's shampoo!* I poured some of the pearly white product out in my hand; the consistency and fragrance seemed the very same as when I had bought it a year ago. Somehow the shampoo now reached within an inch of the top again!

Lord! What are you doing?

To say I felt flabbergasted would be an understatement.

I had no other explanation, except that He had multiplied it for some reason.

Thank You, Lord, but why did You do this? Why did You multiply my shampoo *of all things?*

It seemed pointless and frivolous. However, I heard Him quietly speak: **It's the first of many.**

Oh, really? Thank You, Lord! I'll take any and every multiplication miracle You have for me!

I only know one thing. The next multiplication miracle will probably come when I least expect it.

The shampoo lasted almost another full year. Every time I used it, I marveled at His supernatural intervention in my everyday life, and His awesome promise to do it again in the future. He kept building my faith with increasing expectation in what He could and would do in the future, when it is really needed!

Our God is an awesome God!

A BLESSING

I bless you with sweet gratitude for the smallest provision in your hand. I bless you with His incredible gift of multiplication to bless others when hope seems to be nowhere in sight! I bless you to remember He will clearly lead you in what to do next, WHEN these things happen!

23
PETER WALKS ON THE WATER
Matthew 14:22-33 (Mark 6:45-52, John 6:16-23)

Immediately after feeding the great multitude, Jesus sent His disciples ahead of Him across the lake, toward Capernaum, while He went up on the mountain alone to pray. After the disciples had rowed three or four miles, the wind became fierce. [Greek: the ship was being *tormented* by the billows.]

Around the fourth watch of the night, Jesus began to walk out on the sea towards them; they feared it was a ghost. [Greek: *feared it was a phantom/screamed in terror, feared*.]

He called out, **"Be courageous! It is I. Fear not!"**

Peter cried out, "Lord, if it is You, command me to come to You on the water!"

The Lord answered, **"Come!"**

Peter stepped out of the boat, walking on the water. But as the fierce waves increased, he looked away from Jesus, and began to sink. "Lord, save me!"

Jesus stretched out His hand and caught him, **"O you of little faith, why did you doubt?"** When they stepped back into the boat, the winds ceased.

The disciples worshiped Him, "Truly, You are the Son of God!"

REVELATION, LORD?

(The Lord had completely surprised me seven nights prior to working on this one. I had stayed up late meditating on some of the previous miracles; the clock said 4 a.m. as I turned off the light. As I lay down, I thanked Him again for the visions He had allowed me to see that night in various miracles, though all were brief. Usually, they lasted only a few moments, as a simple birds' eye view.

Lord, would you allow me to see MORE, with longer segments, and more detail? He astonished me, as He answered that request right then! He showed me a much longer scene of the disciples in the boat out on the Sea of Galilee, even though I didn't even have this miracle in mind that night!)

Later I remembered, **"You do not have, because you do not ask."** (James 4:2)

I saw a pitch-black night sky, with an unusual red beam of light letting me see the action in a small field of play, as if looking through binoculars with red lenses. First, I only saw a close-up of a man's face from the side out in the boat; he was peering very intently out to the left of the scene. Then I saw the Lord's face, further away, looking back at the man.

"Peter!" *I heard the Lord cry out! Peter climbed out the side of the boat.*

The scene shifted back to the boat and the rest of the disciples scrambling frantically to stay aboard their vessel, obviously fearing for their lives. Angry waves surged overboard, throwing their equipment all around as they desperately tried to grab hold of anything they could.

In my spirit I heard just then, **It was safer outside the boat with the Lord, than inside the boat without the Lord! Peter's faith was on a Rock, but their faith was in a sinking boat.**

I saw the Lord's sudden joy erase the look of lingering grief over His cousin John's brutal death, as Peter called out his special request. The Father knew just what His sorrowing Son needed—a disciple who was ALL IN! Laughter welled up as the Lord watched His zealous follower take his first watery steps.

Several years later: I received another glimpse into this amazing scene as I was doing another edit of this book. I saw the Lord holding Peter in a long embrace, after he pulled him up out of the water. He held him long enough for all of Peter's fear to leave, and until the peace of the Lord was transferred to him. I heard, **"Aww, Peter!"**

Even though Jesus had to admonish him for his wave of fear, Peter's boldness brought Him wondrous delight. There was no lingering thought of Peter falling, only joy in celebration of Peter's courageous pursuit. Peter's feet had discovered the solid omnipresent Rock that others had missed. What others saw as impossible proved to be such a simple feat in the Kingdom.

As they stepped back into the boat, I noticed that both men appeared to be dry. Reverent awe filled the hearts of all.

ALONG THE WAY

Many life-changing breakthroughs in my life stemmed from the early 1990's. I eagerly went to my first conference in about twenty years, with a lady from church. Several radical missionary speakers led the Spiritual Awakening conference, also mentioned in chapter four. The testimony of one speaker, Avery Willis, moved me greatly.

When the Lord first called him as a missionary, he battled accepting the call. Finally, he told the Lord, *Okay, I'll go, but would you send me someplace where I can see a great revival happen?* He didn't even hope to be a part of it, feeling so underqualified to go.

Not long after he arrived in Indonesia, the great revival of the 1970's broke out all over the islands. Willis shared that he watched a sovereign move of God happen there, as 5 million salvations happened in 5 years. All the churches became filled to overflowing, so that they had to train lay people to lead house churches. First, they trained men, then women, and finally even the youth, as the explosion of souls continued.

Willis encouraged us to read the miraculous account of it that was written by his friend. I found it on the book table there at the conference. What an awe-inspiring book it is! Check out *Like a Mighty Wind*, by Mel Tari.[3]

The author's own sister and her husband led an evangelistic team that walked from village to village sharing the love of Jesus. On one journey, they came to a river at flood stage, with no way to cross. The local people told them to wait a few days. But the team heard the Lord speak to them to cross right then! The locals warned them they would be swept away in the deep waters.

The team began to waver. Mel's cousin who was on the team heard the Lord speak again to **Go NOW!** He decided he would go alone if necessary. Some began to panic as he made his move, fearing his death. But, as he stepped into the water, it seemed to be only about six- to eight-inches deep. It appeared that way the whole time, though it actually plummeted thirty feet deep in the middle. Once the rest of the team saw it happening, they all stepped out in faith, and the Lord let them all cross safely atop the swollen river!

The locals on the shore decided they would do it too. But when they stepped into the rushing flood waters, they sank in and almost

---

[3] Tari, Mel. 1995. *Like a Mighty Wind*. Reprint. Green Forest, AR: New Leaf Press.

drowned! The team rejoiced at this amazing miracle of God, enabling them to all walk across the water.

The Lord reminded them of Isaiah 43:2 (NIV), **"When you pass through the waters, I will be with you … they will not sweep over you."**

I can't leave this subject without also sharing this fascinating dream.

My friend Sharon shared this unusual dream with such joy beaming from her eyes. The opening scene began in her childhood home. Those years had been difficult, as her mother had been a fortune teller and carried unreasonable fears. Sharon had been very restricted from doing normal things, such as learning to ride a bike and going swimming with friends, due to her mother's fear she would get hurt.

As the dream unfolded, she walked out of her mother's house. She thought she would get into her SUV and drive away somewhere. But as she walked up to the vehicle, she noticed it had been wrecked. So, she couldn't go anywhere.

However, as she turned, she unknowingly stepped into some water. As she looked up, she saw a huge lake stretching out before her. To her amazement a pair of strong hands came up under her arms. *How can this be happening?* she thought. Those powerful hands lifted her up and set her on top of the water and she just began to effortlessly walk on top of it!

Sharon kept walking further and further, surprised and enthralled with this blessing. It felt so exhilarating that she walked all the way across to the far side, and then decided to turn around and walk all the way back the way she had just come. The whole scene felt nothing less than incredible! When she awoke, she still felt the awe of her amazing experience in the dream as if it had been real.

As she related the dream to me, she remarked, "Now Peter and I both know what it's like to walk on the water!"

A PERSONAL NOTE...

Perhaps this dream had a deeper symbolic meaning to Sharon, who had left her childhood behind, yet realized her life had become burdened by generational fears from her mother.

Once she saw the Living Waters, Jesus lifted her up and carried her on a new, supernatural journey, which she has enjoyed for many years now in amazement of the ways of the Lord. He set her free from all her fears, allowing her to do many things she once thought impossible.

When the Lord impacts someone with such a powerful dream, I have found that their everyday walk of faith surges to a whole new level!

A BLESSING

I bless you with radical unshakable faith to go where others will not go. I bless you to stand far above your companions in all out steps of obedience, faith, and passion. I bless you to be a forerunner, to cross to the other side, where perhaps none have gone before you.

24
MULTITUDES HEALED IN GENNESARET

Matthew 14:34-36, Mark 6:53-56

Anchoring a few miles east of Capernaum, in the land of Gennesaret, the people immediately recognized Jesus and His disciples as they left the boat. The people realized that Jesus had not been in the boat when the disciples had left the other side of the lake! They ran there to Him from the whole surrounding region, carrying beds of the infirmed. Wherever He went, they laid the sick in front of Him, and begged to *only touch the hem of His garment*. Everyone who touched Him received their miracle! He did not disappoint the multitudes!

REVELATION, LORD?

I heard Him share his heart. ***It was a joy to bring the Kingdom power of heaven to earth! It was an outpouring, a manifestation of both the physical and spiritual restoration that I desire for all creation. Though many were blessed with the physical healings, few could receive the spiritual healing that our Father intended. Seeing eyes were still***

blind. They looked at Me but did not see their Lord. They touched Me but did not comprehend. It took greater faith to receive Me as Lord, than to receive My healing touch. I still touched them and offered My perfect love.

What do You want me to see, Lord?

Immediately, I saw an ordinary hand of a Man reaching out. I saw a Face of love and grace longing to connect deeply with the hearts of the people.

I saw Yahweh in the noisy marketplace throng—walking, blessing, and loving. I saw a picture of **"for God so loved the world."** (John 3:16a)

ALONG THE WAY

In 2011, Gordon and I felt called to start a new initiative called "Pray for Lehigh Valley," to see transformation in our tri-city region. Our first catalyst became the Adopt-A-Street initiative, patterned after a prototype founded by our new friends, Lloyd and Joanne Turner. In just 24 months, all the streets in Newark, New Jersey, had been adopted in daily prayer, as they partnered with only one pastor who seemed willing to think outside the box.

Many "hopeful signs" came about, as they enjoyed huge shifts in the spiritual and economic climates of the city. The light began to push back the darkness. In the year they started, Newark had been the number one city for homicides in the US. But once the daily prayers blanketed the city streets, Newark fell off the Top Ten list for homicides in the US.

Here in the Lehigh Valley, over 36 months, we saw 800 to 900 Streets adopted in daily prayer. For a few years, we led weekly prayer walks in Allentown, praying for the city, as well as some of the people we encountered on the streets. We had many God-orchestrated encounters with strangers along the way.

One young man appeared to be in a huge hurry and kept walking past us when we asked if he needed prayer. He surprised us when he turned his head back and answered "Yes!" over his shoulder!

"For what?" I asked.

"Salvation!" He answered immediately.

"Really?"

"Yeah."

"Wait! Just give me two minutes to pray with you!"

He and his friend halted and came back. "Okay, but I can't be late!" He had to get back to a residency program or he would be given a written violation.

I helped him pray to confess his sins, and ask Jesus into his heart, which he did. He said "Amen!" with a big grin.

"Thanks! I gotta go," as he hurried off smiling.

"Thanks for praying," I called after him.

God had brought the one our way whose heart He had prepared that day! Gordon and I continued to pray for him often, to be discipled by the Savior, through others who the Spirit would place in his path.

Another day, my friend Sharon and I decided to go on a prayer walk down the street to the old post office. We had learned that the Holy Spirit would highlight to us the people we needed to talk to. Once we knew who to speak to, the Lord told us, ***Do it! Don't debate!*** That helped us greatly, to know He would lead us.

That day, the Spirit highlighted one dark-haired man in his fifties. We spoke to him briefly and asked him if he needed prayer for anything. "No thanks," and he hurried away. At the corner, Sharon felt we needed to turn around and walk back the way we had just come. So, we retraced our steps. (I'm noticing an interesting correlation to her dream in the last chapter!)

About halfway up the block, we met the same man again, who had also turned around. We simply said "Hello" again, and smiled as we passed him. But he decided to stop us.

"Okay, I better let you pray for me this time!"

We hadn't even offered that time, but he seemed convicted to stop us and receive prayer! The Holy Spirit knew just what to do!

We asked if he had any pain in his body, as most people do, and would welcome prayer for that. But no, he felt fine. Then I asked the next thing that the Spirit prompted, "Are you carrying any heavy burdens?" That nailed it.

"Oh yeah!" He said with a pained look on his face.

It was all about his ex-wife. We could tell he had a lot of bitterness. Soon we were able to ask him about forgiving her. He didn't think he could. Then we asked if he knew that Jesus had forgiven him of everything. He thought that was impossible. We continued the discussion along those lines. We let him know he could ask the Lord right then to do so and ask Him to come into his heart.

"That's exactly what I need to do," he said excitedly. Then he pointed to a high-rise apartment building a block away, telling us that's where he lived. "I would rather get on my knees and do it there, than here on the street. But I'll do it right away as soon as I get there—in about two minutes!" He reassured us with a sense of urgency and hope. He seemed sincere and off he went.

"And then I'll forgive my wife, too," he blurted out as he hurried away!

We still see the same arm of the Lord reaching out in love along the way, just as He did in days long ago with Jesus. It's clearly the Father's love waiting and watching for the hurting, the lost, and the prodigals to *come home.*

We make it hard sometimes. He makes it simple.

"Surely the arm of the Lord is not too short to save, nor His ear too dull to hear." (Isaiah 59:1 NIV)

A BLESSING

I bless you to touch the one in front of you, among the masses. I bless you with a city vision, as well as a regional, national and global vision. I bless you to help others begin their new journey of faith, hope and reconciliation. I bless you to SO LOVE the world today!

You do not have because you do not ask.

25
DAUGHTER OF A GENTILE WOMAN
Matthew 15:21-28, Mark 7:31-37

Concluding a teaching to the Pharisees about clean and unclean, Jesus and His disciples left Galilee for the Phoenician region of Tyre, in the north. He tried to enter a house privately in Sidon, yet He could no longer keep His presence a secret. As soon as this Canaanite woman heard He had arrived, she came seeking help for her little daughter who was possessed with an evil spirit.

The woman fell down at His feet, begging, "Lord, Son of David, have mercy on me! My daughter is suffering terribly from demon-possession."

He said nothing.

Annoyed, his disciples came and urged Him, "Send her away! She keeps crying out after us."

He replied, "**I was sent only to the lost sheep of Israel.**"

She continued, "Lord, help me!"

He replied again, **"It is not right to take the children's bread and toss it to the dogs."**

She persisted, "Yes, Lord, but even the dogs eat the crumbs that fall from their master's table."

Jesus replied, **"Woman, you have great faith! Your request is granted. For such a reply, you may go; the demon has left your daughter."** And her daughter became whole at that very hour.

REVELATION, LORD?

The Spirit spoke this to me, of both the Father and the Son: Jesus waited to speak, as He did not know yet how to respond to the woman. He needed to wait and listen to the Father. He then processed His understanding out loud.

Three times, He heard this Gentile woman call Him "Lord." And yet, He had just concluded a teaching about "clean and unclean" to the Pharisees. They considered themselves "clean" and would not call Him Lord; they considered her "unclean" and yet she called Him Lord.

The Father demonstrated to His son the stark reality of His own words, spoken just prior to the Pharisees: **"Hear me, everyone and understand. There is nothing that enters a man from outside which can defile him; but the things which come out of him, those are the things that defile a man."** *(Mark 7:14-15)*

What He heard and spoke forth that sounded so harsh, **"It is not right to take the children's bread and toss it to their dogs,"** *drew forth a true revelation of her sincere heart of faith and humility. Amazingly, she did not reply with pride and offense, but with more humility, mixed with more faith!*

The Father had revealed the cleanness of her Gentile heart!

"Yes, Lord," she replied, "but even the dogs eat the crumbs that fall from their Master's table."

I saw Jesus toss His head back and laugh with her unexpected response! Now, He knew she was in line for her miracle, despite the discomfort of the disciples watching and listening. He clearly recognized her great faith and humility as a place of readiness to receive what He had more than enough to give: perfect love and mercy!

Deliverance came forth that day for her young daughter. Seeds of His grace and power began to grow in new places.

ALONG THE WAY

Several years ago, my husband and I travelled to Honduras on short term missions with Mercy Ships, for our 30th anniversary trip. They trained us to help start the eye exams by doing the E charts at the old naval base. The team encouraged the local citizens to come for screening at the free eye clinic. After the exams and fitting the people with free glasses, we always took time to share the gospel. During our two weeks there, Gordon and I saw about 25 salvations between the two of us. *Thank you, Lord!*

One day during the second week, the local jail nearby invited us to bring a mobile clinic inside, to do exams for its entirely male population.

Although we had done prison ministry in Pennsylvania for many years, we had quite a distinct experience stepping into the dank and dreary jail in Honduras. Besides the crowded conditions and the stifling heat, we discovered the guards had a much heavier presence. It startled us to see them sitting casually around the dingy, institutional green rooms, with loaded machine guns in hand, watching over the men and visitors, alike!

We held the eye exams outside in the courtyard area under an awning. But to minister to them personally, we needed to go inside the guarded rooms, where several old card tables had been set up for us. I found myself seated with three young men at my table. As I began to share about the love and mercy of Jesus, two of them seemed eager to learn. But the other one looked deeply depressed and barely able to listen. He appeared to be about 20 years old. Even as I spoke, the Lord informed me that the young man felt he had done something for which he could not be forgiven.

Soon, I told him my impression. Immediately, I had his attention. His head jerked up and He looked me squarely in the eye. With dark torment in his voice, he spoke for the first time, "Of course! I killed a man with a machete! How can I be forgiven for that?"

He explained that he had done it on a "high" and did not know what had happened until he woke up in jail. "I can never bring him back!" Heavy guilt, remorse, hopelessness and despair plagued him.

Amazingly, the Lord had prepared me for this scene about two weeks prior. He had brought to my attention that much of the Bible was authored by men who had killed people: Moses had written the first five books; David, most of the Psalms; Paul (Saul), much of the New Testament. The Lord impressed me that it had been no coincidence; rather He had chosen those very writers to demonstrate that nothing could disqualify people from receiving His love, mercy, and forgiveness!

No one would be set on a shelf as unusable or insignificant. Anyone could still be called to do great things in the Kingdom, no matter what, just like Moses, David, and Paul. As I shared this with the young prisoner, the Lord also had me explain that Jesus became guilty for us on the cross, so that by His mercy we can all stand before Him and be seen as "not guilty!"

I watched his heart melt with new possibilities of hope and grace. He was still too numb to pray to receive Jesus at that moment, but the Lord reassured me the young man would eventually accept His perfect love and mercy.

Meanwhile, my husband had the privilege of doing an eye exam with the prison warden, Oscar, who chose to say "Yes" to Jesus that very day! It was a little ironic because Oscar had been my husband's assigned name in his high school Spanish class. The Lord's signposts can be quite fun.

I prayed for a long time upon our return, that the troubled young "Saul" would soon become a singing "Paul" in that prison in Honduras. I still weep with joy to recall the brightening face of a murderer hearing the good news of God's mercy and hope for the first time ever.

"Blessed are the poor in Spirit, for they shall see God." (Matthew 5:3)

Indeed, I saw seeds of His grace and power begin to grow in new, unexpected places.

A BLESSING

I bless your heart to be filled full to overflowing with compassion for the hardest and least likely hearts. I bless you to always choose love over judgement and condemnation. I bless you to reap the harvest and set those captives free!

He wanted to give them more in their hearts, not just a physical touch.

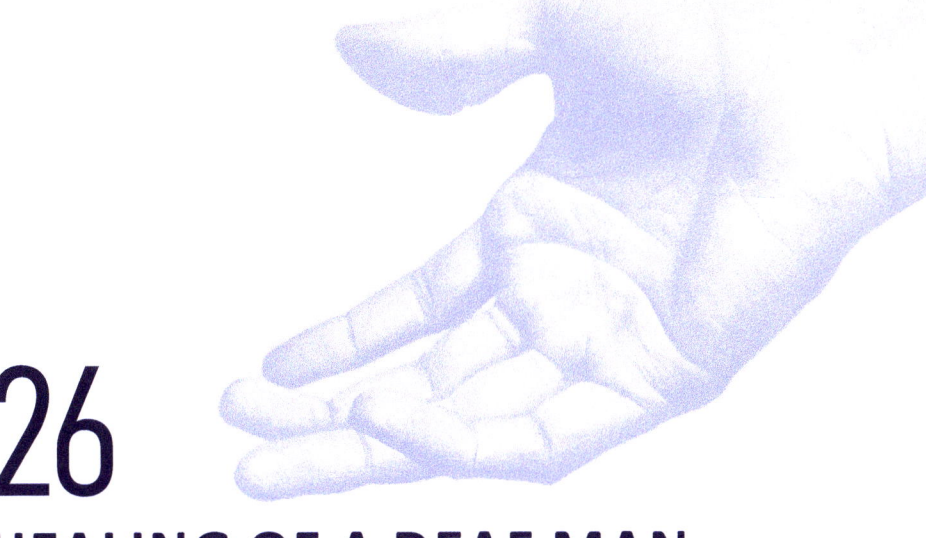

26
HEALING OF A DEAF MAN
Mark 7:31-36

As Jesus departed the region of Tyre, returning to Galilee, by way of the Decapolis (ten Gentile cities), He encountered a deaf man who had a speech impediment. They begged Him to touch him. Taking him aside from the multitude, He put His fingers in the man's ears, then spat and touched his tongue. Looking up to heaven, He sighed, **"Ephphatha,"** that is, **"Be opened!"** Immediately restoration sprang forth and the man spoke clearly.

Jesus commanded the people to tell no one, but they proclaimed it even more widely, astonished beyond measure, saying, "He has done all things well!"

REVELATION, LORD?

I had to ask this burning question: Lord, why did you frequently instruct them to tell no one of their miraculous transformation?

I only spoke that occasionally. Only the Father knew, at the time, when it would have been better (to wait to tell the miracle). **In those cases, He wanted the people who were healed to be still and**

commune with God for a deeper relationship. Instead, as they rushed to tell others, they were missing part of His intended blessing; He wanted to give them more in their hearts, not just a physical touch. This wait needed to be a first step of obedience, as a wait of faith, to teach them a new path of surrender. In time, they would have had more to tell than simply the physical healing.

"'For My thoughts are not your thoughts, nor are your ways My ways,' says the Lord. 'For as the heavens are higher than the earth, so are My ways higher than your ways, and My thoughts than your thoughts.'" (Isaiah 55:8-9)

Thank you for opening my ears to hear this, Lord! Now will you open my eyes?

I saw a grateful man at the feet of Jesus, worshiping Him for this healing, full of wonder of this gift of hearing ears and speech, but astounded at the words to tell no one. His tongue had just been loosed! He felt he must tell the whole world! He could not understand. To not speak about "why" he could speak and hear seemed impossible. He discounted it as unimportant. Everyone would want to know!

ALONG THE WAY

I was sitting in the dentist's chair, just thinking about my day, when the dentist decided to share something that was troubling her. She had just finished my check up and walked around in front of the chair to talk to me. She began to tell me about her daughter, then paused to see what I would say.

Oh! Perhaps she wanted some prayer.

I am always happy to have that privilege! She surprised me though, because we had not spoken of anything serious in any of my prior visits. But as she began to share, I realized she knew that my husband runs a Christian radio station, due to the fact he is usually wearing a lanyard with his station ID. That sparks peoples' curiosity about the station, and it becomes an open door.

She began to share that their baby girl was only a few months old. Sad to say, their baby had failed both of her hearing tests. "However, I don't think she really has a hearing problem!" she stated, with a puzzled look on her face, then waited for my reply. Once I realized this was a prayer request, I took a minute and briefly prayed blessings of agreement with her convictions that all would be well with her daughter.

Another hearing test happened soon after that; once again, the daughter failed it. However, she continued to believe the baby's hearing was good. Gordon and I kept praying and the dentist stood her ground in faith and hope for her daughter. We all pressed on expectantly.

At Christmas time, a couple of months later, we were surprised to receive a handwritten Christmas card from the dentist. In it was a note of thanks for the prayers and a picture of all their sweet children. It felt like a sweet God-hug, for being there, "along the way."

On my next visit, I heard some good news: their daughter finally passed her hearing test! It had been a long wait for these precious parents to see this breakthrough. How wonderful that they had known in their hearts ahead of time, that she would be fine!

As I thought about that long wait for those concerned parents, and the word I heard in the "Revelation" on waiting, a powerful lesson from the Lord came to mind.

Several years ago, the Lord impressed me to look up ALL the Bible verses on the word "Wait." That extensive list took several months to plow through. I highly recommend doing a study on it yourself sometime.

As a result of my immersion into that "unfun" word, I gleaned some rich, life altering concepts. Throughout the Bible, "waiting" is one of the key ways He worked in the lives of all our heroes of the faith.

Every single one went through significant times of waiting. It is a highly intentional teaching tactic of the Lord. All our waiting is to become a "wait of faith," not doubt.

Abraham is our best example of this as he waited 25 years for his promised son to be born. The promise had first come when he was 75 years old!

"Without weakening in his faith, he faced the fact that his body was as good as dead—since he was about a hundred years old—and that Sarah's womb was also dead. Yet he did not waver through unbelief regarding the promise of God but was strengthened in his faith and gave glory to God, being fully persuaded that God had power to do what he had promised." (Romans 4:19-21 NIV)

1. A "wait of doubt" will be longer than a "wait of faith."
2. All our waiting times are important. How we wait in the small things, like in line at a grocery store, indicates how we will wait in the bigger things in life.
3. He is preparing us to receive more at the end of the wait than we could receive today!
4. He taught me to consider those times as my "waiting stage." He loves to use a play on words! He impressed me to see myself as the main character onstage, knowing that all eyes are upon me. He has placed my family and friends on the front rows to watch me under those bright lights of scrutiny, during this trial.

The Lord said, *Be sure to say the right lines on that stage, while the bright lights are upon you. It's your time to SHINE!*

Bravo! Our tenacious dentist mom said all the right lines in her waiting stage. According to James 1, all our trials are to mature us and perfect us.

"Consider it pure joy, my brothers and sisters, whenever you face trials of many kinds, because you know that the testing of your faith produces perseverance. Let perseverance finish its work so that

you may be mature and complete, not lacking anything."
(James 1:19-21 NIV)

Author's Note: Unfortunately, after the book went to publication, the mother in this story gave me some disheartening news. Her daughter had once again failed her audio tests. We continue to cry out to God for the complete restoration of her hearing. The wait of faith continues.

A BLESSING

I bless you to say the right lines in your times of waiting. I bless you with grace to have your ears opened fully, to hear and obey His wise words of wisdom as you move through your life journey. I bless you to be fully persuaded that He is able to meet your every need, in every way, every day!

He healed them all.

27
HEALING AND FEEDING A MULTITUDE AGAIN
Matthew 15:29-39, Mark 8:1-10

Skirting the Sea of Galilee, Jesus went up on a mountain and sat down. A great multitude came to Him, bringing the lame, blind, mute, maimed, and many others—laying them down at Jesus' feet. He healed [Greek: *cured, healed*] them all. The multitude marveled when they saw the mute speaking, the maimed made whole, the lame walking, the blind seeing. They glorified the God of Israel.

Jesus called His disciples to Himself and said, **"I have compassion on the multitude, because they have now continued with Me three days and have nothing to eat. And I do not want to send them away hungry, lest they faint on the way."** Many had come from afar. Seven loaves were gathered, and a few small fish.

He broke the loaves and blessed them, then gave them to the disciples, who gave it to the multitudes, now seated on the ground. They all ate and were filled.

Then they gathered seven large baskets of fragments they had left. This bountiful provision fed 4,000 men, as well as women and children. Then He sent them away and departed on the sea.

REVELATION, LORD?

Is your faith growing? *He asks me, as I follow Him through these miracles.*

Yes, Lord! My expectation is great for what you desire to work through my own hands and feet as one of your modern-day followers!

I then received one of the most unusual visions so far: He gave me a glimpse of something difficult to explain. I saw only His hands and the multiplying bread. Small loaves of bread, connected and flowing in a steady stream, appeared very quickly from inside the flesh of His hands, being transferred out of the unseen, into the seen!

Of course, It matters not how it all transpired. What He impressed in my heart as I received the vision, is that He is daily extruding the Bread of Life, with every word spoken. It is His desire that every healing and miraculous work was meant to open deaf ears and blind eyes for the true Bread of Life that He offers.

The first verse He spoke in His ministry addressed this in Matthew 4:4. **"Man shall not live by bread alone, but by every word that proceeds from the mouth of God."**

ALONG THE WAY

For most of my childhood, my daddy raised beef cattle on our delightful 60-acre farm in northwest Arkansas. He also found it necessary to work full-time as an accountant in Fayetteville, where I would eventually attend the University of Arkansas and meet Gordon. I loved the wide-open spaces of life in the country, there in the scenic Ozark Mountains.

We had moved to our old pre-civil war era house in the summer before my second grade. Besides all the other demands on my daddy's time, he also needed to fully renovate the entire house, including converting the back porch to a bedroom for my sister and me. One of our most joyful childhood memories took place when Trixie, our black German Shephard gave birth to nine puppies! In fact, she chose to have them under our house, and specifically under our bedroom! My sister and I giggled for two weeks listening to them at night, when they seemed most playful. Finally, Daddy crawled under the house in the tiny crawl space to bring them out. We took lots of photos on our outdated box camera Daddy let us use.

About ten years later, we took a rare weekend trip to the State Fair being held three hours south, in Little Rock. Daddy couldn't leave the farm animals alone to travel much at all. A farmer friend from church agreed to come over and do the chores, so off we went.

On our return trip, we received a devastating call that our friend had spotted smoke coming from our house and the fire department had been called. None of us could believe it!

Our friend had been a former fire chief, so the Lord had the right person on the spot at the right time. Although they were able to confine the fire to one room, the horrible black smoke totally damaged the rest.

We lost everything.

Sadly, we soon discovered our insurance proved to be far from adequate, so we had no means to rent a house. Fortunately, that same farmer friend offered us a huge blessing: to come and live with them for a while! They assured us that space would be more than ample, as they lived alone in a large five-bedroom house. It also "just so happened" to be adjacent to the new farm my daddy had recently purchased.

Meanwhile my Daddy lowered the price on our old farm, which had already been for sale. The Lord provided a buyer quickly, so we began to have our new house built. Daddy planned to finish the basement first so we could move in as quickly as possible, then finish the upstairs later.

We lived outside the small town of Prairie Grove with about 2,000 residents at the time, so everyone knew everyone. They all pulled together to help us through the crisis. In fact, the whole town surprised us with a shower to replace our household goods.

I remember we were given 18 pairs of bed pillows! Everything came to us in abundant measure. We had surplus things to exchange for other things we needed. One department store in Fayetteville invited us to come in after hours and select our appliances. Favor seemed to be coming from all directions! My sister attended the University of Arkansas nearby and her large collegiate church even gave us a generous shower, though no one there knew the rest of us.

The most incredible provision was yet to happen. After a month of staying with our friends, they regretted informing us that someone in California had just bought their farm and the house where we had been staying! *No way!* No one locally even knew it was up for sale. They had listed it in the California newspapers on a trial basis, just to see what would happen. So, for the second time in a month, we felt homeless again. However, God had helped us before, so my parents prayed for another miracle.

"God is our refuge and strength, A very present HELP in trouble!" (Psalms 46:1)

The new owners flew out to Arkansas for two weeks to learn the farming business. The man worked as an engineer at NASA and their oldest daughters were college graduates. However, they had been blessed with a baby boy, now 5, and wanted to raise him on a farm. By the time their two- week visit ended, my parents, the former owners and the new owners had all become great friends. Amazingly, all of us also had something significant in common: our love for the Lord. The new family decided to visit our small church in Prairie Grove on their brief trip and said when they moved, they would also be joining there.

Before they left for California to pack and move in thirty days, they dropped a bombshell on us. They told my parents, "We're not going to move in if your family moves out. We want you to stay! We have plenty of extra bedrooms." And they meant it.

At first my parents objected, but soon they recognized the miraculous hand of the Lord at work. I will never forget the night we had that big old native stone farmhouse to ourselves, after one family moved out, and before the next family moved in! How crazy to think, even now, that a NASA engineer and his family would leave California to move into their new home in Arkansas, complete with a homeless family. *Of course!*

Welcome to the Ozarks.

Thank you, Lord for such a multiplication of Your love and provision, to fill our hearts full to overflowing. Our time with both families proved delightful to all of us. As I look back on the three months they hosted us, my heart fills with great joy, in place of any sorrow. We all stayed connected as close friends for many years. In fact, our California family hosted my rehearsal dinner about three years later, in that very house.

Forty years later, my husband and I visited that sweet fellowship in Arkansas, where our California friend had been serving on the church board for many years. I asked the current pastor if he ever heard this story, of their first months in Arkansas, hosting strangers in their new house. No, he had not.

Such love and humility can be so rare today. It should not be. All three of those amazing couples happily reside in heaven today. Writing this account brings sweet tears of immense JOY, even today!

"God works in mysterious way, His wonders to behold."
(A 1773 Hymn by William Cowper (1731-1800.)[4]

---

[4] Cowper, William (1913). Milford, H. S. (ed.). *The Complete Poetical Works.* XXXV Light Shining Out of Darkness. P. 455. London: Oxford University Press.

A BLESSING

I bless you to see the outstretched hands waiting for the bountiful provisions you carry in your basket today, for family, friends, and strangers nearby. I also bless you to freely receive when the need is there. I bless you to see the miraculous ways that ONLY God can orchestrate!

28
BLIND MAN HEALED AT BETHSAIDA
Mark 8:22-26

A blind man was brought to Him in Bethsaida, and they begged Him to touch him. He took the man by the hand and led him out of town. There He spat on his eyes and put His hands on him, asking if he saw anything. He looked up and said, "I see men like trees walking."

He put His hands on his eyes again and had him look again. Restoration came and he saw everyone clearly. He sent him home saying, **"Neither go into town nor tell anyone in the town!"**

REVELATION, LORD?

As *He showed me their hands clasped together, I began seeing an overlay of a transparent red heart covering their hands. The Lord spoke,* **Before his healing, the blind man could see the compassion in My heart that others could not. As we walked out of town, the blind man placed his heart fully in My hands. Brotherly love poured out powerfully between us, healing his wounded heart with every step.**

I wanted him to see his significance, giving him this extra time with me. Hope replaced the barrier of hopelessness that had trapped his bleeding heart in his dark and lonely world. Love changed everything.

ALONG THE WAY

When we say "Yes, Lord," we never know when we wake up each day how He plans to stretch us that day, or what Kingdom assignments He has for us. This is why we're here. We receive the light to shine the light, not to hide it. We receive love to give it away.

One day in a small discount grocery store in Allentown, the Lord alerted me to approach an older teenage boy who I saw walking with a white cane. I had never felt strong enough in my faith to pray for blind eyes, so I confess I began debating that one up and down a few of the isles!

But Lord, You know my faith is not there yet! I can't approach him without any faith to back it up. I tried to convince the Lord it would not be a good idea.

The Lord had an assignment for me and would not let me ignore Him. As the boy kept appearing in front of me in various isles, the Lord kept tapping me on the shoulder, **Pray for him!**

I couldn't. I froze in my unbelief. The Lord placed His strong hand of conviction upon my heart, and now it seemed to be all I could think about.

What list? What groceries? I couldn't even concentrate on my shopping anymore.

But, Lord!

Just then, I turned my grocery cart down the last isle of the store and came to face to face with Jesus! His somber face and eyes peered out from the front of a Chosen book stand and arrested me in my tracks. The title said, *Christ the Healer* by F.F. Bosworth.

Oh no! I knew I could not debate with the Lord any longer.

Okay Lord, if I see him one more time, I'll do it!

But I still had no faith for what I needed to do. As I turned away from the convicting book cover, I almost bumped right into the young man with his mother, standing right there beside me now, near the eggs and cheese!

Of course, I had eggs on my list.

I surrendered my will and approached them out of pure obedience. With a quick smile, and without any small talk, I simply spoke softly to the mother, "Would it be ok to pray for your son?"

"Oh!" She seemed pleasantly surprised and answered with, "I'll ask him."

As she turned to ask him, he immediately smiled in my direction and said, "Sure! And thank you!"

I was relieved at the eager response, and realized such an offer may have been non-existent till now.

Thank you, Lord for leading me, despite my resistance! Now I knew it had been the right thing to do. I thanked Him for helping my spirit to win the battle over my hesitant flesh. Before I prayed, I automatically inquired, "What caused the loss of your eyesight?"

The mother decided to reply, "Oh, he and his twin brother were both born blind!" Wavering faith tried to clobber any boldness in me that had begun to emerge.

The enemy whispered; "You are in double trouble now!"

"Ok, well let's pray for them," I ventured weakly. I asked both the twins' names, in a valiant effort to regain some ground in my fragile faith.

As soon as I finished my brief prayer of blessing, the young man grinned at me happily and whispered something to his mother. I wondered what was up. The mom grinned and said, "He wants to know if you can pray for something else! He doesn't care about his eyes; this is normal for him! But he's losing his hair, and he doesn't want to go bald! Can you pray for that?"

I had to laugh! God knew it all along. All my turmoil about praying for blind eyes had been for nothing. It had never been about the eyes, but about my obedience, and about *hair.*

Well, I did pray for the blind, despite my squawking! So now I simply needed to pray for thinning hair to regrow. No problem! I had once heard a powerful testimony of a man preaching at church who lost most of his hair in his twenties and prayed desperately for regrowth. The Lord answered him and brought it back in twice as thick as ever! As a result, I had often prayed for others who suffered in the same way.

After the hair prayer, my new acquaintance had yet another request! Mom continued, "There's a girl on the bus he likes, but he is afraid to talk to her. He is hoping you will pray for him to be bold!"

What?!

This had all been a Holy Spirit set up! Despite my weak faith, the Lord managed to activate me to do the hard thing, so that to this young man I appeared to be *bold! Ha! Lord, You know how to make me laugh!*

So, my third prayer of the day in the eggs section of the grocery aisle ascended to heaven, and finally my assignment seemed to be completed.

I almost forgot the eggs. I realized the items on my food list had not been as important as the items on this stranger's prayer list.

Lord, You know I still want to see blind eyes opened!

I pray my faith will be in place the next time You give me that opportunity. *Here I am. Use me!*

"Strengthen the feeble hands, steady the knees that give way; say to those with fearful hearts, 'Be strong, do not fear; your God will come...Then will the eyes of the blind be opened, and the ears of the deaf unstopped." (Isaiah 35: 3-5 NIV)

Oh, yes! *Christ the Healer* jumped in my cart that day. Thank you, Lord, and thank you, F.F. Bosworth for penning that amazing book, which dramatically heightened my faith for the healing power of Jesus in my life. I would highly recommend it as a classic from another era, by a miracle worker who actually held several crusades here in Pennsylvania. *Do it again, Lord!*

"I will lead the blind by ways they have not known, along unfamiliar paths I will guide them. I will turn the darkness into light before them and make the rough places smooth. These are the things I will do, and I will not forsake them." (Isaiah 42:16 NIV)

A BLESSING

I bless you with grace to cancel thoughts of fear, selfishness, apathy, and hesitancy. I bless you to cancel any old mindsets of inadequacy, and to fully trust the leadership of the Holy Spirit. I bless you to repent of all that hinders so His compassion and miraculous power may operate freely through you.

All things are possible if you can believe!

29
BOY WITH EPILEPSY
Mathew 17:14-21, Mark 9:14-29, Luke 9:37-42

When Jesus approached the scene, He noticed a great multitude surrounding his disciples. As soon as the people saw Him, they came running up to Him. A man in the crowd called out for Jesus to have compassion on his son. "Teacher, my son has a mute spirit. It seizes him and throws him down; he cries out and convulses, foaming at the mouth, gnashing his teeth, and becoming rigid. It has often thrown him into the fire or the water to destroy him. Help us! I implored Your disciples to cast it out, but they could not."

Jesus answered, **"O faithless and perverse generation, how long shall I be with you? How long shall I bear with you? Bring him here to Me."**

The boy's father implored him, "If you can do anything, take pity on us and help us!"

Jesus echoed him, **"'If you CAN?' All things are possible if *you* can believe!"**

The father cried out in tears, "Lord I believe; help my unbelief!"

As the father and son came to Jesus, the demon threw the boy down in a convulsion. Jesus rebuked the spirit: **"Deaf and dumb spirit, I command you, come out of him and enter him no more!"**

The spirit cried out and came out of him. He lay still as one dead, so that many said, "He is dead." But Jesus took him by the hand and lifted him up.

Later, the disciples asked Him privately, "Why could we not cast it out?"

Jesus said to them, **"Because of your unbelief ... However, this kind does not go out except by prayer and fasting."**

REVELATION, LORD?

I heard ... ***The devil commissions his evil spirits to do anything for attention, to glorify his unholy name. Knowing that the fear of God is the beginning of all wisdom, Satan's goal is to trap people instead with the fear of Satan. With such power displays, he feels honored and glorified. This should not be so within the body of Christ. The unsaved have reason to fear him; My people do not. Do not honor or fear the one who has already been cast down. He is under your feet. Walk freely about, with him firmly under your feet. When others have allowed him free access, it is your task, privilege, and responsibility to demote him to his rightful place, under your feet.***

The Lord continued ... ***I waited for 30 years to be activated into My calling to demonstrate the glory of God on earth. Our Father knows when you are prepared and ready to be activated fully into this calling. When He does, you will need to always be ready. You must walk filled with the Spirit. You cannot walk about in your flesh and bring glory to God. You must slow down and go in the anointing. You must be deliberate in the daily preparation of your heart.***

Are you going on your path, or on My path? Have I fully prepared you for your day? Do you know? Ask Me. I want to fill you. Do not just

prepare to go forth to relay information in teaching. Ministry is much more. Be the more! Go forth to give glory to My Name.

The Vision: *He did not show me the deliverance. Instead, He showed me a child transformed; moments prior the boy had been fearful even to look at, in his wild, tormented state. But now, his face seemed angelic and at peace. Jesus smiled, and lifted the child up, with love beaming upon His face for this precious one and his glorious new life of freedom! Glory!*

First, a quiet hush, then joy erupted all through the multitude! Father and son embraced, with tears of unbelief falling away, making room for tears of joy!

Years Later: *The Lord revealed additional insight regarding the disciples' fledgling faith in this scene. Apparently, they believed God could heal the boy, but not that He would do it through THEM. Our friend Ed Silvoso likes to say, "God has more faith in us, than we do!"*

ALONG THE WAY

Gordon and I had been visiting his sister and her husband in Texas and had decided to visit a family-friendly museum in Galveston. The guys had gone off for a few minutes while she and I stood in line for some tickets. Suddenly all of us in the large foyer were startled by a loud clap on the concrete floor, directly behind me.

As I spun around, I saw a mother crumpled on the floor over her seven or eight-year-old daughter who had just passed out and had been slammed down hard on the polished floor, so strangely. Everyone in the room seemed to freeze for a few moments.

My companion was first to break the silence, *"Someone call 911!"*

She spoke loudly but without panic. My heart sank for the mom, as I knelt beside her. The paramedics responded almost immediately, as if in just the next room. They carried the young girl into a small adjoining room on a stretcher. We found ourselves following the mom into the room, to offer emotional support for the young mother facing this crisis alone.

I knew I needed to offer prayer. The mom nodded "yes" to my offer, with a half-smile. Meanwhile, we all heard the EMT's succinct conversation over her, using the word "seizure." The mom said it had never happened before and was shaken to hear them use that term. Soon, however, the girl awoke, and they reassured her she seemed to be out of imminent danger.

As the Holy Spirit gave us His words of intercession, comfort, and hope, we saw the tension and fear melt away, as if some invisible arms were holding them both. A quiet hush of peace came over the room as the mom took her daughter into her arms, now alert and calm. The EMTs seemed clearly relieved that the startling symptoms had vanished.

We must always be ready. Though we could not know the rest of the story, we had once again seen the power of His right arm to deliver a daughter in great need. Thank you, Lord, for touching this mother and child with your great love. His presence had just filled an unsuspecting place in Galveston, along the way.

And He said to me, **My grace is sufficient for you, for My strength is made perfect in weakness.** (2 Corinthians 12:9 NIV)

Our own pastor's son suffered from seizures since his early childhood. Here is my friend, Ardy's account of them:

"Our youngest son, Ben, started having seizures at the age of eight months. Doctors did not know what caused the seizures to begin, since he had been normal at birth. One day, our son had to be admitted to the hospital to bring the seizures under control. They needed to run tests to find out the cause of them. Tests like spinal taps and CAT scans are never easy to watch a child go through but it felt totally heart wrenching to watch our eight-month-old undergo those. We felt so helpless, but we knew our hope and strength could only come from the Lord who loved him perfectly. We looked to Him for help.

"When they came to administer the CAT scan, we took Ben to the Radiology Waiting Room where we had to hand him over to the doctors and technicians. *Lord, help us!* They were gone for just a short time when one of the technicians came back to request our help. They needed one of us to come back to help calm Ben. The tests could not be done, due to his fearful crying. Gladly, I went back to comfort my son.

"Wearing a lead vest, they allowed me to sit next to Ben's head while they placed him in the CAT scan "tube." Since I could not physically hold him in my arms, I knew I had to surround him with the love of Jesus. He would have to hold him for me. Our "ever present help in time of trouble" gave me the wisdom I needed. **Sing Jesus Loves Me.**

"So, I did the hard thing in that hospital room. I sang over my baby, not caring who heard me. I knew that song had always brought the most comfort and peace to Ben in his moments of crises. As soon as I started singing *Jesus Loves Me*, complete peace and calm came over our sweet son. This momma kept singing and singing the words, over and over as the doctors could now readily run the tests. I could see their relief to see the atmosphere shift. Our Lord had intervened in a way only He could. I breathed my own prayers of gratitude for this supernatural peace. This would be the first of many times we would need such divine intervention by the Prince of Peace for our son."

Prepare us Lord for seeing miraculous deliverances in the growing onslaught of epilepsy, autism, and Alzheimer's. We know nothing is too hard for You, O Lord. Use our hands and feet to set these captives free. Our eyes are upon You, Jehovah Rophe, our Healer.

A BLESSING

I bless you to flow in the path of love, power and obedience that is His desire for you today. I bless you with freedom and courage to step up when no one else will. I bless you to fast and pray as He leads, to see supernatural breakthroughs wherever you go. I bless you to go with His amazing grace.

Our Father loves testing one's faith in every detail.

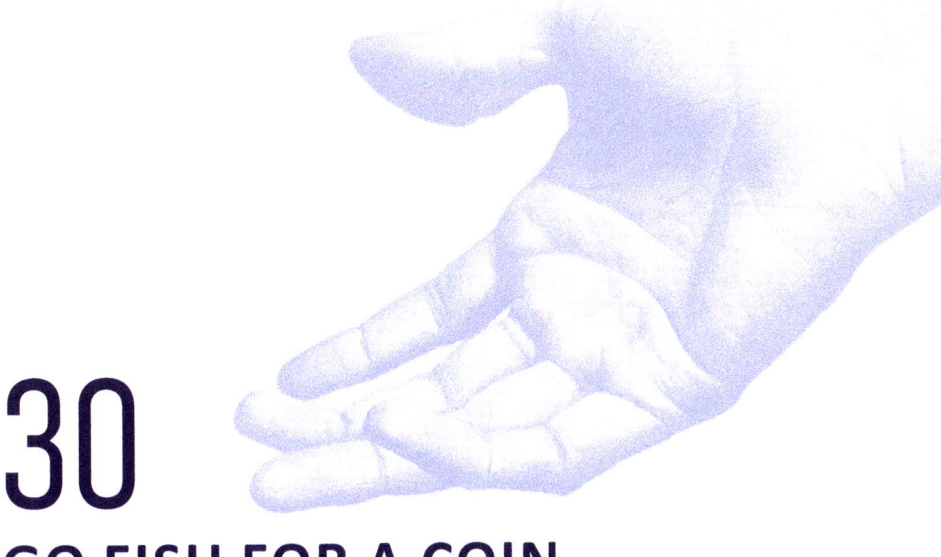

30
GO FISH FOR A COIN
Matthew 17:24-27

The tax collectors confronted Peter regarding Jesus, as they entered Capernaum, by the Sea of Galilee. "Doesn't your teacher pay the temple tax?"

"Yes," Peter replied briefly.

As Peter walked into the house where Jesus was waiting, the Master surprised Peter by addressing the tax concern in his mind before he even voiced it! **"Peter, does a king require his own children to pay the taxes, or strangers?"**

"Strangers," he answered.

"Then his children are exempt. But so that we may not cause offense, go to the lake, cast out a line. Take the first fish you catch; open its mouth, and you will find a ... coin. Take it and give it to them for My tax and yours."

REVELATION, LORD?

He began speaking. . . I laughed when Father showed me Peter's catch, before he even walked through the door the first time! I saw such a small fish, too! Our Father loves testing one's faith in every detail. He loves building up the faith of His children to be a strong substance. He also loves to bring surprises of joy in the midst of the trial.

I couldn't hold back my smile when I told Peter Father's plan to go fish!

As this vision unfolded, I began to see Peter, very scruffy and tanned, with medium brown hair, wiry and unkempt, too busy to think of appearances, walking into the room so somberly. He gave the Lord a furtive look, wondering what to say. Soon that look changed to wonder, as an incredulous grin spread from ear to ear, hearing the Lord's ludicrous instruction!

Turning, he practically ran all the way to the lake for this catch! Next, I saw him pulling in a fairly small fish, about eight inches long. Holding it up in the air, and holding his breath, he pressed its sides to open its mouth. Great laughter erupted as he ran back to the Master, with his hand tightly clutching his outlandish treasure.

That unassuming fish had certainly been Peter's "catch of the day!"

ALONG THE WAY

Gordon gave me some welcome news: He had been given a promotion! It also meant we would be leaving the chilly climate of Minnesota and heading to the sunny climate of Mississippi. It felt like a win-win since I had been raised in the south and would be close to home once again. However, we would greatly miss our new church family there in Owatonna, Minnesota, who had embraced us wonderfully during our 18 months there. Their warm hospitality more than made up for the bitter climate. This move would be our eleventh move in seven states in eleven years due to schooling and job changes. We still wonder how that happened in our early married days with three young boys! Fortunately, we had both worked for United Van Lines and had professional training for packing, loading, and moving! He had been a driver during his summers in college, and I worked as a packer the first summer we had married, as it paid much better than retail!

After our first full year in Mississippi, imagine my delight when Gordon qualified for a free trip to the lush tropics of the Virgin Islands!

As some unusual events unfolded on our trip, we found ourselves taking things a step further, purchasing a new timeshare unit, to keep us going back for 20 years. (And we did!) It felt like a dream-come-true to have a place waiting for us on an island where we could soak up the beauty of the flora and fauna, the sparkling clear Caribbean Sea, and explore several other islands in the USVI chain.

Within a brief time, we fell in love with those islands! We soon became immersed in what became our favorite pastime there, snorkeling and making innumerable underwater discoveries in the pristine bathwaters of St. Thomas and St. John. Swimming with countless species of exotic fish and various other sea creatures, such as urchins, sea cucumbers, rays, and octopuses proved to be our exhilarating highlight each year we went. Most of those underwater creatures appeared to be quite fearful of us as intruders! With the backdrop of neon corals, it caught our breath often, even with our snorkels. Our daily underwater discoveries sparked ongoing worship unto the Creator of the stupendous aquatic array of beauty.

One memorable day at Coki Beach, we laughed because we could barely see each other with all the beautiful Rainbow Parrot fish swimming between us. Then, across the bay, we noticed something new. What looked to us like some coral in an area it shouldn't be, proved to be a giant school of silver fish. Gordon shot some incredible underwater photos while I excitedly plunged into a vortex of a thousand silver minnows. Surreal? No words.

Another time, on a secluded beach on St. John, a small fish adopted us and swam under our chins for about an hour! We stayed longer than we planned, enjoying harmony with God's creation in such an unusual way. I call those times my special "God hugs."

Our favorite beach though, had to be the one closest to our condominium, Magen's Bay. This famous, heart-shaped beach usually ranked first or second in the world's top ten beach destinations. We had read about it in the in-flight magazine on our first flight to St. Thomas, and it did not disappoint! The bay is known for its exceptionally long coastline before merging with the breakers of the Caribbean, providing numerous underwater habitats to explore along the rocky shores.

All set with our sunscreen and t-shirt cover ups, we loved spending the whole afternoon out there, mostly in shallow water along those rocks. One day we made a very unusual discovery; we spotted a sweet galaxy of six-to-seven-inch starfish quite a long way out from the sandy beach. We had left the camera in the car, so I excitedly told Gordon, "I'm taking them in for a quick photo op, but I'll bring them back!"

I carefully draped them all over my forearms and swam back to the beach, relying just on my flippers. They did not mind at all. In fact, they posed beautifully for me! I returned them back to their habitat in a matter of minutes. We never knew what surprises awaited us in those waters.

Later as it began to get dark, we knew we should get out of the water and head back to the condo. Imagine our shock when we got back to the rental car on the beach only to discover that the car key had fallen off Gordon's suit somewhere in the ocean! That had never happened! We could not believe it.

We faced quite a serious dilemma. We couldn't reach the rental office after hours and a locksmith would be impossible to find. We watched the sky grow darker by the minute. The whole thing felt very overwhelming.

Gordon totally surprised me as he stated very matter of fact, "Well, we just have to find the key!"

That was preposterous! I knew there was no way to find a lost car key in the vast ocean, after dark, after swimming four hours or more. *No way!*

"What? We will never find it!" I argued.

But Gordon had already headed back into the water.

"Okay, okay!" I gave in reluctantly. "But we have to pray!" I called out after him, in exasperation.

He paused briefly and yelled out his quick SOS into the heavens:

"Lord, You know right where that key is! Protect it. Don't let it wash out to sea. Lead us right to it! "

And off we went.

With the white Caribbean sand, we noticed we could see better underwater now than above, with the darkening skies.

Apparently, Gordon's desperate SOS resounded in the ears of our "ever present" Helper. After swimming only a few yards, I heard the Lord say, **Go to "the rock!"** I knew exactly what He meant! About 70 to 80 yards out was a huge flat landmark rock jutted upward about eight to nine feet, shaped like a giant arrowhead. We usually enjoyed relaxing a while on the warm sand of the tiny private beach. *It must be there!* My minuscule faith began to think about growing.

As soon as I reached the giant arrowhead, I hurried out of the water and looked all around. *Oh no!* I found nothing! That was strange; I knew I had heard the Lord send me to the rock. Finally, I got back in the water, more dejected than ever in the darkness. The sunset had even faded by now.

Wait—what is that?

Almost immediately as I got back in the water, I saw something I had missed, in my hurry to get out.

There was our key!

What I saw absolutely stunned me. I just floated motionless for a while staring at the underwater scene through my goggles before even telling Gordon. I will never forget this image!

I saw our precious key stuck straight down into the sand like a stake in about three feet of water. But there's more! Someone had barricaded our key with four sand dollars stuck vertically in the sand all around it, like four beautifully designed walls. The current could not possibly carry it away.

"Gordon—you will not believe this!"

Finally, I had to click the picture into my memory bank, grab the key, some special sand dollars and go. As I swam back, I had some pondering to do.

No one else had been around the area where we had been that afternoon. We had it all to ourselves. Our key had been surreptitiously placed there, but by whom? The Lord? A covert ministering angel? A friendly fish on special assignment?

We would never know.

But I did know this: Explosions of unprecedented faith reverberated through my being with every stroke back to the beach. *Our God reigns!*

How could I have doubted He would help us?

I'm sure the Lord had the same smile on His face as when Peter found the coin in the fish's mouth. He had done it again—pulling treasure out of the sea for some unsuspecting followers.

We thanked the Lord many times for His incredible rescue that day on a dark island, far from home. What a great and mighty, caring, and compassionate, infinite loving God we serve. Interestingly, we had never seen sand dollars there before that day, or since, in our many years of returning to Magen's Bay.

About 20 years later we found ourselves back in St. Thomas and were blessed to attend our first ever Sunday morning service right there on the beach at Magen's Bay. Afterwards, I told our incredible key story to one of the local members; she looked stunned by it. She too had never ever seen sand dollars there.

RECENTLY...

One of our sons lost his key ring for several hours in Ocean City, New Jersey. They had scoured their vacation beach house thoroughly and retraced their steps on the boardwalk back to the beach. They found nothing. He finally called a locksmith to estimate the cost of replacing the key fob and key to the cargo carrier. Sky-high prices made that a last resort!

He texted us, "Please pray!" but finally called us to pray over the phone. It just so happened I was at my computer working on this manuscript. I prayed briefly with him on the phone and hung up. Just then, I glanced at the screen and saw that the "lost key" story (above) would be the next one to edit! Ha!

I knew immediately his lost keys would be found and God would do something amazing, again! Just two minutes later he texted a photo with the keys in his hand! Though they'd searched everywhere for hours, including all the couch cushions, right after we hung up he reached his hand down in the cushions again, and felt his missing keys.

"With God, all things are possible!" (Matthew 19:26)

A BLESSING

I bless you with childlike faith and wonder to ask, seek, knock, and go! I bless you with joy and laughter on the journey. May you take great delight in confidently pursuing your glory stories with your creative Friend and His fun-filled surprises!

Who is blind but My servant or deaf as My messenger?

31
BLIND MAN HEALED ON THE SABBATH
John 9:1-41

Jesus passed by a man who had been born blind. His disciples asked, "Rabbi, who sinned, this man or his parents, that he was born blind?"

Jesus answered, **"Neither this man nor his parents sinned, but that the works of God should be revealed in him."** He spat on the ground, made clay with His saliva, then anointed the man's eyes with the clay. **"Go wash in the Pool of Siloam. "**

He obeyed and came back seeing. This all happened on the Sabbath. The Pharisees said, "This man is not from God, because He does not keep the Sabbath."

Others said, "How can a man who is a sinner do such signs?" Much division clouded the onlookers.

The blind man answered and said, "Whether He is a sinner or not I do not know. One thing I know: that though I was blind, now I see... Why, this is a marvelous thing that you do not know where He is from; yet

He has opened my eyes! Now we know that God does not hear sinners; but if anyone is a worshiper of God and does His will, He hears him. Since the world began it has been unheard of anyone opening the eyes of one who was born blind. If this Man were not from God, He could do nothing."

They answered, "You were completely born in sin, and are you teaching us?"

And they cast him out. Jesus found him and asked, "Do you believe in the Son of God?"

"Who is He, Lord, that I may believe in Him?"

"You have both seen Him and it is He who is talking with you."

Then he said, "Lord, I believe!" And he worshiped Him.

And Jesus said, **"For judgment I have come into this world, that those who do not see may see, and that those who see may be made blind."**

Some Pharisees asked Him, "Are we blind also?"

Jesus said to them, **"If you were blind, you would have no sin; but now you say, 'We see.' Therefore, your sin remains."**

REVELATION, LORD?

Appearing large in my view was an intense Jesus, extremely close to the man's face in their second meeting, with an urgent query, **"Do you believe in the Son of God?"**

This time He had come to open the eyes of his heart. His gift of sight must bring him into the Light. Darkness must flee!

"Lord, I believe," the man replied.

His heart had been won; it had been the greater miracle.

In this case, seeing meant believing! Yet we know that many who had seeing eyes did not believe. It occurred to me that even in the days of watching Jesus do His miracles, it took MORE faith to believe that the Messiah himself stood in their midst. The "proof" (seeing actual miracles) still took faith to get beyond the mental objection of "this man is only a carpenter!"

ALONG THE WAY

In Chapter 6 I shared the incredible story of Harry Gomes, healed of skin disease, finding Jesus, then being called into evangelism for the masses, capped off with God's love through countless miracles. One phenomenal outpouring of God's power came one day when seven young men from a "blind school" came to hear him speak.

I watched the video testimony sent to me by his sister, of all seven of the young men having their sight restored. With great joy and delight, Gomes tested each one, by holding up fingers for them to match with their own hands, while standing three to four feet away. Just imagine those seven beaming faces and their bright and shining eyes!

I smile as I am reminded by the Spirit of the one verse that Pastor Gomes had prayed over Gordon and I years ago at our church: **"Call to me, and I will ... Show you great and mighty things, which you do not know!"** (Jeremiah 33:3)

MISSION TRIP...

As I mentioned previously, Gordon and I were thrilled to go on some short-term mission trips to Honduras several years ago with Mercy Ships. The ministry provided free exams by our ophthalmologists, who then sent the eyeglass prescriptions back to us to find the right glasses. Incredibly, the ship had 22,000 pairs of glasses to select from, all donated by the Lions Club!

In our free time, we also learned how to "read" them and notate their strength, to then be sorted by male, female, and children's sizes and styles. The clients usually had three to four pairs to choose from.

Some of the locals had never been able to afford an exam or glasses, so they felt incredibly blessed by our generosity. Older people with poor vision suddenly saw the world coming into focus before them for the first time ever. Joy lit their faces, from ear to ear. We loved watching their joy and wonder at seeing clearly for the first time in years!

The best part came after that. Every appointment allowed for extra time afterwards to take them to another table and offer to pray for them. We would find out if they knew Jesus or not. Because of their gratitude for their new gift of sight, we saw complete openness to our prayer and sharing time.

On our first trip to Honduras, Gordon and I saw 25 people accept Jesus during those two weeks, between the two of us. He usually worked with the men while I worked with the ladies. Many left the clinic seeing perfectly with both their physical and their spiritual eyes.

Gordon had a special blessing one day, getting to help two brothers, both in their 50's, both truck drivers, both practically blind! The ship also offered many free medical procedures. We knew they had one last appointment for cataract surgery available. When the brothers arrived one day, both had great need of this procedure. The older brother wanted his younger brother to have it done, since he would live longer. But the younger brother wanted to honor his older brother to have it done. As the ship staff observed the debate, they knew they had to work late that day, and do both! So, they did!

Gordon got to finish up with them and find the right glasses. He laughed as he told me the story later, saying that many lives were probably saved on the highway, as bad as their eyesight had been! Miracles come in many assorted and precious packages in many lands.

ANOTHER MEMORY...

As I worked on this chapter and continued to contemplate the opening of blind eyes, the Lord caught me off guard with a memory of my own, of quite a different nature. He reminded me of a verse He had shown me many years prior in Isaiah 42:19, **"Who is blind but My servant, or deaf as My messenger."** It jarred me the first time I set eyes on it.

I can still see and feel the scene that happened that day between the Lord and me. When I made myself comfortable on our blue tweed couch by the picture window, little did I know how soon I would become uncomfortable! The Lord had something to show me very pointedly. I didn't really like this verse staring me in the face and began to squirm.

Lord, what does it mean? The verse called out blindness and deafness in His servants. The room suddenly felt stuffy and confining. *Who me, Lord?*

As an on-fire Christian believer, I never considered having any blindness. I knew Truth, and I could see very well, or at least I thought. But now, for the first time ever, the Holy Spirit prompted me to seriously ask, *Do I have any blindness, Lord?*

Wow, what deep insights He had awaiting me! He didn't waste any time downloading a list of ten different areas right then, where He saw blindness in my heart. To say I felt stunned would be an understatement.

That hour is etched in my mind as a humbling reality check in my core being, yet His correction clearly had been gracious. Perfect love did not want me to dwell in any darkness. He is a God of mercy!

The two blind men had called out to Jesus, "Lord, have mercy on us!" As He showed me my blindness that day in His great mercy, the Lord was opening my eyes to see beyond the places where I had been stuck! My darkness gladly succumbed to the Light that day. Suddenly my heart began to soar with new expectancy, freedom, and grace.

This has now become a regular part of my prayers: *Lord, remove any blindness You see in me!*

I fully trust His heart of love. On the first day I enjoyed this new sight, He gave me a miracle I had not even requested! Such grace.

A BLESSING

I bless you to not hesitate to go into difficult places, in the Name of Jesus! I bless you with eyes to see as He sees. I bless you with courage to freely ask this hard question—*Lord, do you see any blindness in my life today*?

32
MIRACLE OF IMPARTATION TO THE SEVENTY

Luke 10:1-9, 17-24

The Lord appointed 70 others also and sent them two by two into every city and place where He Himself was about to go.

Then He said to them, **"The harvest truly is great, but the laborers are few; therefore, pray the Lord of the harvest to send out laborers into His harvest. Go your way; I send you out as lambs among wolves. Do not take a purse or bag.** [Greek: bag, beggar's bag]

But whatever house you enter, first say, 'Peace to this house.' And remain in the same house, eating and drinking...and heal the sick there, and say to them, 'The kingdom of God has come near to you.'"

Then the 70 returned with joy, saying, "Lord, even the demons are subject to us in Your name!"

The Lord said to them, **I saw Satan fall like lightning from heaven. Behold, I give you the authority to trample on serpents and scorpions, and over all the power of the enemy, and nothing shall by any means**

hurt you. Nevertheless, do not rejoice that the spirits are subject to you, but rather rejoice because your names are written in heaven.

Jesus rejoiced in the Spirit, "I thank You, Father, Lord of heaven and earth, that You have hidden these things from the wise and prudent and revealed them to babes."

REVELATION, LORD?

Immediately, I saw a gathering of Jesus with the Twelve, surprised but pleased with His sudden appointing of these seventy new workers. The Twelve beamed with happy grins and nodded in affirmation when He began His discourse to the newest sent ones. Truly the Twelve would agree, "the workers were few!"

Relief seemed to settle over them, as they watched the Lord sending forth more laborers. The twelve disciples looked with wonder, back and forth from the Lord to the newest ones being commissioned, awed by the birthing that they witnessed. Soon, they began to tell them a few of their own experiences before the new workers went forth.

ALONG THE WAY

For over twenty years, I served as Prayer Leader at New Beginnings Fellowship in Allentown, Pennsylvania. As I have learned to reach out and bless strangers along the way, I have shared many testimonies on Sunday morning. Over time, others wanted to learn to do the same. Several times, we have set up "Treasure Hunts" for people to gain boldness and confidence to go out and pray for strangers. It's a fun way to learn.

Before we go, we pray and ask the Lord to give us clues ahead of time about who we need to pray for and where to go. Someone may get a mental image of a man with black hair, a red shirt and black running shoes. Someone else may see a sign for a store, restaurant or business.

Before we go out, we have always prayed over everyone to impart faith and courage, then we head out with our clues.

We have gone to shopping centers, parking lots, farmers markets, the malls, and other places. As we find the people that we saw in prayer, it increases our confidence that God has a special plan of healing or blessing. Sometimes, we even tell the person after we pray, about the clues we had. They feel even more special, to find out God had highlighted them ahead of time. Most people are very receptive. We have always returned with some special stories to share.

One time, our church invited a group from out of state to help us grow in reaching out, by drawing creative pictures and/or writing words of encouragement to share. One of the leaders suggested that a group contact a police station or local businesses, instead of simply finding strangers on the street.

JOEL'S STORY...

Joel took the time to call ahead and struck out with his request to visit the police station but got the okay to go to a local fire station. He simply stated that a group from church would like to stop by and release some blessings. The fireman who answered had been a bit hesitant but very cordial. He probably hung up the phone, scratching his head about what he had just agreed to do.

In Joel's words, "Before we left the church that day, once the leaders prayed over us, we were to ask the Holy Spirit to give us a picture for someone and draw it in a card with a message. After an awkward time of having no idea what to draw I finally got a picture of a man sitting on a swing with a small boy on his lap. The message for this person was about the calling he had on his life to simply be a good Father to his soon-to-come son.

"It was great to finally have something to draw but having no artistic talent, I struggled how to translate on paper what I saw in my mind. I managed to draw some type of outlined form of a father and son on a swing with a paragraph or two with a special message. We drove to the fire station and were met by one of the people who helped manage the station. He told us that most of the firefighters were sleeping and didn't know who we could hand the cards to. We resigned to leaving the cards for them for when they woke up.

"As we turned to go, a different fireman came out and seemed kind of irritated that we had come. We lamely tried to explain why we had come, but it didn't seem like he bought our story. I finally got up the courage to ask if anyone there was expecting a baby soon, and that I had a card for him. The irritation of the fireman suddenly turned to surprise and shock as he realized I had a card for him!

"He told us that he and his wife recently found out they were going to have a baby and he hadn't even told his mother yet. He sternly told the older fireman that he better keep this a secret! After talking more with him about the revelation of this news, his countenance completely changed. He even began joking around and became extremely warm and friendly.

"Before we left, he invited one of us to come back and ride on the fire truck at Christmas with Santa. Suddenly, a whole bunch of other firemen came out who we enjoyed talking with. They even let us take a group picture in front of one of their trucks.

"What a great feeling to know that God would choose to speak to this young firefighter through my terrible drawing! I still love to think back and imagine what the message of my card meant to him and the encouragement it may have brought him during that transitional season of his life."

ARDY'S STORY...

"One of the nights we went out on a Treasure Hunt proved to be especially memorable for me. Before we went out, we asked the Lord to impart His power, and any specific clues He had for us ahead of time. I got a specific description of a woman the Lord wanted to highlight for me. I saw a picture of her wearing a leopard top with a black belt around her waist. I saw her at Ice Cream World, near the church. I felt impressed that she had issues with back pain. I remember being surprised at all those specific details.

"Kent and I and three others left together and headed a block away to the ice cream shop. As we drove up, we saw lots of people sitting out front on their green benches, with happy faces and the usual drippy ice cream. I couldn't believe what I saw! Right there in front of the shop, I saw a woman sitting there in a leopard top and a black belt around her waist!

"Silently, I prayed and asked the Lord for the right words. As I approached her, I decided to be forthright with why I was there. 'Excuse me ... ' and I proceeded to tell why I had come, and that God had impressed me she suffered with back pain.

'Yes, I do!' she answered in amazement.

"I asked her if she minded if I would place my hand on her back and pray for healing. She said that would be fine. When I finished praying, I asked her how she felt. She looked at me smiling, and she said, "The pain is gone!" She stood up then and started moving around, to be sure. No more pain!

"That was quite memorable for me! Now I have no doubt the Lord will use me to reach out even to strangers, if I am willing, and seek His direction."

Those are two examples. Thank you, Lord, you know exactly how to prepare and equip us, for healing, blessing, or encouragement, all done in love, grace and humility. No pride allowed! Thank you for choosing ordinary people to do extraordinary works in the Name of Jesus!

Additionally, we desire to be his obedient disciples to go forth as sent ones. Hopefully, it has become apparent in this book that my husband

and I have given the Lord our "Yes" to always be available wherever we go.

We have made it a habit to pray ahead of time for all of this—releasing peace, fellowshipping, meeting needs in divine appointments, and bringing people into the Kingdom.

At first it seemed awkward and intimidating. We wondered, *what will they think? Will we do it right? Will we offend someone? Will we be rejected?*

Those are normal questions to wrestle in the beginning, but all are simply tactics of the enemy to stop us from loving. Once we press in, and simply learn to love people in a deeper way, it becomes noticeably easier. Eventually, sharing the light and blessing people feels quite natural and adds greater purpose to our day-to-day routines.

We realized over time that all those type questions (above) are fear-based. **"Perfect love casts out fear."** *(1 John 4:18).* As we allow the Lord to perfect our hearts, love shuts down those fears and doubts. We care more about helping people than our discomfort. The Lord sets us free to flow in the stream of His perfect love for the hurting people all around us.

Gordon and I have learned through the ministry of *Transform Our World*, that reaching out in these ways is for building the Kingdom (as Jesus instructed the 70), not about building up our own local fellowship. We simply bless, heal, and let the Holy Spirit lead people where to go. If they ask us about our place of worship, then we will share that information. But that is not to be our motivation. We have learned to "Think Kingdom!"

Praying for our server in the restaurant has become our standard procedure. We care. They need prayer. We are going to pray for our meal soon anyway, so we ask if we can pray anything for them. If they are receptive, we will take a minute (quickly!) and pray while they are present. If not, we pray for them on our own. If they say no, we pray for them anyway after they leave.

CANADIAN TRIP...

Here is one of our special memories, from a trip to Canada. The Lord had us order business cards that simply said,

BLESSINGS

with graphics of a road in the middle of wheat fields and our phone number at the bottom.

We left one of those cards with a tip for the housekeeper in a Niagara Falls hotel one time. After saying a quick prayer of blessing, we laid it on the dresser in an envelope. About an hour later as we stood in line for a Ferris wheel, we suddenly realized we had left something valuable behind. Back to the hotel we rushed! The manager called housekeeping, and the housekeeper who cleaned our room seemed especially thrilled to see us.

She began to share that God had spoken something special to her through our BLESSINGS card!

Her husband had moved a few months prior to work in another Canadian province about a two-days' drive from home. She had not wanted to move, so they had been separated since then. When she saw the card and saw the open road in the graphics, she felt God saying to her:

Take the road to go be with your husband!

And with that unexpected word, she now planned to move!

Such peace and joy covered her face as she spoke! When we had ordered those cards, we never dreamed God would impart His Spirit through a simple picture to convict someone's heart so powerfully in a foreign country. We released our small blessing, and He imparted His great blessing. She never mentioned the money in the envelope. His blessing of light trumped everything else.

A BLESSING

I bless you with an impartation of His sweet, unexplainable anointing as an eager worker in the harvest! I impart to you the zeal of the Lord He has placed in my heart, and the fire of His anointing to impact your family, community, nation and beyond! I bless you to walk daily in this expansion of fresh anointing, arrested and guided by His love .

33

18-YEAR INFIRMITY HEALED ON THE SABBATH

Luke 13:10-17

As Jesus taught in the synagogue on the Sabbath, He saw a woman who had been stooped over for 18 years, from a "spirit of infirmity." He called her over and said, **"Woman, you are loosed from your infirmity!"**

He laid hands on her, and immediately she glorified God, fully healed. The ruler of the synagogue became indignant because Jesus had broken the Sabbath.

Jesus answered, **"Hypocrite! Does not each one of you on the Sabbath loose his ox or donkey from the stall, and lead it away to water it? So ought not this woman, being a daughter of Abraham, whom Satan has bound—think of it—for 18 years, be loosed from this bond on the Sabbath?"**

When He said these things, He put His adversaries to shame while the multitude rejoiced for all the glorious things He had done.

REVELATION, LORD?

He began, **How happy and eager I was to release love to this daughter, as our Father kept "showing Me" her frame, before My own eyes fell upon her. I knew My teaching would once again be cut short. What a joy to stand in My sacrifice that day. Such a demonstration of our love had been pent up so long! Knowing the persecution that would come only intensified the yearning for love's encounter.*

Then the Lord opened my eyes:

I saw the Teacher speaking, but with eyes glancing here and there, then resting on one small woman. Love's tender smile lit the darkened synagogue. As the woman walked haltingly towards Him in obedience, the wonder and faith of a few believers nearby sparked a soft glimmer of hope in her eyes.

Old seeds of faith buried long ago would suddenly break through the hardened soil of her heart. The heavy yoke had lifted! Faith and Love stood tall for other hearts to touch and see the goodness of the Lord!

ALONG THE WAY

I felt stooped over for many years, as burdens in life weighed heavily upon my heart, year after year. Though mine had not been not physical, the weight of those heavy burdens kept me weary for about 20 years. There is a passage in the Bible I used to object to, as it did not seem to work in my life.

My paraphrase of Matthew 11:28-30, **"Come to Me all who are weary and heavy burdened, and I will give you rest. Take My yoke upon you and learn from me, for I am gentle and lowly in heart, and you will find rest for your souls. For My yoke is easy and my burden is light."**

None of my yokes or burdens seemed light; they all felt heavy! So, I would simply turn the page when I saw that passage, and go on, ignoring it completely.

But, one day the Lord stopped me and would not let me leave it; they became neon verses. I began to confess, *Lord, you know I don't like these verses. They don't work for me!*

But the Lord decided to shine a bright new light on the verses for me:

If it's heavy, it's not yours!

What?!

Okay, Lord, I resign! I resign from carrying heavy burdens ever again!

And I did.

I understood immediately. Wow, after all those years, in just one moment, my daily life changed dramatically! Yes, life has many challenges and burdens that the enemy uses to weigh us down. But Jesus says to 'cast all our cares upon Him because He cares for us' (paraphrasing 1 Peter 5:7). I fully understood those truths, finally! *Thank you, Lord!*

I felt lighter than I had felt in years. After a few weeks of enjoying this new Way of freedom, I thought about the end of that passage. *Lord, what exactly do you mean by* **"My yoke is easy, and My burden is light?"**

It sounded contradictory. Thankfully, He had more amazing insight for me!

He graciously unfolded this awesome insight in a simple vision: I saw an old heavy wooden beam being lifted off my back by Someone, and a new yoke of a Plexiglas type material, filled with light, being placed on my back. I saw life-giving words on the yoke, such as wisdom, peace, grace, hope, strength, and courage. So, He carries the heavy part, and I need to only carry the light part!

Once I release the old heavy yokes and burdens that the enemy wants me to carry forever, I'm free to receive only God's yokes!

What a dramatic difference this has made! I hope you will try it.

Since that day, I have remained free of heavy burdens. I recognize them immediately when they try to come and hang over me. I process them by saying, *NO! I will not come under this heavy burden. I cast it off to you Lord, and I only choose to come under Your yoke of peace, or whatever is needed.*

If I have done this for an hour or two, and the heaviness lingers, I have learned to call a friend who understands this concept and ask her, "Please pray about heaviness for me!" Even if I don't tell her any details, she will pray for me, and all heaviness will leave in about one to two minutes while we are on the phone. The Lord has taught me that sometimes He wants us to humble ourselves and let others know that we are struggling and need their help.

Like the woman who had been stooped for 18 years, I can now stand tall, straight, and free. I am no longer bowed down, except to worship my Lord!

I am eternally grateful.

"It is for freedom that Christ has set us free. Stand firm, then, and do not let yourselves be burdened again by a yoke of slavery." (Galatians 5:1 NIV)

The Lord has led me to teach a class at church on Sunday mornings for over 20 years, called The Overcomers' Class. I have learned more than anyone else, in teaching concepts for victory week after week! One simple word of instruction He gave me was: ***I don't want you under it. I want you over it!*** That fits in perfectly with the heavy burdens that try to hang over our heads.

"The God of peace will soon crush satan under your feet." (Romans 16:20 NIV) He impressed me at one time that I am to walk ***crushing the enemy under my feet all day long.***

The Lord has amazed me countless times with some unique illustrations about overcoming. My favorite one is this: ***If you attend a track meet and watch the high hurdlers perform, you would not clap*** *for them if they only jumped over a three-inch hurdle. Rather, the higher the hurdle, the more you would cheer.*

He added this: ***When you face the highest hurdle you have ever faced before, you need to know it is never intended by me to hit you in the face and knock you down. No, that is the plan of the enemy. My plan is this: This is your time to go higher than you have ever been before! I will stand beside it to clap and cheer for you, as you soar above it!***

Thank you, Lord!

These revelations have set me free to stand tall, walk free, and soar above whatever comes my way.

"Everyone born of God overcomes the world. This is the victory that has overcome the world, even our faith. Who is it that overcomes the world? Only the one who believes that Jesus is the Son of God." (1 John 5:4-5 NIV)

A BLESSING

I bless you with freedom to cast off every heavy burden, to truly walk in freedom and help set other captives free! I also bless you with a heart to see His transforming work waiting to manifest in the lives of others, before it is done, and to be that powerful catalyst for breakthrough. I bless you to soar higher than you ever have before, when facing your hurdles, knowing He is right there cheering for you!

Who was this man, Jesus?

34

DROPSY HEALED ON THE SABBATH

Luke 14:1-6

The Pharisees scrutinized Jesus avidly as He went into one of their houses to eat some bread. He noticed another guest there who suffered dropsy, (an archaic term for edema or swelling). [Greek: internal swelling from water retention].

Jesus asked them, **"Is it lawful to heal on the Sabbath?"**
Noone answered Him.

He healed the man and sent him on his way. Then He asked the others, **"Which of you, having a donkey or an ox that has fallen into a pit, will not immediately pull him out on the Sabbath day?"**

They could not answer Him.

REVELATION, LORD?

I immediately saw an exceptionally large man with grayish brown hair, in a light tawny garment that revealed his large arms and jowls. He never expected to see a change in his weight and mobility. As Jesus approached him with His hands outstretched, grasping the man's upper arms, the man gasped, as transforming power surged through his body! Disbelief covered his face.

A few years were suddenly erased from his face, along with the weight.

Eagerly, he scurried away unencumbered to see his family, with a massive heart of gratitude and amazement. They wouldn't believe what happened! He wondered if they would even recognize him.

As the Pharisees stood there speechless, seeing the impossible, with weight vanishing, and their comrade's clothes now draping gracefully, they were torn by indecision about Jesus this time and had no rebuttal to the unexpected scene they witnessed.

Many would lose sleep that night, wrestling with issues of light and darkness. Who was this man, Jesus?!

ALONG THE WAY

Our church announced an upcoming healing conference being held in our region. I hoped we could go, though at the time, we had never attended any except for a small marriage conference once. Gordon never had peace about the cost factor, so we didn't register. However, just a few days before the event, we heard they needed people to man the video cameras and the cost would be waived! So, we both volunteered to cover two of the three large video cameras. The Lord knew how to make a way!

The Lord gave us plenty to see! We excitedly observed countless healings: all kinds of pain removed, deaf ears and blind eyes opened, and even some trauma healed. Above all, our own faith grew to expect Him to use our own hands more! For the first time ever, when I had the opportunity to pray over one young lady, the power of the Spirit caused her to slump down to the floor.

The Bible gives us several instances of this; I had never been exposed to that until my adulthood. When I first observed it, I had no interest.

In fact, my skepticism had blocked that possibility completely. The Lord decided to personally educate me about that!

He gave me a dream one night where a lady in a tourist store at the beach prayed over me. She held up both her hands as in a "high five" position, and I touched my palms to her palms as she prayed. Suddenly in the dream, I felt electricity course all through my body as she prayed. My legs grew weak, and I knew I could no longer stand up. I realized I didn't care if I looked foolish, because I could feel the power of God, and knew that had to be a good thing. I felt complete peace and joy, confirming His sweet Holy Spirit's presence.

I heard a voice in the dream tell me, as I lay on the floor, under His power, that if I reached out and touched anyone else, they too would be blessed by His Spirit. It seemed very difficult to open my eyes in the dream, but I faintly did so and saw two ladies walking by. I touched them and saw them slowly falling, as if in slow motion. I woke up soon after that, and still felt the *electricity, peace, and joy all through my body*, as in the dream! The Lord kindly let me know to trust Him as He works in His own supernatural ways, and not to limit Him to my understanding.

One noteworthy speaker at the conference especially caught our attention, because of his winsomeness. He could not stop grinning as he spoke. My husband told me, "He has contagious Christianity!" Gordon even asked our pastor if we could invite him to speak at our church sometime. He accepted our invitation to come not only once, but three times!

He shared that his burden for a healing ministry on the streets had been deeply ingrained by the Lord in the core of his being. He has become so radical in his faith that he told of several occasions when he literally ran one or two blocks to chase down a wheelchair when the Lord pointed out someone for healing. He has also become drawn to anyone with a turban, as he has found that the Lord would almost always heal that person to display His love to a lost soul.

We marveled as he shared a puzzling account of a malady that occurred in his own body one time. For no particular reason that he ever knew, one leg began to suddenly swell drastically. Meanwhile, he had some healing engagements to fulfill. He asked the Lord what to do. ***Go ahead and speak,*** the Lord indicated to him.

Off he went, dragging one leg behind, and speaking about healing! People came for prayer and got healed. After the meetings, he would drag his leg back home each time. All the while, the swelling kept increasing, even though a growing number of people prayed for him.

He finally went to the doctor after two or three weeks since his leg continued to get worse. When the nurse came in and saw it, she became alarmed, and prematurely spoke her mind. She abruptly stated that since he had waited dangerously long, the condition could even take his life. She told him the doctor would likely send him to the hospital to remove his leg in order to save his life.

He stood up and said, "Ma'am, it's not yours to take, or mine to give, so I'm ready to go now!" He stood up and walked out, still dragging his ballooned leg behind him.

Later that week, on Sunday morning, he told the Lord, *You know I'm so tired of all the questions everyone asks about my leg. I'll just stay home today, Lord, and spend time with You.*

The Lord had another idea. To this man who only wore casual shirts and jeans to church, He said, ***No, you need to go to church today, and I want you to wear a suit and tie.***

What? He really wanted to object to both going and wearing a suit, but he knew the Lord had spoken, so he knew he must be obedient in all things. Reluctantly, he put on his jacket and began to tie the tie. Just as he pulled the knot tight, he felt the power of God surge all through his body, and electricity travelled down his swollen leg!

All the swelling miraculously left his body in just an instant!

He could walk normally again. When he showed up at church in a suit and tie, everyone noticed him right away, of course. The Lord had him ready to share his amazing testimony with everyone.

All glory to our God!

"This poor man cried out, and the Lord heard *him*, and saved him out of all his troubles." (Psalms 34:6)

It was a few days after I had written this story, that I noticed the correlation with this chapter's title: Dropsy Healed on the Sabbath!

At the end of his speaking engagement at our church, one of our sons began to unload some heavy burdens to his listening ear. With great compassion and humility, the speaker showed no desire to rush off to lunch, but rather listened intently. After a while, he sat cross-legged on the floor to continue to minister to our son who had sat down in the front row. Eventually, our visitor amazed us further by stretching out on his side, propped up on one elbow, as if he had all the time in the world to listen. They both shared deeply as if they were old friends. We marveled at the deep compassion of Jesus that flowed from this well-known minister's heart.

I realized He wasn't even ministering; he was "being Love."

A BLESSING

I bless you to expect breakthroughs in all areas, and especially when others cannot believe for a change. I bless you with obedience and faith without limits, not needing to explain or understand. I bless you to relax and let Jesus *shine* His love through you.

Love had come their way, not to pass them by.

35
TEN LEPERS CLEANSED
Luke 17:11-19

On the way to Jerusalem, Jesus passed through Samaria and Galilee. Ten lepers stood afar off, and lifted their voices to Him, "Jesus, Master, have mercy on us!"

When He saw them, He called out, **"Go show yourselves to the priests!"**

As they went, they became whole. When one of them saw it, he returned to Jesus and glorified God with a loud voice, giving Him thanks.

Jesus asked this Samaritan, **"Were there not ten cleansed? Where are the nine? Has only this foreigner returned to give glory to God? Arise, go your way. Your faith has made you well!"**

REVELATION, LORD?

Jesus, Master, have mercy on us! Jesus, Master, have mercy on us! Jesus, Master, have mercy on us!

They cried loudly over and over with their voices of desperation! They could not let this Man of Hope simply pass them by. Faith and fragile hope cried out for Love. It seemed to be music to His ears. Love had come their way, not to pass them by.

If only they could know the love bursting in My heart, the Lord said. **My love exploded in my heart for them. I saw each one standing there whole, so I could instruct them: Go show yourselves to the priests!**

I saw this Man of Grace standing there blessing them with His few smiling words as He first saw this motley crew from afar, staggering in their pain, yet still beautiful in His eyes. He saw them whole, redeemed, and free. They would never be the same!

Afterwards, He stood watching and waiting as they hurriedly left for the temple, much like the Father watching for the prodigal son. Only one would return. Love longed for ALL their hearts.

ALONG THE WAY

The Holy Spirit may lead us to stop for a group at times, like Jesus did in this miracle account. In my weekly Bible study at the Lehigh County Jail, I usually prayed for physical healing for one person at a time. But as time and my faith progressed, I eventually found myself praying over entire groups.

One day only eight had come, rather than the usual fifteen to twenty. That day I will never forget. The Lord had plans to do a deep work among them. Sadly, many women there had been sexually abused during their childhood. The Lord surprised me that day by leading me to approach that painful topic with the whole group. He had not shown me this ahead of time. He orchestrated it all very naturally—no, supernaturally! He surprised me with His leading to take them all through a group healing session for their childhood abuse and trauma.

At my request, each one willingly shared the various emotions they had experienced for years, tied in with their sexual abuse trauma. I eventually had a composite list of about thirty various emotions written on the board. They had carried those emotional wounds for many years. Those old wounds continually impacted all their other emotions.

I reminded them of this encouraging word: *Nothing is too hard for the Lord* (paraphrasing Jeremiah 32:17).

It's as if the Lord looked upon our small group of precious ladies with their eight bleeding hearts, and said, **Enough is enough.** As the Healer walked us through this group session, a few tears began to flow, but overall, they seemed relieved that someone, rather Someone, wanted to help them find healing.

In my training for praying about emotional healing for others, I learned that it's helpful to ask them to visualize Jesus as we pray to forgive the offenders and release the painful memories and emotions. I help them to understand they have carried those wounds long enough, and it is no longer necessary.

"The Spirit of the Sovereign Lord is on me,
because the Lord has anointed me
to proclaim good news to the poor.
He has sent me to bind up [heal] the brokenhearted,
to proclaim freedom for the captives
and release from darkness for the prisoners." (Isaiah 61:1 NIV)

No matter what one has gone through, the Healer comes to heal each heart once He comes to dwell within us as Savior. That is called good news!

He is also our "ever present help in trouble," according to Psalms 46:1. Learning to visualize Him in prayer is helpful to grasp His nearness when needing His comfort.

As I walked the women through this process, the Holy Spirit enabled each one to see Jesus standing nearby as they prayed, as they gladly released the painful memories. Soon, I began to see the light of peace and healing replacing the pain on their faces. They looked around at the others in amazement, seeing new smiles emerging on almost every face.

When they finished casting all their hurts upon Jesus, all but one said they felt they had been set free from their deep, traumatic pain, once and for all. None of them had thought that would ever be possible. The one remaining lady felt somewhat better, although she had not been able to visualize the Lord. I knew I needed to help her more in the future, and hoped she would keep coming.

"Cast all your anxiety [care] upon Him, for He cares for you."
(1 Peter 5:7)

Before we finished our group healing time, the Lord gave me a unique way to help them to further understand what He had done. Jesus prompted me to ask them to close their eyes and let Him show them each of their hearts being held in His hands.

Again, each one saw Him holding their heart, except for the one lady. I asked if any of them would like to share what they saw. Surprisingly, they all wanted to do so, and had some poignant ways to describe what the Lord had shown them. They each described colorful and unique visions of healthy hearts that had been healed! We all rejoiced in the power of God to touch them so powerfully as a group that day, even for such a traumatic issue that had plagued them for years.

In Jesus' healing of the lepers, there had been one set apart who took the time to thank Him. In this case, I saw one who could not yet receive her healing. I am impressed that even when the Lord touches a group of people, He is still keenly aware of the journey of each one.

Each one is seen by Him.

Each one is significant.

Each one is precious in His sight.

> **"Surely, he took up our pain and bore our suffering,**
> **yet we considered him punished by God,**

stricken by him and afflicted.

But He was pierced for our transgressions,
He was crushed for our iniquities;
the punishment that brought us peace was on Him, and by his wounds we are healed." (Isaiah 53:4-5 NIV)

"I will restore you to health and heal your wounds, declares the Lord." (Jeremiah 30:17)

A BLESSING

I bless you with growing freedom to stop for the one or the ten, whoever the Lord may place in your path. I bless you to be the one who will not turn your gaze away from the hurting ones who may be shunned by others. I bless you to see Perfect Love embrace each heart, as you pray.

This sickness is not unto death, but for the glory of God. . .

36
RESURRECTION OF LAZARUS
John 11:1-54, 12:10-11

Mary of Bethany had once anointed Jesus' feet with costly ointment, using her hair. Now, she and her sister Martha sent word to Jesus that their brother, Lazarus of Bethany, had become very sick, and could possibly be dying. Jesus replied, **"This sickness is not unto death, but for the glory of God, that the Son of God may be glorified through it."**

He lingered two more days, before responding to their plea. Then, despite the personal danger of going to Bethany (only two miles from Jerusalem where they were waiting to arrest Him), He told His disciples, **"Our friend Lazarus sleeps, but I go that I may wake him up."**

They didn't understand, so He explained further, **"Lazarus is dead. I am glad for your sakes that I was not there, that you may believe. Nevertheless, let us go to him."**

Lazarus had been in the tomb for four days. Martha met Him. "Lord, if You had been here, my brother would not have died. But even now I know that whatever You ask of God, God will give You."

"Your brother will rise again," He stated.

Martha replied, "I know that he will rise again in the resurrection at the last day."

"I am the resurrection and the life. He who believes in Me, though he may die, he shall live. And whoever lives and believes in Me shall never die. Do you believe this?" He asked.

"Yes, Lord, I believe that You are the Christ, the Son of God, who is to come into the world."

When Mary joined them, she echoed her sister's words. He groaned in the spirit and was troubled. **"Where have you laid him?"**

Jesus wept. As He came to the tomb, He called out, **"Take away the stone!"** Jesus lifted His eyes, **"Father, I thank You that You have heard Me. I know that You always hear Me, but because of the people who are standing by I said this, that they may believe that You sent Me."**

He cried with a loud voice, **"Lazarus! Come forth!"**

Lazarus came out of the tomb, though bound hand and foot with grave clothes, with his face still wrapped with a cloth. Jesus instructed them, **"Loose him and let him go!"**

Many of the Jews who had come and seen the things Jesus did, believed in Him. But some of them went away to the Pharisees and told them the things Jesus did. The chief priests and the Pharisees gathered a council, "What shall we do? For this Man works many signs. If we let Him alone like this, everyone will believe in Him. "

From that day on, they plotted to put Him to death, so that Jesus no longer walked openly among the Jews, but went from there into the country with His disciples.

REVELATION, LORD?

What do you want to show me, Lord?

This was so unexpected... I was looking over Jesus' shoulder, as He looked at the white stone in front of Lazarus' tomb, seeing a brown cross superimposed over the stone. Apparently, the Father was giving Him a vision of what was coming, wanting Him to see past the cross, to the empty tomb.

In only a brief time, the Father would be giving the directive to the angels, **Remove the stone—Loose Him!**

Jesus was now standing in the place of authority for Lazarus, the same place the Father would soon be for Jesus. It seemed to be heart preparation for Jesus.

But for now, He received the joy of seeing Lazarus come forth, and the joy of others ecstatically surrounding him. Underneath, the Father had reassured Him, about what would soon transpire in Jerusalem.

"Looking unto Jesus…who for the joy that was set before Him endured the cross." (Hebrews 12:2)

Resurrection would be worth the agony.

ALONG THE WAY

Our intercessory prayer team received an urgent life and death prayer request for a friend of a friend in our church. I'll call our friend who requested prayer, Jaxson, and his friend who had slipped into a coma I'll call Barry. The physicians told the family that they now considered Barry to be brain dead. Jaxson and his wife went to the hospital as soon as possible, wanting to pray for healing over their friend, despite the bleak picture. He and his wife phoned another bold intercessor, Shelly, and our prayer team to join their heart cries of faith for Barry's life.

Once we received the request, everyone came into agreement for his healing, decreeing life and life abundant! John 10:10 tells us (my paraphrase) the thief comes to rob, kill, and destroy, but He came to give life and life more abundantly! We also prayed Psalms 118:17 (NIV) over Barry: **"I will not die but live and will proclaim what the Lord has done,"** and other similar decrees for life.

Shelly heard the news about Barry from Jaxson on her answering machine. Immediately she felt the urgency in her spirit to also intercede for life! Soon afterwards, she had to make a quick trip to the bank, and ignored her old sweatpants and messy hair, thinking no one would see her at the drive-through. However, as she left the bank, the Lord startled her by saying,

Go see Barry's wife now!

But Lord, I'm a mess. Look at me! Besides it's been about 10 years since I went there. I don't even remember their address. Silence filled her car. The Lord meant business and would not debate with her.

Reluctantly, she drove several miles to the adjacent town, vaguely remembering how to find the neighborhood. But once she found it, none of the houses looked familiar. After ten or fifteen minutes, she gave up. *I can't find it, Lord! I'm going home.*

Just then she noticed two men on the sidewalk ahead of her. *Oh! I'll ask them,* she decided. "Excuse me, do you happen to know where Barry and Rea live?" They smiled and pointed. "You are parked right in front of their house!"

Wow Lord, you brought me right to it! You amaze me.

Now I really know I'm supposed to be here.

When she rang the doorbell, Rea answered the door. *"Rea, can I come in?"* she blurted out, despite the ten-year lapse in seeing her.

"Come in." Rea wearily stepped aside and took her into the living room. She began telling her how Barry had gotten addicted to one of his prescription meds, and they suspected it led to his recent heart attack. She explained that he had basically died fourteen days ago, as there had been no brain activity since. Only life support had kept him here on Earth those two long weeks. She explained how the doctors had wanted to remove life support this very day, but she had insisted they wait until tomorrow. She told the staff, "He's going to go home to Jesus, and the family needs to all be with me to say goodbye and release him."

Shelly spoke boldly what the Lord wanted her to tell Rea, "He has not died! Your husband is coming back!" Rea didn't know what to think about that. Shelly felt some resistance from Rea to think that could be possible, but she admitted she had seen a little movement in one hand that week. Apparently, the doctors put no merit in his movement, but Shelly did.

"That's great!" Shelly responded. That small glimmer of life fueled Shelly to keep going. "I tell you, he's coming back," she reiterated one more time. At first, Rea couldn't grasp the hope that Shelly had, but explained how concerned she felt for their son, who stayed alone upstairs, being totally devastated about losing his dad.

"But Barry has no brain activity," she kept reminding Shelly. Finally, she agreed to pray with Shelly for Barry's miraculous recovery, and they did. Afterwards, Rea needed to check on supper she had started in the kitchen. Shelly felt free to leave, knowing she had been obedient to the Lord's leading.

Back in the car, she panicked, *Oh my gosh! What have I done? Why did I say all that? I can't tell people someone is coming back like that!* The enemy of her faith tried to rob her bold stand, by heaping piles of doubt upon her.

Ok, Lord, help me now! I don't want to give into doubt. I can't worry about what I said, or my reputation. I know YOU took me there, right there to that house, and gave me those words!

The Spirit reminded her of Philippians 2:7-8, **"But [Christ] made Himself of no reputation, and took upon Him the form of a servant, and was made in the likeness of men ... humbled Himself and became obedient unto death.** She realized she needed to stay more concerned about her obedience than her reputation.

Meanwhile back at Jaxson's house, right before bedtime, he suddenly heard a surprising word from the Lord: **Lazarus!**

It jolted him so powerfully that immediately his faith exploded off the charts, far beyond where it had been. He told his wife that now he knew that even if Barry died, God would bring him back!

The next morning, he called the prayer team to share that powerful word with us! Then he knew he had to call Rea. "I heard the Lord say **'Lazarus!'** So even if Barry dies, I know the Lord is going to raise him back up!" Rea again didn't know how to respond but told him Shelly had also told her Barry would live.

That same morning at Shelly's house she felt led to pray in an unusual way: "Barry, I call your spirit to attention, to the front, up above your soul, to hang out with the Holy Spirit now. I call your mind, body, will and emotions to all come into 'kingdom alignment' with the Lord Jesus Christ!"

Her words surprised even herself, but the next part, even more. She heard the bold prompting of the Lord: **Call him forth like Lazarus! Call him by name!**

"Barry! Come forth! Rise up from that bed!"

Next, she had to phone Jaxson and his wife, to tell them what she had prayed. Jaxson excitedly exclaimed, *"I got the same thing!"* They couldn't believe they both heard the Lord say **"Lazarus!"**

Shelly added, "When Barry wakes up, he's going to say, *'Get this stuff off me!'*"

Meanwhile, at the hospital, the doctors took Barry off life support. The doctors did not expect him to ever breathe again on his own, as they had considered him brain dead for about two weeks.

Despite all the odds, Barry began to breathe, "Get this stuff off me!"

In a few minutes, Rea called Jaxson's house on a different line, while Shelly was still on the phone with Jaxson, with the miracle report, "He came back, just as you both said!"

To the shock of everyone, Barry had no brain damage. In a few days he left the hospital, fully recovered. Before long, he began serving in prison ministry with a powerful testimony to share about hope and the power of prayer. With God, it's never too late! **"Where, O Death, is your victory? Where, O Death, is your sting?"**
(1 Corinthians 15:55 NIV)

The Lord had called forth another *Lazarus!*

Barry's longevity continues to amaze his family, over ten years later.

A BLESSING

I bless you with increased faith, boldness, joy and power, to see the sick healed and the dead raised! I bless you with courage to hear the words of LIFE from the life-giver residing inside of you. I bless you to fully yield your hands, feet and words to the Master.

Jesus, Son of David, have mercy on me!

37
BLIND BARTIMAEUS AT JERICHO
Mark 10:46-52, Luke 18:35-43

A great multitude followed Him out of Jericho. Blind Bartimaeus sat by the road, begging. Hearing Jesus of Nazareth, he cried out, "Jesus, Son of David, have mercy on me!"

The people warned him to be quiet, but he cried out even more. Jesus stood still and called for him. They told the man, "Be of good cheer. Rise, He is calling you." [Greek: *fone*, calling]

Throwing aside his garment, he rose and came to Jesus.

He asked him, **"What do you want Me to do for you?"**

"Rabboni, that I may receive my sight!"

Jesus said, **"Go your way; your faith has made you well."** Immediately he received his sight and followed Jesus on the road.

REVELATION, LORD?

Quite surprisingly, I saw Bartimaeus practically galloping his way to Jesus, with the intense look of a wild horse in his dark unseeing eyes!

He knew his destiny was just a few leaps and bounds away, and nothing would hold him back now! His long dark hair stood out straight behind him, like a horse's mane flying in the wind!

The Lord then spoke this to me: **As I heard his desperate cry off to My side some distance away, the Father showed Me, My healing hands over the face of a trusting soul. What a joy to turn and see that man leaping towards Me as if he could already see! He knew where I stood waiting for him.**

The crowd parted like the Red Sea, so that Bartimaeus could freely make his way to Me. **"Go your way; your faith has made you well!"**

The blessing was released.

ALONG THE WAY

When the young lady walked into the room for our Transformation Prison Ministry one Tuesday morning, I immediately noticed one of her eyes swollen shut. She looked down in embarrassment. Soon, we all put her at ease, and she started to share. She had come that day because the girls on the pod told her to come get prayer from "that miracle lady!" I laughed, as I had never heard them say that before. "What?" I asked with a grin.

One of the regular gals said, "Well you always pray, and miracles always happen, so it's true! "

That was music to my ears! I knew then that God would heal her, since she came with such a bold and desperate hope. *Hallelujah!*

We prayed over her right away. I asked one of the girls who had been healed the week before to go lay hands on her. We both prayed a brief prayer to stop the swelling and bring full restoration.

She said she felt something odd when we prayed. Within about ten minutes, someone said, "Look it's getting better!"

Every few minutes, someone else would notice some improvement again. By the time our Bible study was over, her eye was open and almost completely normal. She could look around and see again with both eyes. She was incredulous and kept saying, "I didn't really think anything would happen!"

Several of the other girls said, "Oh, we knew it would happen!"

Lord, I pray for the day when I will see blind eyes open!

SHARON'S STORY...

Previously, I shared an amazing "walking on the water" dream that my friend Sharon relayed to me in chapter 23. About two years ago, she had a routine visit to the dermatologist that uncovered some suspicious tissue just below her right eye. She felt uncomfortable having to set up an appointment for a biopsy. Filling her days with appointments, tests and medications sat squarely at the bottom of her list of things to do. But as she shared the news with me and others for prayer, she voiced great optimism for favorable results. The diagnosis, unfortunately, proved to be squamous cell skin cancer. Her stubborn faith would not accept this. That cancer had to go!

Reluctantly, she made an appointment to remove it. When her first doctor examined it, he decided it was too close to her eye for him to safely perform the procedure. He referred her to the Cancer Center to remove it. That meant the procedure needed to be postponed for about six to eight more weeks. We both agreed we shouldn't be concerned about the delay, rather, it simply gave more time for it to be healed!

All her close friends kept praying daily it would be healed. We also anointed her with oil one night at church. We witnessed her unwavering faith that it would be healed. The Lord had impressed her one day that **cancer could not live where peace lived.** She guarded her heart to walk in that peace.

When the day came to have the surgery, the growth had not changed in appearance. Sharon called me, however, and said, "I feel strongly I need to ask the doctor to do another biopsy before they do surgery." I could hear faith and boldness welling up inside of her and penetrating every word.

I quickly agreed. "I can tell you feel strongly about that, so you should definitely stand your ground."

When the doctor walked in to do the procedure, she told him she did not want to do the surgery without another biopsy. He indicated that would be a waste of time, as nothing had changed. She insisted. He showed her the paperwork once again, reiterating what type of cancer she had. With uncharacteristic courage she told him she had received prayer for it and would not relent. He made no effort to hide his irritation.

Reluctantly, he cancelled the surgery that day, and performed another biopsy. He informed her it would now delay the surgery another week.

A week later, as she waited to see the doctor, she kept praising God for His faithfulness. As she laid on the table, the doctor walked in and announced from the doorway, "Well your suspicions were correct; there is nothing there!" He didn't know what else to say!

She had hoped, she had prayed, and she had believed. But now that it happened, she was shocked! *"Thank you, Jesus! Thank you for healing me! Thank you for giving me boldness to stand my ground with the doctor!"* She ran down to her car and called me with the awesome news. God had given her a precious miracle after all! We excitedly praised the Lord for His healing hand! All at once, I thought about her paperwork.

"Did they give you anything that states the two different test results?"

"No, they didn't." She realized.

"Well, you need this documentation for your miracle. You should go back upstairs and get it!" I encouraged her.

She agreed and called the office from her car. They complied. She left armed and dangerous with her miracle testimony and the paperwork to prove it. For days, Sharon couldn't stop thanking her amazing God for the healing He purchased for her on the cross.

Hallelujah!

"Because of the Lord's great love, we are not consumed, for his compassions never fail. They are new every morning; great is your faithfulness." (Lamentations 3:22-23 NIV)

A BLESSING

I bless you to never doubt when a supernatural need is thrust into your path unexpectedly. I bless you with new levels of faith to rise to meet any occasion. I bless you to enjoy a lifestyle bathed in the supernatural.

I am He! Those whom He spoke to fell to the ground!

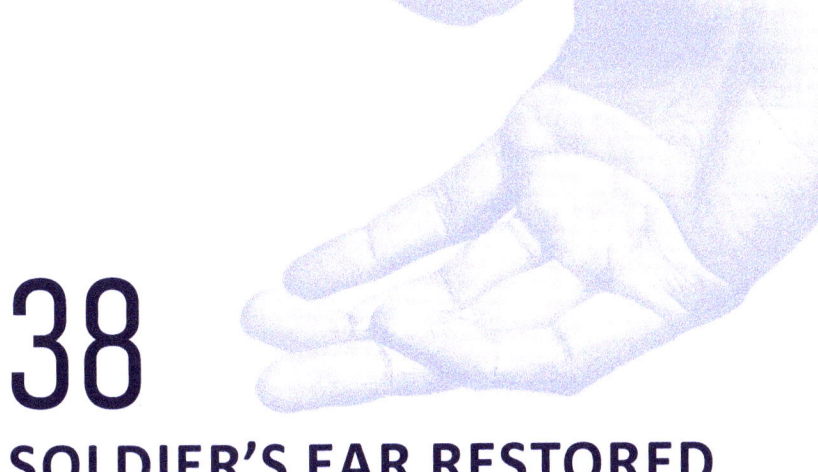

38
SOLDIER'S EAR RESTORED
Luke 22:47-53

Following Jesus' prayers in Gethsemane, He led His disciples across the Kidron Brook, to another familiar garden. Judas arrived shortly, leading a detachment of troops and officers from the chief priest and Pharisees, coming with lanterns, torches, and weapons. Jesus knew everything that was about to transpire, but simply asked,

"Who are you seeking?"

Jesus of Nazareth. **"I am He!"**

When He said this, those whom He spoke to fell to the ground!

"I have told you that I am He. If you seek Me, let these go their way," He entreated, hoping to spare His beloved followers.

With the kiss of Jesus' betrayer, Judas Iscariot, the soldiers laid hands on Him to arrest Him. His disciples queried, "Lord, shall we strike with the sword?" Before Jesus could respond, Peter drew his sword and struck Malchus, the high priest's servant, badly slicing his right ear.

Jesus quickly intervened, **"Permit even this."** He touched His ear and healed him, rebuking Peter.

"Put your sword in its place, for all who take the sword will perish by the sword ... Shall I not drink the cup which My Father has given Me? Do you not think I can pray to My Father and He will provide Me with more than twelve legions of angels? How then could the Scriptures be fulfilled, that this must happen?"

All this was done so that the Scriptures of the prophets might be fulfilled. Jesus asked His captors, **"Have you come out against a robber, with swords and clubs? When I was with you daily in the temple, you did not try to seize Me. But this is your hour, and the power of darkness."** Then all the disciples forsook Him and fled.

A PERSONAL NOTE...

Before starting this chapter, the Lord showed me an interesting contrast in two seemingly unrelated accounts.

Chapter 5: At the end of the miraculous catch of fish,

they forsook *all* and followed Him.

Chapter 38: At the end of Jesus' arrest in the garden,

they forsook *Him* and fled!

I went to bed that night, and the Lord gave me a dream where I saw myself typing and heard the Lord speaking.

Who will you forsake? Who will you follow?

When trials arise, will you follow Me or flee?

How sad that in the *beginning* of Jesus' ministry, His young disciples had *followed* Him freely, but in the *end*, His well-trained disciples and close friends had *fled*.

May you find us faithful followers to the end, O Lord!

REVELATION, LORD?

I saw the moment of Jesus healing Malchus' ear. The wounded servant had fallen on his knees, holding his head in agony. The Lord reached down with his hand, with the most compassionate and tender look of love beaming from His eyes, as if nurturing a young child.

There in His last miraculous touch prior to the resurrection, I witnessed the proof of His powerful words soon to be spoken from the cross: **Father, forgive them, they know not what they do!**

He not only forgave but healed His pursuer. This would be Love's proof, speaking to Malchus's troubled heart daily. (Hopefully he made his peace with the Lord one day, and we will meet him in heaven.)

Then I saw the Lord's head lift from Malchus and His eyes cloud with pain, as He watched His close comrades flee in fear in all directions, even John.

Years later, John would write this profound truth: **"Perfect love casts out fear."** (1 John 4:18)

ALONG THE WAY

The sun shone brightly as our eight-year-old son rode his bike to a friend's house. Suddenly an oncoming car veered over the center line, causing him to swerve out of the way, crashing in the gravel at the side of the road. As his feet came off the pedals, his downward momentum only stopped when his face met the ground. Fortunately, the woman driving stopped to help. Surprisingly, our young son could recall his dad's phone number, despite the pain and trauma of his injuries. The shaken driver made the call.

Gordon reached the scene quickly while I drove to the hospital about fifteen minutes away to meet them. Gordon told me the bad news that his ear was detached partway at the bottom. When I saw our son in the ER, a huge gash extending from his ear to his chin caused my heart to sink.

Oh no—he'll have a scar on his face for the rest of his life! Then I remembered Gordon's question about his torn ear. "Will his hearing be affected?" No one knew yet.

Our church prayer line went on high alert, as well as family and others. The ER team wisely called in a plastic surgeon to handle all the procedures, after the initial wound cleaning. The Lord's hand clearly guided the surgeon's hand, so that the ear was reattached perfectly. The doctor gave us great news; there would be no hearing impairment!

It took many stitches to close the deep gash on his face. Once the plastic surgeon finished, he gave us some much-needed encouragement and guidance. He told us that as soon as the new skin grew over the wound, to start applying Vitamin E oil daily and scarring should be greatly minimalized.

The extended family and prayer team kept bombarding heaven with healing prayers. None of us expected the results, however. In only three to four weeks, the light pink scar faded away completely! His ear and face had healed perfectly!

When that scar disappeared, we all agreed we had been given a miracle! Today you would never know he had that accident. *Thank You, Lord that your* **"compassion is new every morning, so great is your faithfulness"** *(paraphrasing Lamentations 3:22-23)!*

TWENTY YEARS LATER…

He seemed to hear the United States Air Force calling his name. He had been surprised that he sailed through the entrance exam and had his option of any career field. His recruiter in Nashville suggested going into "Intel." He happily agreed. On Friday afternoon, he finalized his paperwork. On Monday, he would board the bus for boot camp in San Antonio, Texas.

On Saturday evening, his older brother and a bunch of friends honored him with a going-away party. Before sunset, several of the guys went out in the backyard, tossing some small boulders off the small wooden bridge into a gurgling creek. Somehow, he lost his footing, and his boulder took him down into the water. When he landed in the riverbed, his thumb became sandwiched between two unforgiving boulders. His smashed thumbnail came off instantly.

We got the call as his brother drove him to the emergency room. They gave us one piece of good news: a registered nurse there at the party had immediately washed it. She insisted that she must clean it thoroughly right away, despite the pain. Done!

The news they got at the ER went from bad to worse. We found out much later that night that the doctor told him he likely had a bone infection from the dirty creek water. He warned him that people could die from that within a few days. He wanted to amputate his thumb to eliminate the threat of death.

"No, I need my thumb! I play guitar, and I'm going into the military." Our son wouldn't consider the possibility of losing his thumb.

The doctor went on to say if he ignored the gravity of the situation, he might have to amputate his hand instead, in a few days. He became quite adamant. Our son stood his ground. The staff required him to sign papers to not hold the doctor responsible if he died. He informed the doc he would take his chances, and he would be keeping his thumb. After he and his brother left the ER, they called us to tell us everything. *Oh!*

The news hit hard, but we trusted our son's judgement, and began to pray over him for no infection. The RN's wise intervention proved to be a lifesaver, literally, and a godsend!

He suffered no infection! When he went back the next week, the doctor seemed genuinely surprised that our son appeared to be fine. He then informed him, "By the way, your thumbnail will never grow back, as the nailbed has been destroyed."

The USAF recruiter had said, "Call us when you have a thumbnail again," and placed him on the inactive list.

The next time the Dr. examined him, the thumbnail had grown in halfway! Faith kept winning this battle! "Well, it will never be a normal nail; it will always be deformed," Doc insisted. Of course, the nail grew back completely normal. Jehovah Rapha, our Healer, faithfully took care of His young follower who did not flee or give in to fear in his time of crises.

But there's more miracles in this story. During his recovery, the Lord opened some unexpected opportunities "on the road" with his brother and various bands. Soon, they began asking him to fill in at venues without lighting engineers, with only "on the job training," and being self-taught. Thanks to his brother's connections in Nashville, he eventually had the opportunity to go on the road for three months as a new lighting engineer for a famous Christian band. This time, they trained him at the factory on high-end lighting sets, including how to repair any that would malfunction.

Finally, one year after the accident, he boarded the bus to boot camp with a perfectly new thumbnail! After he finished his training, they assigned him to Honolulu, Oahu, in the vicinity of Pearl Harbor. Within four months he received an email stating the USAF needed a lighting man to go on a one-year world tour with the Tops 'n Blue singers. The tour would encompass every USAF base in the world to rally the troops, as well as holding some public relation concerts.

When he applied, the Commander over the tour called him excitedly: "We need you! You are by far the most qualified."

His own commander released him to go. Thanks to a smashed thumb and the courage to stand by faith and keep that thumb, he enjoyed a one-year world tour in the performing arts field of the USAF! His lighting training (due to his injury) proved to be *the key* to unlocking this incredible new chapter. Yes, the Lord works in mysterious ways!

"And we know that ALL things work together for good to those who love God, to those who are the called, according to His purpose." (Romans 8:28)

A BLESSING

I bless you with courage to overcome fleshly emotions even in the face of grave danger and uncertainty. I bless you to faithfully stand, immovable and unshakable in your faith, hope, trust, and love. I bless you to walk faithfully in every storm, able to soar above the crises—in confidence that *all is well!*

Why do doubts arise in your hearts?

39
RESURRECTION OF JESUS!
Matt 28:1-10, Mark 16:1-8, Luke 24:1-12, 25-46, John 20:1-18

When the first day of the week began to dawn, Mary Magdalene and the other Mary went to the tomb, bringing the spices which they had prepared. *Who will roll away the stone*, they wondered. An angel of the Lord descended from heaven, with a great earthquake that rolled back the stone, and he sat upon it. His face shone like lightning, and his clothes were white as snow. The guards shook in fear and fell as though dead.

The angel spoke to the women: "Why do you seek the living among the dead? Do not be afraid, for I know that you seek Jesus who was crucified. He is not here; for He is risen, as He said! Remember how He spoke to you when He was still in Galilee saying, 'The Son of Man must be delivered into the hands of sinful men, and be crucified, and the third day rise again.' Come see the place where the Lord lay! Then go quickly and tell His disciples, and Peter, that He is risen from the dead, and indeed He is going before you into Galilee—there you will see Him!"

They remembered His words and left the tomb with fear and great joy, running to bring this word to the Eleven. As they went, Jesus met them, saying, **"Rejoice!"** They held Him by His feet and worshiped Him. Jesus said to them, **"Do not be afraid! Go and tell My brethren to go to Galilee, and there they will see Me."**

Trembling, they hurried off and found the disciples, mourning and weeping. When the men heard their report that He was alive, they did not believe the women. But Peter and John both raced to the tomb. John outran Peter and stooped down to look in; he saw the linen cloths lying there, yet he did not go in. When Peter came, he hurried right into the tomb. He also saw the linen cloths lying there, and the handkerchief that had been around His head, not lying with the linen cloths but folded together in a place by itself. Then John followed him in, saw and believed.

For as yet they did not understand the Scriptures, that He must rise again from the dead. Then the disciples went away again to their own homes, marveling at what had happened!

[Luke] Later in a home in Emmaus, the Lord admonished Simon Peter, and another disciple: **"O foolish ones, slow of heart to believe in all that the prophets have spoken! Ought not the Christ to have suffered these things and to enter into His glory?"**

They rose up that very hour and returned to Jerusalem, and found the others gathered together saying, "The Lord is risen indeed, and has appeared to Simon!" They told about the things that had happened on the road, and how He was known to them through the breaking of bread at a meal.

Now as they said these things, Jesus Himself appeared in the midst of them, and said to them, **"Peace to you!"**

They were terrified and supposed they had just seen a ghost! He asked, **"Why are you troubled? And why do doubts arise in your hearts?**

Look at My hands and My feet, that it is I Myself. Handle Me and see, for a spirit does not have flesh and bones as you see I have."

When He had said this, He showed them His hands and His feet. They still did not believe, but marveled, so He said, **"Have you any food here?"** So, they gave Him a piece of a broiled fish and some honeycomb, which He took and ate in their presence.

Then He said to them, **"These are the words which I spoke to you while I was still with you, that all things must be fulfilled which were written in the Law of Moses and the Prophets and the Psalms concerning Me."**

And He opened their understanding, that they might comprehend the Scriptures. **"It is written...it was necessary for Christ to suffer and rise from the dead the third day, that repentance and remission of sins should be preached in His name to all nations, beginning at Jerusalem. And you are witnesses of these things...**

Behold, I send the promise of My Father upon you; but tarry in the city of Jerusalem until you are endued with power from on high."

REVELATION, LORD?

I saw the two women named Mary huddled together in fear and dismay, their brown eyes wide in shock and unbelief, riveted by the first sight of the open tomb!

What happened?! Who had taken the body of the Lord?

It was unbearable to try to conceive what was going on.

Their hearts were broken once again.

Next, I saw the eyes of unbelief of the disciples, when Mary came to tell them the good news.

They had been chosen. They had been entrusted. They had been taught. They had been prepared. And yet, their hearts now became hardened with fear and their eyes blinded, despite their great privilege of walking with Him daily for three years.

What happened to their faith?

It would take the absence of the Lord to train their hearts and renew their sight, to walk by faith. Soon, however, Perfect Love reappeared to them and cast out their fear and doubts!

I saw Him there— as bright, shining Love—standing and beaming in their midst, amidst their first response of terror. Deep pools of unquenchable love surveyed the hearts of His dear disciples and soon they became fully immersed. Love prevailed and fear lost its unholy grip!

I saw love, joy and peace overtake each countenance. Once again, they chose to be ALL IN, ready to rise on wings of eagles and take the good news to their world! Glorious transformation swept through the room, and the world would never be the same.

ALONG THE WAY

We had met Tom and his wife when the four of us were being interviewed on TV60 by Pastor Larry Burd in 2011. One of his stories he shared on the air had been the gripping story centered around his parents in their latter stages of life.

His father, Walter, resided in Kingston, New York and suffered from cancer. It had begun in his lungs but progressed to his neck. It had greatly impacted his voice box, so that he could barely speak. His weight had fallen from 250 pounds to about 90 pounds, and he required oxygen around the clock.

Tom's parents had been divorced for over thirty years, as his dad had a severe alcohol problem and didn't work much. Finally, Frieda decided she had had enough, took the kids and left. The two of them never talked after that and never wanted to see each other. They even shopped at different grocery stores so they wouldn't accidentally run into one another.

On weekends, Tom and his son would drive up north three hours from Easton, Pennsylvania to do some work for his dad. They had just finished roofing his house one Saturday when his dad called him back inside. Walt asked Tom if they could stay overnight and take him to get his X-ray the next day at the hospital in Albany. But since Tom already had a teaching commitment for his Sunday School class, he felt he should leave. Walt became irate and flung out his usual expletives. Nevertheless, some tender tears flowed as Tom prayed for his dad before they left.

Tom got in and out of the car several times, debating what he should do. His son finally told him to make up his mind, and they left. Tom kept reflecting on his unusual prayer that had rolled off his lips, moments before. He had heard himself asking Jesus to "give his dad one more year."

The next day when Tom got home from church, the phone was ringing. Tom answered it and heard a strong male voice like his dad's old voice. "Come home! I want to see you!" Tom asked, "Who is this?" He knew it couldn't be his dad since he no longer had a voice.

As a lot of loud expletives jarred his eardrums, he realized it had to be his dad! He agreed to drive back home right away to find out how his dad's voice restoration had suddenly happened! When he arrived, his dad walked out to the car in his favorite dress suit! Tom couldn't believe it: no walker, no wheelchair, and no oxygen! It had been such a long time since he had walked unassisted!

His dad slid into the passenger side and asked Tom to take him back to the hospital to see what explanation the doctors might have for him. Meanwhile, he demanded Tom give him some answers. "How did this happen?!" His dad seemed truly mystified!

"It's a miracle! I can't explain a miracle." Tom didn't know what else to say. "How does a black and white cow eat green grass and give white milk?!"

Walt told him to quit talking double talk. "Just explain this," he yelled over and over as they drove.

According to the doctors, his brother and sister had brought him in to get the new x-ray. "Go with the pretty nurse," they told him. Meanwhile, they went out to smoke. After the x-ray, the doctors said Walt suddenly took off his oxygen.

"What are you doing?" the doctor asked him alarmingly.

"Well, Doc, it's like this. My son prayed for me for twenty-five years, and I decided it's time to believe God!" He stood up and suddenly got out of his wheelchair! Then he turned and walked away, down some stairs, to the elevator, and out to the truck to drive home. He left his brother and sister on their own, still outside smoking!

The doctor had no more explanation for either of them. Before they left to drive back home, the doctor asked Tom, "Why would God heal a crusty old man like him, when there's lots of good people much younger than him that I have to watch die?"

"God is 'no respecter of persons,'" Tom explained, referring to Acts 10:34 (KJV).

They drove the one hour back to Walt's home in silence. Tom had never seen his dad so speechless. When he stopped the car, Walt quietly asked his son, "What should I do?"

"I don't want to get yelled at, but you see what God has done for you. If I were you, I would give my heart to Jesus, and start forgiving people." The old familiar tirade erupted again.

"Wait, you asked me what you should do," Tom replied calmly. The yelling stopped. Walt asked his son to help him pray. Tom prayed a very simple prayer.

"That's it?" Walt asked.

"Yes, that's it."

The next day, no one at church could believe it when they saw Walt walking unassisted and also heard him talking with a strong voice. But then, he shocked them even more. In front of everyone, he got on his knees and asked a lady to forgive him, whom he had ridiculed each week for years. He felt she talked too much during the testimony time. She forgave him.

His new kindness stunned everyone. Soon, he even started raising both hands high in the air during the worship, though he had often made fun of his son for that. Tom even heard him *yodeling* during worship a few times! He didn't care what others thought now that he had Jesus.

That first week, Tom's mom called and asked, "What did you do to your dad?"

"Nothing, Mom. God touched him," he tried to explain.

His mom began to unfold what had happened. "He came over here and rang my doorbell. Then he got down on his knees and asked me to forgive him!" she said disgustingly. "I told him to go to ----!"

"Well, I only had to ask you that," Walt had responded to her, as he stood up to leave. He realized her response had to be her own choice. He then went all over town, to see more family members and others he had offended, to ask them to forgive him.

One Sunday at church, a lady asked the pastor if Walt could come up and pray healing for her cancer, since God had healed him of cancer. The pastor agreed. Walt hesitated because he didn't know how to do that. Tom was there that day and said, "Just tell Jesus you want Him to do the same thing for her that He did for you." So, that's what Walt did, and they all said amen.

When he sat back down, he asked Tom if that would work. "I hope so," he replied honestly.

That made Walt mad, "Well, it better!"

That Wednesday night at church, the woman stood up and testified that she had been completely healed of cancer! Walt called his son to tell him the news, "You won't believe it! It worked!"

Tom watched incredulously as his dad made a complete 180-degrees change in his life, not just physically, but emotionally and spiritually. To God be the glory!

The Lord granted Walter one more year to the exact date of Tom's unusual prayer request, "Lord, please give my dad one more year!"

I'm reminded of the prodigal son story as related in Luke 15:11-32. In verse 23, the father said, **"Bring the fattened calf and kill it. Let's have a feast and celebrate. For this son of mine was *dead and is alive again*; he was lost and is found.'"**

There's still more to the story!

Five years later, Tom's mother Frieda went into hospice, due to a tumor that began to suffocate her. Doctors said they needed to call her kids, to let each one come spend an hour with her. Tom and his mom had had a broken relationship for many years since he had converted from Catholicism to Protestantism. When he walked into her room, she said she didn't want to see him. "It's okay, I'll just sit with you awhile from this corner over here."

"You know I don't have you in my will," she reminded him.

"I know Mom. I don't care about that," he responded quietly.

She became silent, just staring at the TV. After a while she tossed an unexpected question his way. "So, what would you want me to pray?"

"Oh! Just 'God save me, in Jesus' name,'" he offered with a sliver of hope.

She repeated his words. "What else?" she asked.

"Nothing else, just 'Amen!'"

"Amen," she concluded. She turned her head toward the wall for about three minutes, in loud silence.

Soon, one lone tear ran down her face, and splashed off her glasses onto her gown.

"So, Jesus is real?" she asked in a soft, kind voice, so different than before.

"Yes, Mom."

With sincere conviction, she began to confess all the ways she had wronged him through the years.

"It's over, Mom. And it's all under the blood. It doesn't matter anymore," he reassured her with the Lord's mercy flowing.

Just then, his brother walked in and saw her tears.

"How did you get the Rock to cry?!" he asked jokingly.

She lived one more hour after her prayer of faith.

Another five years passed. Tom and his wife were facing some financial issues that had mounted up over the years to about $100,000. They were grappling with how it could ever be resolved. One day when he went to the mailbox, there was a check for $50,000 from the law firm that handled his mom's estate. He wondered how that could be possible, as she had stressed, she never put him in her will. He called his sister to say, "We can't accept this. I told Mom it wasn't about the money. I just cared about her heart."

They met together in the next few days, and Tom heard something quite amazing. After he had prayed with his mom that day and left the room, she had spent her last hour with his brother making calls to her different lawyers, adding Tom into her will. When all had been finalized, they awarded him over $100,000.

Tom had wondered if his mom's prayer had truly been sincere. Now he knew. The Lord had softened her heart, and just like his dad, she had found new life just in time. Love had been resurrected out of all their broken hearts.

"Where, O death, is your sting?" (1 Corinthians 15:55 NIV)

A BLESSING

I bless you to be the voice of faith when others are silent. I bless you with the power of His perfect love and mercy, to rise again after any attack of the enemy! I bless you to soar in bold faith and anointing, *to never give up.* I bless you to always press on in HOPE, in Jesus Name.

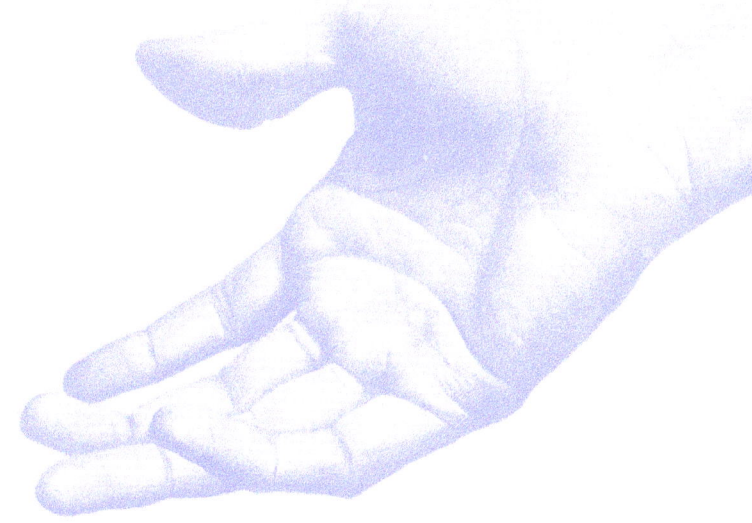

40
ANOTHER MIRACULOUS CATCH OF FISH
John 21:1-25

Peter, Thomas, Nathanael, John, and another disciple decided to go fishing on the Sea of Tiberias. They fished all night and caught nothing.

In the morning, Jesus stood on the shore and called to them, **"Children, have you any food?"**

"No," they answered.

"Cast the net on the right side of the boat, and you will find some."

So, they cast again, and they were unable to draw it in because of the multitude of fish. John said to Peter, "It is the Lord!"

Peter plunged into the sea, eagerly swimming to the shore. The other disciples came back with the boat, dragging the net full of fish. As soon as they reached the shore, they saw a fire of coals there, with fish and bread on it.

"Bring some of the fish which you have just caught," the Lord called to them. Peter dragged the bulging net to land, filled with 153 large fish!

"Come and eat breakfast!" Jesus took the bread and fish and gave it to them. For the third time Jesus showed Himself to His disciples after He was raised from the dead.

After breakfast, Jesus said to Peter, **"Simon, son of Jonah, do you love Me more than these?"**

Peter replied, "Yes, Lord, You know that I love You."

Jesus said to him, **"Feed My lambs."** Jesus repeated the same question two more times. Peter was grieved because He said to him the third time, **"Do you love Me? "**

He replied, "Lord, You know all things; You know that I love You."

Jesus said to him, **"Feed My sheep."** And when He had spoken all these things, He said to him, **"Follow Me!"**

"And there are also many other things that Jesus did, which if they were written one by one, I suppose that even the world itself could not contain the books that would be written." (John 21:25)

REVELATION, LORD?

The Lord began... *In the beginning, I gave My call clearly to some fishermen chosen by the Father, to "follow Me and I will make you fishers of men!"*

The arrest and crucifixion left their faith reeling. My resurrection became yet another challenge for them to grasp. Their world had been turned upside down twice—first when they left all, then when I "left."

Now what? They had no idea. Nothing made sense to them, not life or death or anything. They all seemed to be in a quandary. No one had any real answers: what should we do? They came together often but didn't have many words.

A great storm had come. Once again, Peter climbed out of the boat. He couldn't reach My side fast enough!

As the Lord gave me a glimpse into this final scene, I saw the hungry eyes of Peter, as he stood drenched and panting from his exuberant plunge, now standing before the Lord on the shore. Peter felt parched and hungry, not for fish, but for the presence of His Lord.

None could take their eyes off the Lord, as they came ashore. They all quickly obeyed His simple request.

"Bring some fish!"

All appeared hungry to receive whatever fresh manna would fall from the Master's lips. Their myriad of questions melted away as they simply enjoyed the presence of this Holy One they had been longing for, and now here He stood! They looked cautiously ecstatic.

The other disciples sensed Peter's heart of remorse getting squeezed by the poignant interaction with the Lord. They marveled as they heard his call being renewed, hearing those powerful words came forth once again:

"Follow Me!"

All eyes gazed upon Peter and the Lord. The painful sorrow filling Peter's eyes gave way to joy and revelation: he could continue his blessed mission!

I just observed another loving rescue by the Lord, after Peter's fall.

He dropped to his knees in loving gratitude, weeping for joy before his Lord. The hand of the Lord caressed the wet hair of this fisherman who was ALL IN.

ALONG THE WAY

Many of us have been praying for years for the last Great Awakening throughout the world, indicated in Revelation. I asked the Lord one day to show me His "reaping angels." (Revelation 14:15)

I saw a line-up of angels immobile in a waiting position, with their reaping sickles held down at their sides, tips resting on the ground. (vision, 2021)

Lord, why have they not gone forth?

They have in some lands, but not where you are, He replied.

Why not?

I am preparing them. They are ready to go when they are released.

Why the delay?

People's hearts are not ready yet. Division shows there is a people-focus, not a God-focus.

Bless. Bless. Bless your enemies. Bless and do not curse.

Call them forth to turn. Your focus must be Me. Sing and praise and bless. Do not fight, accuse and condemn. Bless with love.

Hear the Word of the Lord. Love is calling out to you.

Let them see love and compassion.

Love will win, only love.

Love is the oil that must burn brightly so the light of My face can be seen in you. Nothing else.

Then, I heard Him be specific to the land where I live: **To whom much is given, America, much is required. I am requiring love.**

I realized we must choose love, to propel the work of the harvest in the Greatest Awakening we so desire.

A few days later, the Lord surprised me with a phrase early in the morning that would not leave me until I sat down to write what He had to say about it. The words flowed rapidly.

Please apply it to the land where you reside.

I DECREE: A MIRACLE IN AMERICA

A miracle to LOVE the Lord our God with all our hearts.

A miracle to LOVE our neighbor as ourselves.

A miracle to LOVE the Giver of Life, eternal and abundant.

A miracle to LOVE one another.

A miracle to LOVE the light and turn from darkness.

A miracle to LOVE grace, mercy, compassion and kindness.

A miracle to LOVE and cherish the life of every man/woman/child.

A miracle to LOVE and honor our family, friends, strangers.

A miracle to LOVE our "enemies," to bless and not curse.

A miracle to LOVE and invest my time to lift up the weak and weary.

A miracle to LOVE and listen to the one in front of me today.

A miracle to LOVE and forgive those who have wounded me.

A miracle to LOVE and apply healing balm to the wounds of others.

A miracle to LOVE and cover every offense.

A miracle to LOVE and overcome every downfall.

A miracle to LOVE and serve others with sincerity and delight.

A miracle to LOVE and to soar above the highest obstacles.

A miracle of LOVE to put defeat under our feet.

A miracle of LOVE that sees destiny in the broken.

A miracle of LOVE to weep with those who weep.

A miracle of LOVE to seek to understand what we missed yesterday.

A miracle of LOVE to surrender our sorrows.

A miracle of LOVE to seek and find the lost.

A miracle of LOVE to celebrate the purifying of our souls.

A miracle of LOVE to press in, press through, and never give up.

A miracle of LOVE that smiles past the storm.

A miracle of LOVE that shifts catastrophes into milestones.

A miracle of LOVE that keeps seeking the Face of Grace.

A miracle of LOVE that sings a new song in the fire.

A miracle of LOVE that contends for greater love.

A miracle of LOVE that mandates hope in place of despair.

A miracle of LOVE that speaks words to refresh and nourish.

A miracle of LOVE to fear not and to faint not.

A miracle of LOVE to be unshakable in faith, hope and love.

A miracle of LOVE to be undeterred by disappointments.

A miracle of LOVE that speaks courage amidst uncertainties.

A miracle of LOVE that is not threatened by disagreement.

A miracle of LOVE that reduces monumental differences to minimal.

A miracle of LOVE that journeys in shoes of peace.

A miracle of LOVE that treads lightly with the unstable.

A miracle of LOVE that rescues souls from hatred.

A miracle of LOVE that elevates and edifies my brothers/sisters.

A miracle of LOVE to persevere through the birth pangs.

A miracle of LOVE to build new bridges in impassable places.

A miracle of LOVE that is seen and not just heard.

A miracle of LOVE that will lift heavy burdens.

A miracle of LOVE that will empower the uneducated.

A miracle of LOVE that will eradicate injustice.

A miracle of LOVE that will rebuild in the place of destruction.

A miracle of LOVE that will prepare the way for a new day.

A miracle of LOVE that dissipates oppression.

A miracle of LOVE that will resurrect life and hope.

A miracle of LOVE that beautifies and renews.

A miracle of LOVE to hear past the pain.

A miracle of LOVE to know you and be your friend.

A miracle of LOVE to wait for your heart.

A miracle of LOVE to walk with you today as my great privilege.

A miracle of LOVE to open my heart and my home to you.

A miracle of LOVE to deny myself for you.

A miracle of LOVE that sees greatness in your eyes.

A miracle of LOVE that stomps on the head of the serpent for you.

A miracle of LOVE to repent for not loving.

A miracle of LOVE that knows love will win in the end.

A miracle to LOVE our neighbor as ourselves.

A miracle of LOVE to believe—

> **With man this is impossible,**
> **but with God ALL THINGS ARE POSSIBLE!**

As I heard line after line, I identified many shortcomings in my life. Change me, Lord!

A BLESSING

I bless you as a precious son or daughter of His to know this and to never doubt it. *His grace is sufficient for you and His mercy endures forever!* I bless you to stand, walk, run, and soar in His unfathomable mercy, and to heal your hurting world with powerful love, grace, peace and hope.

I bless your life to be seen as a miracle of love!

EPILOGUE

This concludes the original 40 miracles of Jesus that we are to emulate in various ways, to magnify His Name. Thank you for going on this extensive spiritual journey of miracles with me!

My hope has been that as we *follow Him* and carefully observe His love and miracle working power, we would go and do likewise, as His hands and feet. It is clear He wants to use us. It's either us – His body residing here on earth – or no one! That includes all of us who will.

There are other supernatural events recorded in the Bible that did not fall into the healing category (to emulate), so they were not considered for this book.

After working on the manuscript off and on for several years, I finally finished the 40 chapters. They were all typed and ready to take along on a trip across the country, where a dear friend would receive the manuscript to edit.

About one week before that trip, the Lord surprised me by bringing up the following five events, with instructions to add them at the end of the book.

Really, Lord?!

None of them seemed like ones to emulate, but He was quick to convey the applications that He had for me to glean and share.

It all made sense then.

Be ready to stretch your faith even more!

HIS HANDS, MY FEET

PART 2

1. Sudden Boat Transport
2. Transfiguration
3. Cursing of the Fig Tree
4. Jesus' Crucifixion
5. Kingdom Come!

Is anything too hard for the Lord?

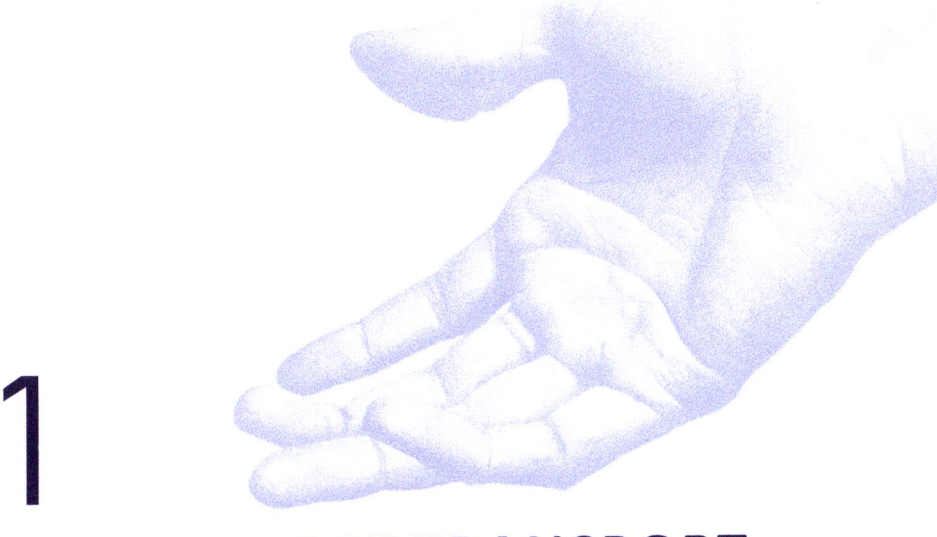

1
SUDDEN BOAT TRANSPORT
John 6:16-21

At the end of a long day, Jesus' disciples left a remote area where they had just fed the five thousand, to go across the Sea of Galilee, about eight miles. The seas soon became rough, so it became a long arduous journey. Would they make it?

About halfway across, something strange startled them out on the water. Could it be a ghost? Just then, they heard a familiar voice, **"Don't be afraid!"** *Jesus!*

Their miracle worker's appearance terrified them this time. After taking Him into the boat, they found they had *suddenly reached the distant shore!*

REVELATION, LORD?

He began speaking... *I needed to train the disciples to fully perceive the limitless power of God on behalf of all the people upon the earth. These chosen followers had begun to witness various facets of the supernatural, water to wine (substance and time) and the sick being healed (physical dominion). That very day they had witnessed food multiplying (seen from the unseen), My walking on the water*

(defying laws of gravity), and now their boat itself being transported four miles in a moment (time and space).

Is anything too hard for the Lord? *In the vision, I then saw John standing mesmerized in the boat as it suddenly arrived at water's edge, saying to the others—"Look! We shouldn't be here! We were just out there in the middle of the lake!"*

The others appeared numb and drained, simply unloading the boat. They were only glad to call it a day. The Lord put His arm around John, smiled and nodded. John continued to stand immobile as the others scurried off the boat.

I realized the Lord had just planted this story in the book of *John*.

ALONG THE WAY

I have not yet had a transport miracle. But He reminded me of an unusual dream that is fitting:

At the time of the dream, I drove a red PT Cruiser convertible. In the dream, I saw myself driving it around and around a giant oval, like a racetrack. However, I knew that I was driving fairly fast on a highway along with many other drivers, yet we seemed to be going nowhere. This went on for quite a while, until I finally noticed an exit. I knew the next time I got back around the track, I should take the exit.

When I did, I pulled over and parked, but I'm not sure why. As I did, a man came over, got in the passenger side, and shut the door. He demanded that I back the car up. At first, I started to do so. But I had an uneasy feeling about this stranger. As I looked in the rearview mirror, I realized I was backing onto some huge, jagged rocks along the edge of a lake. I hit the brakes and stopped abruptly. As I did, he grabbed the keys from me.

"No!" I said and took the keys back. He got out and left.

When the door shut, I was surprised my car had instantly been transported to my destination. I found myself parked in front of a red brick building at a college in Bethlehem, Pennsylvania, about 30 miles away. Apparently, I had gone there to take a ballet class. I don't need to tell all the rest of the story, as it is too involved to write, but some supernatural things happened there in the class, by the power of the Holy Spirit.

When I awoke, I immediately knew the devil had come to bring me harm and prevent me from reaching my destination (destiny). As I simply took my authority, he had to back off. The Holy Spirit intervened, blessed my wise discerning actions, and transported me suddenly to where He wanted me to be, to be blessed by the supernatural in a new way.

I could feel something of the surprise that John and Phillip must have felt. The Lord taught me several things, including the *possibility* of a transport miracle in my life!

The dream had such a dramatic effect on me that for several months, I did a prophetic act anytime I drove anywhere. Odd as it may sound, I would intentionally pull over to the side of the road on the way to my destination and say "No!" to the enemy and "Yes!" to the Holy Spirit. I wanted to be sure I would not fall into the old trap of "going nowhere fast" that He had demonstrated to me so powerfully. I wanted to fully honor and follow the Holy Spirit, to operate in His anointing. It became a powerful training season, to be sure to be in alignment, driving *along the way!*

As mentioned in Chapter 21, the Lord gave me interesting insight that I would like to review here.

He gave me **Three A's** one day as some overarching insights that cover all our life situations:

ALIGNMENT + ACTIVATION = ACCELERATION

Alignment means to agree with Him and His word, and not to doubt.
Activation means to be obedient to act on our faith.
Acceleration means the results will happen more quickly!

I smile when I think about Him reminding me of this subject! I suppose the inference is that if supernatural transport is ever to happen in our lives, we must be fully aligned, in the right place at the right time, for His sovereign intervention and kingdom purposes!

There are other examples of biblical transport miracles, as well:

"Then Philip opened his mouth, and beginning at this Scripture, preached Jesus to him. Now as they went down the road, they came to some water. And the eunuch said, "See, *here is* **water. What hinders me from being baptized?"**

Then Philip said, "If you believe with all your heart, you may."

And he answered and said, "I believe that Jesus Christ is the Son of God."

So, he commanded the chariot to stand still. And both Philip and the eunuch went down into the water, and he baptized him. Now when they came up out of the water, the Spirit of the Lord <u>caught Philip away</u>, so that the eunuch saw him no more; and he went on his way rejoicing. But Philip was found at Azotus. And passing through, he preached in all the cities till he came to Caesarea." (Acts 8:35-40, [verses 26-40, entire account]) (Various historians report the distance to be between 20-50 miles.)

Ezekiel's experience: **"Then the Spirit lifted me up and brought me to the gate of the house of the Lord that faces east."** (Ezekiel 11:1)

A BLESSING

I bless you with this new realm of transport possibility invading your mind that is accustomed to operating with more "normal" mindsets. I bless you to allow a new normal set of beliefs to include what has previously been unthinkable. I bless you to be a son or daughter of the King who operates in growing faith for the supernatural each day, each week, each year.

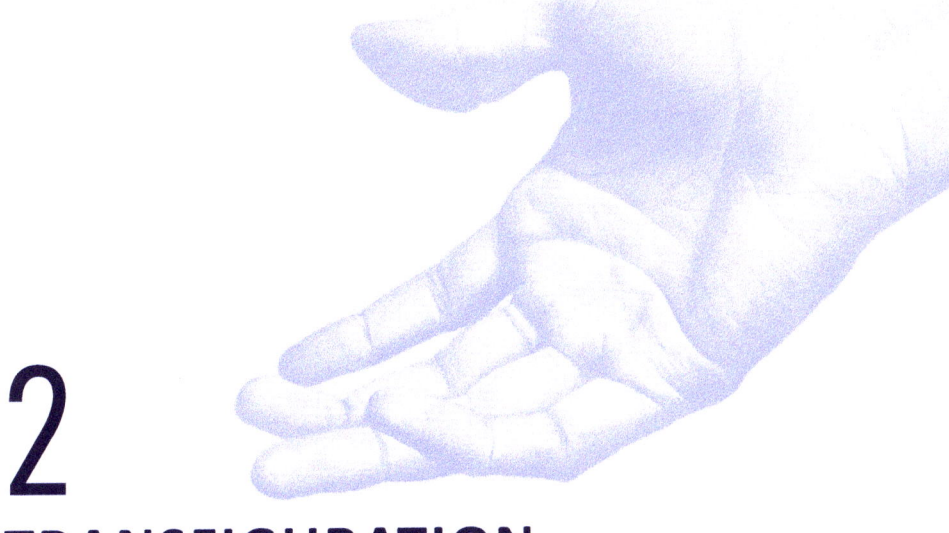

2
TRANSFIGURATION
Matthew 17:1-13

Peter, James, and John climbed up a high mountain with the Lord. Once there, something happened that totally shocked their senses: Jesus *transformed* before them into an unbelievable state of GLORY! His face shone like the sun and His clothes became white as light! Suddenly, two great Bible heroes appeared there with them, and began talking with Jesus: Moses and Elijah. *Wow!*

Peter became so excited that he (as usual) said the first thing that came to mind—"*Lord, it is good for us to be here; if You wish, let us make here three tabernacles.*" Peter's words were cut short by a bright cloud appearing that over-shadowed them.

The Father's voice spoke from the cloud, startling the disciples with, **"This is My beloved Son, in whom I am well pleased. Hear Him!"**

Upon hearing this Voice, the disciples fell on their faces, "vehemently afraid," according to the Greek. As the sound subsided and the cloud vanished, they cautiously lifted their faces from the ground. Elijah and Moses had disappeared with the cloud. Jesus touched them and said, **"Arise, and do not be afraid."**

As they got up to follow their master back down the mountain, He gave them a clear directive not to tell anyone about this until the **"Son of Man is risen from the dead."**

REVELATION, LORD?

Never before had Peter, James or John felt the majestic power of God's presence, as when the almighty voice of the Father invaded the earth! They felt undone and powerless! Their strength and their legs gave way in this unexpected realm of glory. They had been given a foretaste of the power they would know in heaven one day in the presence of the Godhead—Father, Son and Holy Spirit. It would give new meaning to **"Your Kingdom come, Your will be done on earth as it is in heaven!"** (Matthew 6:10)

Although Peter, James and John laid low on their faces, overcome and fearful of this power, at the same time they never wanted this blessing to end. Once the cloud lifted, they found the weightiness of the lingering glory causing them to get up rather slowly. Next, they had to gather extra effort to scramble after the Lord, as He was heading back down the mountain. They were "ruined for the ordinary" now and could only think to ask about Elijah returning again.

At this point, the Lord suddenly flashed a recent dream back into my mind. The night that I first began working on these epilogue chapters, He had given me a brief dream: I had seen His eyes in a way I never had before with a very bright hue of amber irises. He quickly explained to me in the dream, **It's because they wouldn't have been able to endure seeing His eyes of fire.**

When I woke, I knew that **"they"** *was referring to the disciples who had witnessed the transfiguration. (I was later startled to see similar eye color in pictures of the Golden Eagle's eyes—also a bright amber hue!) And now as I write about the men's descent down the mountain, He impresses me that His glowing eyes were the last tangible glory to fade away, before they would meet anyone else along the way.*

ALONG THE WAY

Gordon and I left on a getaway for his birthday. That night I became wide awake, after only two hours of sleep. As I lay there in the dark, the Lord began to amaze me with the most incredible experience. A vision unfolded, with Jesus interacting with me in my backyard.

First, I saw the two of us sitting in the bright sunlight at my patio garden table by the myriad of blue, yellow and white flowers bending gently in the breeze. He smiled, observing me absorbed in my daily journaling. Soon, He got up and decided to hoe for me, while I continued to write. My heart tried to comprehend the depth of His servant heart to demonstrate such love to me, hoeing my garden. Soon, we began walking and talking, side by side in the backyard, as He responded to the love and hunger in my heart for Him. He seemed intent on revealing the continuous interaction He desires with us in our daily lives.

Something had been on my mind when I woke up in the night, and He knew it fully. I remembered hearing a speaker who had shared his many visionary ascents to heaven, as he learned to seek the Lord in deeper ways. God had opened his eyes and heart to see into the heavenlies on a regular basis, with ongoing visualization and interaction at the throne room. I thought of Jeremiah 29:13, **"And you will seek Me and find Me, when you search for Me with all your heart."**

With these thoughts uppermost in my mind, I surprised myself, suddenly blurting out a question to the Lord: "Could we go up now?" Oh, no! How could I be so blunt like that? Wait, I didn't know I was going to say that.

I realized He had orchestrated that, as He knew the desires of my heart. But I still felt embarrassed at my bluntness.

In answer to my huge request, however, a large white staircase suddenly appeared in the grass, extending about 40-feet up into some white clouds! They landed on the ground right in front of a 30-year-old oak tree my husband's dad had planted in our yard on his first visit to our house decades ago. The Lord knew how to blow my mind with sensory overload in countless ways, all at once.

As soon as the stairs appeared, Jesus began to quickly walk up the steps so that His head was already in the clouds while I was still on the second step. "Wait for me," I wanted to say, but before I could, He responded to my thoughts and appeared back down on the ground behind me.

Now I was quick to object out loud, "No, I want to go up!"

Oh no! I embarrassed myself again. The Lord was so gracious. He simply extended His hand and said, **We can go up together.** As I placed my hand in His, the stairs disappeared, and we began to float up effortlessly together!

As we floated into the throne room, I saw the Father there on His throne, in a hazy way, without much detail. Everything else had been as real as everyday life. The Lord knew my thoughts again, and prompted my next embarrassing question, much to my chagrin.

"Could I see my mansion now?" The Lord seemed in a playful yet revelatory mode that I had never known before. I didn't know how to respond to the way He put all those demanding words in my mouth. Ahhhhh, I guess He knows me all too well, and wanted to demonstrate how He anticipates my heart desires. This interaction astounded me.

"Yes, it's right over there, on the cliff by the waterfall!" He informed me, pointing to a large indescribable structure about 75-feet away. My mouth fell open.

Next, He let me meet a Bible character. This amazing encounter began an ongoing series of heavenly interactions I never dreamed possible.

"For our citizenship is in heaven, from which we also eagerly wait for a Savior, the Lord Jesus Christ." (Philippians 3:20)

Through all these experiences, the Lord has clearly convinced me that we have been granted dual citizenship or heavenly access, His way, in His time. But I now know that it can also be granted readily at our request made with faith and expectation, along with our willingness to be stretched!

Whereas in the past these things rarely happened, they are occurring much more frequently today, in the lives of others, as well as mine. There are numerous testimonies I have read or watched, with heavenly dreams, visions, and visitations. He seems to be pulling back the veil and engaging His people dramatically in both realms—heaven and earth.

We often mouth the familiar words of the Lord's prayer, *Your Kingdom come on earth as it is in heaven,* barely grasping what that may look like when He allows it! (See Matthew 6:9-10)

A BLESSING

I bless you with a great lifestyle of pursuit, going from glory to glory with the Lord, as you begin now to *take your rightful place* in the heavenlies in prayer. I bless you with eyes to see and ears to hear. I bless you to seek Him and find Him in times of ascending to the throne in prayer. I bless your face to shine His glory, and your life to lead others up to new heights!

He changed the subject from figs to faith. . . **_Have faith in God._**

3
CURSING OF THE FIG TREE
Matthew 21:18-22, Mark 11:12-25

Mark 11 begins with the triumphal entry of Jesus into Jerusalem. Once there, He looked around the temple, but it was late in the day, and they left. The next day, walking back into Jerusalem, He spotted a fig tree in the distance and being hungry, hoped for some fruit. But none grew there as it was not yet the season for figs.

"May no one ever eat fruit from you again," He simply stated, addressing the tree. Upon reaching Jerusalem, they returned to the temple, and Jesus began driving out the money changers. This felt like such an abrupt shift in the normal compassion of His ministry. Amazingly, He remained there awhile and did some teaching, not leaving until nightfall.

The third day as they headed back into Jerusalem, Peter noticed the fig tree and saw that it had withered to the roots. "Rabbi, look! The fig tree You cursed has withered!"

The other disciples chimed in, "How did it wither so quickly?!"

He changed the subject from figs to faith, hoping to plunge them deeper in their faith journey. **"Have faith in God,"** Jesus answered.

"Truly I tell you, if anyone says to this mountain, 'Go, throw yourself into the sea,' and does not doubt in their heart but believes that what they say will happen, it will be done for them. Therefore, I tell you, whatever you ask for in prayer, believe that you have received it, and it will be yours."

REVELATION, LORD?

I saw the incredulous look on Peter's face as he discovered the withered tree. As he interacted with the Lord, that look never left. Looking around, Peter saw the other disciples' faces mirrored the same. Clearly nothing made sense: the curse when the figs had been out of season, the withered tree, and the incredible instructions that followed.

The Lord's newest faith teaching seemed perplexing. The implications had their thoughts reeling. Looking at the withered fig tree forced their minds to even consider processing His words "cast the mountain into the sea" quite literally.

ALONG THE WAY

This book on the miracles of Jesus was first started in 2013. He had me writing this manuscript off and on with other projects in between. For two whole years, from 2017-2019, He had me lay this manuscript aside while He released a new download of revelation regarding Eden. He taught me twelve new paradigms that I have begun teaching from Genesis 1-3 and John 1. One of the key paradigms has been about walking in dominion over ALL things. *That will be another book and study guide!*

Romans 8:19-22 (NIV) is key:

"For the creation waits in eager expectation for the children of God to be revealed. For the creation was subjected to frustration, not by its own choice, but by the will of the one who subjected it, in hope that the creation itself will be liberated from its bondage to decay

and brought into the freedom and glory of the children of God. We know that the whole creation has been groaning as in the pains of childbirth right up to the present time."

We have vastly overlooked His incredible plan for our dominion over all of creation. The body of Christ needs to step into this great plan! We must realize our authority in Jesus Name has no limits. As we read in the last chapter, Ephesians 2:6 says we are **"raised up and seated with Christ in heavenly places."**

One day as I was delving into the Eden revelations, He instructed me to start praying daily blessings over creation in my region, where the Lord has instructed me to pray for revival and transformation, in correlation with the *seven days of creation*. The following are some excerpts of the decrees I use on a continuous basis.

Day 1: Light and Dark
Let there be light over _____! (Name your city, state, or nation) Darkness must flee. I release the first light into the darkness here. Let all chaos be overtaken by the eternal light and love of God the Father, Son, and Holy Spirit.

Day 2: Sky
I bless the heavenlies over _____. (city, state or nation) *Jesus is Lord!* Reign and rule in the atmosphere. I shut down the enemy, the prince and power of the air. Enough is enough. I decree a shift in the atmosphere. *Your Kingdom come!* I align with the atmosphere of heaven: HOLY, HOLY, HOLY.

Day 3: Seas, Land and Vegetation
"The Earth is the Lord's and the fullness thereof!" (Psalms 24:1) I bless all the seas around the globe. The land of _____ belongs to you! I bless the land, the vegetation, the trees and the water here with abundant Life! I shut down all disease, drought, thorns and thistles.

Day 4: Sun, Moon and Stars
I decree your Kingdom come, your will be done here in _____ as it is in heaven. I thank You for the blessing of time as a gift to your children to advance your Kingdom on earth. I bless this land and atmosphere to flourish under the Kingdom of light, where Jesus shines over everyone continuously, as in heaven!

Day 5: Fish and Birds
Lord, I bless all our birds and fish here in _____. I bless them with life and fruitfulness, and I say "No" to disease. I bless the birds and fish to be in harmony with us and to serve us in new ways, bringing joy and delight, as in Eden.

Day 6: Animals
Abba Father, Jesus, Holy Spirit—thank You for calling forth such unfathomable creation in the animal kingdom. I bless all creatures great and small in this city and region to be safe and be kind.

Day 6: Man
I also bless every man, woman and child with the breath of Abba Father, breathing eternal abundant Life into everyone. I bless all of you to walk in your dominion and God given destiny for greatness. I also bless you to be a blessing to your fellow man, and to walk in obedience to Elohim, your Creator God, Alpha and Omega.

Day 7: Rest
I decree that this entire region chooses to honor the Sabbath as a holy day. We the people of this land all choose to enter Your Rest and will no longer break the Sabbath Day. We all align with You, Lord, and surrender all! Make us holy as You are.

I began to gain much greater confidence to operate in my dominion over creation, in praying for these daily blessings.

BACKYARD CONFIRMATION...

As I walked barefoot in the grass one gorgeous spring morning, the Lord interrupted my words of blessing over the land, with a unique assignment. *Go into the house and get your olive oil, to anoint your garden. Call your two friends, Sharon and Karen, and tell them to also get their olive oil to be ready do the same when you call them back on a conference call. Then the three of you can simultaneously anoint your land, forming a triangle that will be a first fruit blessing of restoration for the Lehigh Valley.*

What a great idea, I thought, as I pictured our three homes in different parts of the valley: Gordon and I in the eastern part, Karen and Jim in the western part, and Sharon in the southern part. Yes, it would be a perfect triangle! Excitedly, I called my friends, as I hurried inside to get the oil. Both answered and loved the unexpected assignment before us. We agreed to be ready in about five minutes.

As we joined our voices and hearts on the Holy Spirit conference call, we eagerly anointed all our gardens for full restoration, back to the original design, like the garden of Eden. With one united voice, we sprinkled the earth in three directions with the oil and sprinkled our powerful words of blessing into the atmosphere. We knew they all merged in the unity of Father, Son, and Spirit as our God had directed this triune blessing.

Our expectancy for Him to do a mighty work in this land flowed as effortlessly as the oil. Later in the summer, two of us saw exponential results from our ordinary flower seeds. Karen and I had both planted Zinnia seeds for the first time in many years. By mid-summer, we both took photos of their amazingly abnormal growth rates. My red Zinnias that should have only been 2-3 ft tall, were all at eye-level! Karen had several of her dainty pink ones surpassing the roof of her garden shed, about seven- to eight-feet tall! The flowers themselves still appeared to be about the same size, but they certainly had been given supernatural growth spurts by the Master Gardener! I had also planted semi-dwarf marigolds that came up to my waist! They had been a $1 bargain box and should have been about six-inches tall.

We took great delight that He had given us tangible proof that our prayers of blessing and restoration for the land would reap huge benefits in the days, months, and years to come.

Hallelujah!

A BLESSING

I bless you with a servant heart that is wide open to hear and to yield to growing faith. I bless you to begin to speak these same blessings over creation itself and to see things shift under your authority wherever you live. I bless you with great grace to listen for His unique and supernatural promptings, and the boldness to obey!

4
JESUS' CRUCIFIXION
Matthew 27:32-56, Mark 15:16-32,
Luke 23:26-43, John 19:16-27

Perfection left glory and came down: **Jesus, My Lord!**

Humility took Him to a womb, a manger, a carpenter's shop, dusty roads, the garden, the cross, and a tomb.

Ridicule assaulted Perfect Love:

THIS IS JESUS, KING OF THE JEWS.

It was a sign.

> Love suffered, bled and wept for me, for you.
>
> Crucifixion dripped holy blood onto the ground.
>
> Suffocation came, but Love could not die.
>
> Love arose, more glorious than before!
>
> *Grace exploded! It was a new eternal day!*
>
> *Mercy over sin and victory over death! Hallelujah!*

REVELATION, LORD?

I heard Him say, **Unless a seed falls into the ground and dies, it cannot produce more life! First, the Father chose to plant this Seed into the womb of a woman, by the Holy Spirit. That planting of the Seed was both a season of** [a type of] **"death," or separation from My eternal realm of glory, perfection, peace, joy and honor in heaven—as well as a season of new life, as Perfection entered the earth realm. For the joy of those who would receive Me, I endured the sorrow of that separation from my glorious home.**

I looked up the passage of the seed in John 12:23-24 (TPT) and discovered the context is literally His upcoming death on the cross!

Jesus replied, **Now is the time for the Son of Man to be glorified. Let me make this clear: A single grain of wheat will never be more than a single grain of wheat unless it drops into the ground and dies. Because then it sprouts and produces a great harvest of wheat—all because one grain died.**

The Lord continued speaking to me: **Do you see the many cycles of life and death? My glorified life suffered a death** [not physically, but separation from the glory] **to be planted in the womb as a seed. That Seed came forth and flourished as the Tree of Life upon the earth, with all its leaves for healing... Soon it became time for the ax to be laid to the base of that Tree. Crucifixion planted the Seed of Life back into the soil of the earth in Jerusalem, where it would now spring forth with even greater Life—resurrection, grace, and rebirth now possible for all!**

Much as the first Adam was formed out of the dust, now this New Life, the second Adam, sprang up from the dust of death, the grave, and Hades, to plant this Tree of Life all over the earth, in countless earthen vessels, for hundreds and hundreds of years.

I saw the Lord Jesus in heaven, being placed (long ago) in the palm of His Heavenly Father, being reduced to a miniscule, formless being. He *then became as nothing—and changed into a tiny seed I could barely see. The Father lifted His hand and blew upon the seed. I saw the Wind of the Spirit carry it down to earth—where I knew it had been planted into the womb of Mary's earth-clad sanctuary.*

These had been our pre-determined choices, He continued, **all for Life and love! So vital it was, that Life must be seen triumphing over death, to display it's all sustaining eternal power.**

"Death is swallowed up by a triumphant victory! So, death, tell me, where is your victory? Tell me death, where is your sting?"
(1 Corinthians 15:54-55 TPT)

ALONG THE WAY

I found myself in tears one day, many years ago, due to some ongoing challenges we were facing. As I stood alone in a dark hallway, the Lord spoke His wisdom to me gently.

I am taking you through the fire. Everyone goes through fire. It is always for refining, to purify the gold in you. He paused, then asked, *Which fire would you choose: health, loss, finances, pain, persecution?*

None, Lord. I would choose none!

I know, so I will choose. But I bring you through to be stronger than before.

I was reminded of Isaiah 43:2, **"When you pass through the waters, I will be with you; and through the rivers, they shall not overflow you. When you walk through the fire, you shall not be burned."**

He reassured me that His ways would work for my good. Dying was difficult, but it would be followed by new life. No fiery flames would be wasted!

I love the Greek meaning of resurrection, *"Anastasis," to stand again.* Hallelujah, Lord, nothing is wasted!

The Lord is eager to break through stony places in our hearts at any place, at any time. His revelation about my heart jolted me another day as I sat among two-thousand women in New York City. Several ladies from our church in Allentown, Pennsylvania had been invited by a former member who now lived near the Big Apple. She had hoped we would join her in a one-day women's retreat at the Brooklyn Tabernacle.

We laughed and joked around like schoolgirls as we drove the eighty miles to Janette's house in New Providence, New Jersey. We then took the nearby commuter train into the bustling city. When we stepped out of the subway, our hostess had our full attention, as she wove confidently through the plethora of people on the city sidewalks. Fortunately, we only had about two-to-three blocks to follow her to our destination. Janette delivered her bundle of hungry hearts seamlessly.

Our speaker delivered just as powerfully, helping us do some overdue housecleaning in our hearts throughout the day. At one point, she spun a challenge for us that would be life changing. She posed a question for each of us to ask the Lord, as we sat in solitude before Him: *What is one thing, Lord, that You want to show me about my heart, that I have never seen?*

Though it was a heavy question, I felt no trepidation or expectation of hearing much when I asked Him. I simply repeated the words and waited in silence. Quite abruptly, Abba Father unleashed a startling vision in response.

I saw something I had never seen before: Jesus hanging on the cross!

In this uncanny scene, I saw myself kneeling before Him, under his nail-pierced feet, only a short distance away. For unknown reasons, I appeared normal in size, while the Lord appeared about three times my size. My heart began to pound; I had no words, only awe and shock, as if I had been present. Finally, I queried, W*hat are you showing me about my heart, Abba Father?*

He said nothing. Rather, He added another element to the vision. All at once, He dropped another cross (normal size) between me and Jesus on the cross. I couldn't believe what I saw, *my husband hanging on the cross!*

Why is Gordon hanging on a cross?

Abba Father immediately responded. **He's giving his life for you.**

What? How? I felt incredulous at the thought of that. My brain couldn't wrap itself around any part of this scene.

He never wanted to be an insurance salesman, He reminded me. **He would rather be doing many other things, but he's doing all this for you, to provide for you. He is being a living sacrifice.**

I felt stunned to the core. I had prayed that verse numerous times for Gordon, never realizing he had already been doing it: **"Husbands, love your wives, just as Christ loved the church and gave himself up for her."** (Ephesians 5:26)

The Lord broke my heart with the fact that I had carried such ingratitude toward his work, along with the lack of appreciation for his sacrifice. My heart had been totally blind to see any of that. Now my Abba helped me see it so powerfully while He gently transformed my heart. Admittedly I had a critical perspective, focusing on things I wanted to be different between us, completely oblivious to the incredible way the Lord saw my husband's life.

Forgive me, Lord.

I repented and asked for His grace to let this new perspective fully permeate my heart, words, and attitude each day. After those ten eternally elongated minutes of solitude, the speaker instructed us to share what He had shown us with someone nearby.

Oh dear! Now the Lord had deeper waters of humility for me to plunge into. *Help me, Lord!* As my friend Crystal and I shared vulnerably together and prayed, our hearts grew lighter. We realized we would now be more accountable to the Lord and one another in our new revelations. He graciously rewarded us both with new peace.

I left New York as a different woman, humble and thankful for His work in my heart. I knew our marriage would be greatly strengthened. Coincidentally, Gordon had recently lost his office assistant, which meant I needed to be his assistant until a replacement could be found. Working side-by-side at the office seemed to be our greatest times of challenge, trying to keep our peace and overcome stress.

As I walked down the lack-luster green hallway to his downtown office in Allentown on Monday morning, I carefully reminded myself of the sobering vision on Saturday. As I grasped the antique doorknob, my heart received another jolt. The design of the six-panel door had once been described to me by someone as representing a cross on top (4-panels) and the open Bible at the bottom (2 panels). There on the crossbeam of the "cross" hung my husband's name on the name plate. Of course, I had never noticed it that way, until now, when the whole vision flashed back into my mind, when I saw him hanging on the cross.

Yes, Lord, I remember.

I would see this blatant reminder, daily thereafter, that Gordon continued to lay down his life for me. That afternoon, as we worked on some files, I grimaced as he made a negative comment about a situation. As my old critical thoughts began to surface, the Spirit quickly intervened before I could speak. **Don't look down at him; look up at him!**

I knew He referred to the scene where I had to peer up at him hanging on that cross. Then the Spirit gave me the convicting verse, **"God resists the proud, but gives grace to the humble."** (James 4:6.) Wow, I knew that looking down on someone revealed a heart attitude of pride. I didn't want God to resist me.

I had more repenting *to do. Yes, Lord, but how do I look up to him when he has a wrong attitude?*

Honor his position. Thank Me for bringing him to you as your husband, and that he is giving his life for you. Then you can <u>bless</u> him.

The Spirit made it all so simple and clear.

I surrendered to this grace and wisdom. I experienced true freedom to bless him with sincerity. In about two minutes, Gordon leaned back in his chair with a sheepish grin and offered some words of kindness, "I really should not have said that. I'm sorry."

I stared with amazement at this man I hardly knew after all these years.

"Thanks." I had no other words. My mind reeled over the speedy results of my small obedient act. What sounded so hard had been so simple, when I let my heart come into alignment with His will.

The name of the women's conference was: *Open Heart, Open Home.*

"For My thoughts are not your thoughts,

neither are your ways My ways," declares the Lord.

"As the heavens are higher than the earth,

so are My ways higher than your ways,

My thoughts than your thoughts."

(Isaiah 55:8-9)

A BLESSING

I bless you to peacefully yield to Him, with a heart cry of *"not my will, Yours be done!"* I bless you to surrender daily in laying everything down before the Lord. I bless you to yield to His plan for exhibiting His powerful resurrection LIFE through you.

POWER OF THE CROSS

My husband has been impressed to remind me that the greatest miracle of all is the power of Jesus' loving sacrifice on the cross to save us all from our sins. Amen and hallelujah!

Thank you, Lord, for Your great mercy, to forgive us of everything!

If you never prayed to be forgiven, today can be your day!

Or perhaps you need this guide to help catch others, as you become a fisher of men.

I have a simple **prayer of salvation** offered on the next page.

Know that the Lord can use ANY of us to help people receive His gift of salvation. If you want to help someone receive Jesus, you can remember this simplistic approach:

Please... and thank You!

(Please save me and thank You!)

Of course, anyone can use their own words, too.

**Picture a child lifting his arms up to his Daddy.
That's the heart the Father is seeking!**

A SALVATION PRAYER

Lord thank you for dying on the cross for all my sins.

I confess I am a sinner. I ask you to forgive me of all my sins.

Thank you for coming to earth to take my guilt away.

I receive Your great gift of love and mercy.

Come into my heart now and live, Lord Jesus!

THANK YOU, LORD, *for hearing my prayer and saving me!*

I also pray now that you will: Heal me, in my body, soul, and spirit.

Holy Spirit, fill me and baptize me with Your holy fire.

Teach me now to follow You.

Come, be Lord of my life.

Thank You for this promise in Romans 10:9 –

"If you declare with your mouth Jesus is Lord,

and believe in your heart that God raised him from the dead,

you will be saved!"

"EVERYONE
who calls on the name of the Lord will be saved!"
Romans 10:13

Follow Me!

5
KINGDOM COME!

Matthew 28:19-20, Mark 16:15-20, Acts 1:3-11, 2:1-21, 37-43, 9:1-9, 18:9-11, 2 Corinthians 12:9

T he love journey of a humble king.

Miracles of love.

Crucifixion of love.

Love placed in a tomb.

Love arose.

Ascension!

"After the Lord Jesus had spoken to them, He was taken UP into heaven where He sat down at the right hand of God. Then the disciples went out and preached everywhere, and the <u>Lord worked</u> with them and confirmed His word by the signs that accompanied it." (Mark 16:19-20)

What an incredible plan of the Lord, His supernatural ministry upon the earth. This would not be the ending, rather, He would simply continue His miraculous activities *through the hands and feet* of His believers.

REVELATION, LORD?

I heard: The beautiful day became accentuated by the beloved Master appearing to the disciples once again—this time in quite the memorable place, the Mount of Olives. The disciples' hearts quickened every time He reappeared to them since His startling resurrection.

Recently they had ventured to ask, **"Lord are You at this time going to restore the Kingdom to Israel?"** *(Acts 1:6)*

No longer could they hold back inquiring about this. Why else would He have returned from the dead? Even the Jewish leaders who had sought to crucify Him would have to view Him differently, they reasoned. Hope began to soar!

He replied to them, **"It is not for you to know the times or dates the Father has set,"** *(Acts 1:7 NIV). His reply did not sound encouraging; instead, it sounded like they faced more waiting! It didn't make sense. The longer He waited after the crucifixion and resurrection, the less anyone would remember all the recent events, they reasoned.*

But now they wondered if this would be the day! However, He carefully drew the attention off Himself, and focused on them as His witnesses. Their ears heard the words, but their hearts longed for their Messiah to be known as the King of Kings, just as the sign had read at the cross. Well, maybe it would happen next week, or...

Wait!

This couldn't be happening! Jesus had begun floating up in the air! He had disappeared before, but never like this! Was He leaving them for good? But what about the Kingdom? What about everything yet to be done?! What about proving His deity?!!

Bewildered and breathless, they felt as stunned as the day they heard "Crucify Him!" They had never anticipated a heavenly departure like this. Since death couldn't keep Him, they thought, surely, they would continue working with Him as long as they had life and breath! And

He had just said, **"Surely, I am with you always, to the very end of the age."**

I was shown their faces—shock, wonder, disbelief, dismay, as they looked up at Him and around at one other.

What is He doing?! Where is He going?!

They wanted to yell, **"JESUS!"**

Most were speechless. They couldn't have been more perplexed.

Their hopes for establishing the new Kingdom on earth with Jesus fell to the ground, as surely as He vanished into thin air over their heads!

Thus, Mark ended his book with this report in a far different way than they had hoped—as Jesus never physically reappeared after that day.

> **"After the Lord Jesus had spoken to them,**
> **He was taken UP into heaven**
> **where He sat down at the right hand of God.**
> **Then the disciples went out and preached everywhere,**
> **and the LORD WORKED WITH THEM and**
> **confirmed His word by the signs that accompanied it."**
> Mark 16:19-20

ALONG THE WAY

The Lord led me to organize my first prayer vigil in our region, from 6 pm to midnight, on October 31, 1990. We marveled at our incredible night flowing in love, peace and power, shining the Light in a traditionally dark night. We witnessed such united prayer happening with passionate intercessors from several different churches in the Lehigh Valley.

The next day, the precious awe of those rich hours together continued to permeate my spirit. Being home alone, I found myself bowing low, thanking Jesus over and over for what we had experienced together.

After a few minutes, His presence hovered so strongly, I found that I could only speak His name: *"Jesus, Jesus, Jesus."* His name became so holy and precious! It seemed musical each time I spoke it. *"Jesus, Jesus, Jesus."*

At that point, my first ever heavenly encounter began, totally expected!

I saw myself bowed low, in the same way I was kneeling on the floor of our bedroom, but now in a white gown, near the throne of God! I saw Jesus from the side, as He intently interceded at the throne before our Father ... I continued to simply speak His name, *"Jesus, Jesus, Jesus."*

I suddenly realized I was being allowed to watch my prayer happening!

As I kept speaking His name, the Lord turned toward me, looking down at me with a huge, wonderful smile. Wow, I had just seen His intense intercession, and now His face radiated pure joy! I realized that through my own praise and adoration He is able to pause from His work to fully receive my praise with joy!

A random thought flew through my head just then: *I better enjoy this while I can, as it may not last long!*

The Lord immediately reassured me, however, **No, you may tarry!**

That amazed me. I continued to worship for a few more minutes. Then I began to pray about some things, but in a few more minutes, I heard, "You must go now!"

I felt disappointed, as it hadn't been very long, after all.

Wait a minute! The Lord had said I could "tarry," I reminded myself. I suddenly realized the admonition to leave had been the voice of the enemy trying to shut me down! Immediately, I saw myself get up and run over to hide behind Jesus' white flowing garment. I looked like a young child, peering out from behind Him. He was pointing to a hazy green spirit form, and spoke firmly, **"You must go now!"**

The green hazy spirit disappeared at once! I then felt free to simply enjoy being in this awesome place. As I walked around, I felt like I had truly arrived HOME where I belonged! I felt the strongest sense of *love and acceptance* that I had ever known. Perfection permeated the air and all my senses.

After a while I thought of a question that had been on my mind a few days, regarding 1 Corinthians 2:16 which says, **"But we have the mind of Christ."** I decided to ask Jesus about that perplexing verse. I turned to Him, and we now stood face to face.

"Lord, do I have 'the mind of Christ?'"

He responded with one simple word, **"YES!"**

I then saw Him place His hand on my forehead. I noticed a large patch of blood on His palm about the size of a half dollar. As He touched my forehead, I saw that same patch of blood appear briefly on my skin, then gradually fade, as it permeated my skin and disappeared.

Oh! I replied, as I suddenly understood it perfectly. When He came to live inside of me as Savior, through His great sacrifice on the cross, He came in fully as Himself. All that He is, resides here in me, in my bodily temple. I thus have full access to His mind. I simply need to yield my thoughts to His, to allow His mind to take over mine.

After some further dialogue, the vision ended. When I glanced at the clock afterwards, I realized it had lasted about 30 minutes. The Lord had taken me up there with Him that day, even without my request. It started as a vision, but afterwards, I felt I had actually made a visit to the throne. I could still feel the perfection of the atmosphere that I had been breathing, with perfect love and acceptance saturating my being, from another realm.

As I later shared it with my parents, my daddy was quite intrigued and shook his head in amazement. He thought of Paul's unusual account in 2 Corinthians 12:1-4 (NIV).

"I will go on to visions and revelations from the Lord—I know a man in Christ who 14 years ago was caught up to the third heaven. Whether it was in the body or out, I do not know, God knows.

And I know that this man... was caught up to paradise and heard inexpressible things."

Lord, transform our small thinking to yield, welcome and engage in Your ways, so that the supernatural becomes natural in us and through us.

Not only did Jesus ascend that remarkable day so long ago, but He is wanting *us to ascend* to the throne room to commune with Him! This happened many years ago in my life, but it is still vivid in my mind, like an unexpected seed that germinated for even greater heavenly blessings that would unfold over time.

A BLESSING

I bless you to relax and breathe, to enjoy the journey for which you were destined before time began. I bless you to pursue Him UP as a citizen of heaven now! I bless you to no longer doubt that He has chosen to release His powerful miracles through you. *I bless you with ears to hear His daily invitation:* **"Follow Me!"**

> **"He who says he abides in Him ought...
> to WALK JUST AS HE WALKED."**
> (1 John 2:6)

PRAYER OF SURRENDER

Your Kingdom come,
Your will be done in me today!

I surrender all.
I lay aside all that hinders
and fully yield to your Holy Spirit.
Not my will, Yours be done.

Fill my heart with Your compassion
to "so love" the world,
that I will give my time, my energy,
and my life for others.
I give you my heart,
My hands, my feet.

I receive Your anointing to go forth in Jesus Name,
to be

"GOING yet BE PROCLAIMING
saying that the kingdom of the heavens has neared,
be CURING the ones being infirm...
dead ones BE ROUSING!"
Matthew 10:7 Greek Interlinear

So be it!

INDEX
"ALONG THE WAY" STORIES

1	Water to Wine	**Baptism of Spirit**
2	"Unclean spirit"	**Spirit of Addiction**
3	Peter's Mother-in-law	**Anointing our Son**
4	City Seeks Jesus	**New Prison Ministry**
5	Miraculous Catch	**Fish Jumping on Beach**
6	Healing the Leper	**Muslim's Skin Disease**
7	Paralytic Through the Roof	**Kidney Stones**
8	Healing of Withered Hand	**Crooked Arm**
9	Healing the Multitude	**Many Backs Healed**
11	Resurrection: A Son	**Resurrection at Jordan**
12	Nobleman's Son	**Miracles: Son & Wife**
13	Casting out demon	**Divided Home United**
14	Wind and Waves	**Authority over Storms**
15	Casting out Legion	**Authority over Demonic**
16	Twelve Year Infirmity	**Years of Pain Healed**
17	Daughter's Resurrection	**Man's Resurrection**
18	Restoring the Blind	**Eyes: Africa & USA**
19	Mute Speaks	**Mute & Shyness Overcome**

20	Pool of Bethesda	**Crippled Man**
21	Impartation to the 12	**Impartation of Anointing**
22	Feeding the 5000	**Two Multiplications**
23	Peter Walks on Water	**Walking on Water**
24	Multitudes in Gennesaret	**Street Ministry**
25	Daughter of Gentile	**Honduran Murderer**
26	Healing Deaf Man	**Baby Girl's Ears**
27	Healing and Multiplication	**Fire! Blessings Multiplied**
28	Blind Healed	**Twin Blind Boys**
29	Boy with Epilepsy	**Children with Seizures**
30	Go Fish for a Coin	**Ocean Miracle**
31	Blind Man on Sabbath	**Eyes: Honduras & India**
32	Impartation to the 70	**Going Forth by Faith**
33	18-Year Infirmity	**20 Year Burdens**
34	Dropsy Healed, Sabbath	**Swelling on Sabbath**
35	Ten Lepers	**Trauma Group**
36	Lazarus' Resurrection	**Lazarus Miracle**
37	Blind Bartimaeus	**Eyesight & Cancer**
38	Soldier's Ear	**Son's Accidents**
39	Resurrection of Jesus	**Love Resurrected**
40	Last Miraculous Catch	**Miracle in America**

EPILOGUE

1	Boat Transport	**Car Transport Dream**
2	Transfiguration	**Vision: Taken UP!**
3	Cursing Fig Tree	**Blessing 7 Days of Creation**
4	Jesus' Crucifixion	**Our Refining Fire**
5	Kingdom Come	**Heavenly Visit**

AUTHOR'S NOTE

I am delighted that you have taken this journey with me!

As I followed Jesus through a study of His miracles, I thought it would be for my own benefit alone. The Lord surprised me as He led me to share it with the world, and now you have followed my journey.

Let my journey become your journey!

If you have not done so, I would invite you to plunge into the *His Hands, My Feet: Study Journal,* where I share the Applications and Observations from my original Bible study (before it became a book).

I have good news! A sample chapter is provided for you on the following pages. Take a few moments to pause and personally commune with the Lord. See what the Holy Spirit will plant in your heart, to prepare you for greater fruitfulness.

My passion is to see the entire body of Christ GROW in compassion, surrender, and a daily demonstration of His power being released in each one of us!

If you would like to share a part of your journey from studying these accounts, I would love to hear your amazing stories from "Along the Way" with Him!

Blessings from your sister in the Lord,

Gail Okuley

HisHandsMyFeet@Outlook.com

HIS HANDS, MY FEET
Journey through the Miracles of Jesus
STUDY JOURNAL (Sample Chapter)

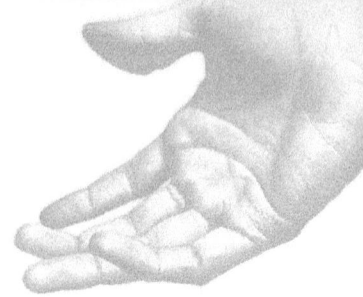

1
WATER TO WINE AT THE WEDDING
John 2:1-11

APPLICATION

Jesus' first miraculous word was: **FILL!** [Greek: *replete,* fill to the brim, or overflowing] Jesus came to pour the supernatural into the natural. He came to be emptied and poured out to fill us. *Our time has come!*

We are that blessed bride, receiving the new wine of His blood! Drink and be filled—full to overflowing! He lives within us now in His full resurrection power. It is our privilege and responsibility now to serve Him with that God-given supernatural power and to respond obediently as those humble servants did to Mary's instructions: **"Whatever He says to you, do it!"** (John 2:5)

OBSERVATIONS OF THE BIBLICAL ACCOUNT

1. John 2:1 begins with **"On the third day."** This timing amplifies the prophetic significance of the entire miracle. In the resurrection, His earthen vessel became glorified on the third day, just as water became wine, representing the blood of Jesus.

2. How significant it is that the first blessing from His hands was reserved for a **bride**, though she knew it not. Today, we are that blessed bride, receiving the new wine of His blood!

3. Another symbolic fact to note is the **six stone pots**: the number six represents man, and stone can represent our earthen vessels. He provided enough new wine to fill ALL the earthen vessels of mankind.

COMMUNION

Open my heart, Holy Spirit, to be still and listen to Your heart. Help me to receive and believe. Prepare me for powerful new activation.

Biblical Applications and Observations

ALONG THE WAY Reflections (on the author's story)

CONTEMPLATIONS

When did I receive the new wine of His spirit?
When have I responded to His voice lately?
What supernatural works of the Lord have I observed in recent weeks?

Contemplations Response

Lord, what would You desire to say to me today?

ACTIVATION PRAYER

Lord, I receive the new wine You desire for me! Help me to press in close to Your heart and follow You passionately. Empower me to be Your hands and feet, to pour out Your lavish love and grace for others. I yield fully to your Holy Spirit. Release Your miraculous power through me today!

MY "ALONG THE WAY" STORIES

Keep this journal ready to fill in your stories when they happen!

"He who says he abides in Him ought…to WALK JUST AS HE WALKED."
1 John 2:6

ABOUT THE AUTHOR

Gail is a passionate author, speaker, thought leader, intercessor and worshipper, who pursues the miraculous daily from her home state of Pennsylvania, and in their extensive travels as "snowbirds."

When the Lord unexpectedly plunged her into a 30-year prison ministry, the ladies soon began to refer to her as "the Miracle Lady." Gail and her husband were the co-founders of the *Transformation Prison Ministry*, in Allentown, Pennsylvania. New outlets emerged for ministry in the miraculous, including ministry at the *Mosaic House of Prayer*, *Healing Rooms*, and teaching the *Overcomer's* class at her church.

She and her husband are also co-founders of *Pray for Lehigh Valley*, (under the umbrella of Dr. Ed Silvoso's *Transform Our World*), to impact their tri-city region for personal and city transformation. They are privileged to have served on the Global Prayer Presbytery for Dr. Silvoso for over 10 years.

Gail is a graduate of the University of Arkansas, with a Bachelor of Science in Education. She and Gordon celebrated their 50th anniversary in 2021. They excitedly share their life motto: *The best is yet to be!* Her husband serves as station manager for WJCS, 89.3 FM, in Allentown, a Moody affiliate. They reside in Florida in the winters, and in Pennsylvania in the summers, where they are members of New Beginnings Fellowship. They are blessed with three grown sons and eight grandchildren.

Email: HisHandsMyFeet@Outlook.com

www.ingramcontent.com/pod-product-compliance
Lightning Source LLC
Chambersburg PA
CBHW040251090526
44586CB00041B/2744